MW01678362

Coaching Behavior Change

AMERICAN COUNCIL ON EXERCISE®

EDITORS

Natalie Digate Muth, M.D., M.P.H., R.D., FAAP

Daniel J. Green

ACE®

Library of Congress Control Number: 2014945564

ISBN: 978-1-890720-57-5

Printed in the United States of America

B C D E

Distributed by:
American Council on Exercise
4851 Paramount Drive
San Diego, CA 92123
(858) 576-6500
FAX: (858) 576-6464
ACEfitness.org

Project Editor: Daniel J. Green
Technical Editor: Natalie Digate Muth, M.D., M.P.H., R.D., FAAP
Creative Direction: Ian Jensen
Art Direction: Eric Lucatero
Production: Nancy Garcia
Stock photo images: iStock
Index: Kathi Unger

Acknowledgments:
Thanks to the entire American Council on Exercise staff for their support and guidance through the process of creating this guide.

C16-039

TABLE OF CONTENTS

INTRODUCTION

Health coaching works. Studies have shown that effectively implemented health coaching interventions contribute to long-term behavioral changes (reviewed in Miller & Rollnick, 2013; Olsen & Nesbitt, 2010; Stober & Grant, 2006), especially when combined with broad-based efforts to support healthier communities. These changes are critical in the treatment and prevention of numerous diseases, including those typically categorized as "lifestyle diseases," which result from a chronic imbalance of nutrition and physical activity, smoking, stress, and other factors. Individuals who have developed expertise in effective coaching skills are well positioned to play an important role in helping individuals and groups adopt permanent behavioral changes that lead to lasting improved health outcomes.

While earning a nationally accredited certification is critical to enter the profession of health coaching, developing practical skills in behavioral change is equally important, both for professional health coaches and for individuals from other professions who include coaching as part of their practices such as physicians, nurses, dietitians, and personal trainers, for example. It is for this reason that the American Council on Exercise has developed the Behavior Change Specialist credential, which is intended to accompany the ACE Health Coach Certification for the full health coach training experience. These educational offerings may also stand separately to help professionals from all disciplines and walks of life develop the skills they need to help support meaningful lifestyle changes.

COACHING CORE COMPETENCIES

This program is based on the Core Competencies established by the International Coach Federation (ICF). The 11 ICF Core Competencies are grouped into four clusters:

- Setting the foundation, including (1) meeting ethical guidelines and professional standards and (2) establishing the coaching agreement
- Co-creating the relationship, including (3) establishing trust and intimacy with the client and (4) coaching presence
- Communicating effectively, including (5) active listening, (6) powerful questioning, and (7) direct communication
- Facilitating learning and results, including (8) creating awareness, (9) designing actions, (10) planning and goal setting, and (11) managing progress and accountability

These 11 core competencies are developed and supported throughout the training program. For a more complete description of each of the core competencies and skills that a coach is expected to master in each area, refer to Chapter 1 and Appendix A.

COACHING FUNDAMENTALS

Communication is at the heart of coaching, and effective communication is critical for a coach and his or her clients to be successful in making behavioral changes. This first section of this manual begins with a chapter to help coaches develop the applied and specific communication skills required for an effective client–coach relationship and development of a coaching plan. The next two chapters support the coach in improving communication skills in general through discussion and application of emotional intelligence. It also strongly advocates that coaches take a positive strength-based approach to helping their clients that is rooted in positive psychology.

THE ACE CYCLE OF CHANGE

Understanding human behaviors—and more, how to help humans change ingrained, long-standing behaviors—is complex. In the text *Evidence-Based Coaching,* psychologist and executive coach Dianne Stober, Ph.D., describes the ACE (awareness, choice, execution) cycle of change to help simplify the process of coaching a client toward longstanding behavioral change (Stober & Grant, 2006). The ACE cycle of change is the model within which the ACE Behavior Change Specialist program is rooted and within which each of the 11 ICF Core Competencies will be addressed.

Awareness refers to the process by which a client first comes to identify that a behavior change is needed, and explores the advantages and disadvantages of beginning to pursue change. It is during the awareness phase of change that ambivalence is explored and communication approaches such as motivational interviewing are particularly effective. Other coaching techniques and behavior-change strategies, including identifying a client's stage of change and visioning, are also important in this phase of coaching.

Choice describes the process by which a client who already has decided or intends to make a change actually commits to the change. Identifying strengths and assets and SMART goal setting can help a client successfully navigate the choice phase of the ACE cycle of change.

Execution describes the process by which a client is engaging in the activities required to successfully achieve and maintain the desired change. Here, action plans, accountability, and evaluation are important to help solidify the change. The coach may also use a variety of adult learning techniques and strategies to help arm the client with the foundational information and skills needed to achieve success.

LET'S GET GOING!

It is an exciting time to embark on the journey to become a skilled coach. Over the course of this experience, you will be challenged to think differently about your communication style and how to adapt it to most effectively help individuals and groups experience lasting behavioral change. You will be challenged to engage in activities and skill-building exercises to enhance your effectiveness. You also will be exposed to tools and resources to help you structure your coaching sessions and develop as a coach in each of the ICF Core Competencies. We recommend the following advice provided by Stephen Covey (1990) in *The 7 Habits of Highly Effective People:* "Share with your loved ones what you are learning. And most important, start applying what you are learning. Because, remember, to learn and not to do, is really not to learn. To know and not to do, is really not to know." We hope you will engage 100% in the process. As you do, you and the others around you will recognize in you a transformation of style and skill as you become a more effective instigator of change.

—Natalie Digate Muth, M.D., M.P.H., R.D., FAAP

—Daniel J. Green

References

Covey, S.R. (1990). *The 7 Habits of Highly Effective People.* London: Simon & Schuster.

Miller, W.R. & Rollnick, S. (2013). *Motivational Interviewing: Helping People Change* (3rd ed.). New York: The Guilford Press.

Olsen, J.M. & Nesbitt, B.J. (2010). Health coaching to improve healthy lifestyle behaviors: An integrative review. *American Journal of Health Promotion,* 25, 1, e1–e12.

Stober, D.S. & Grant, A.M. (Eds.) (2006). *Evidence-Based Coaching.* Hoboken, N.J.: John Wiley & Sons.

EXPAND TO THE FULL BEHAVIOR CHANGE SPECIALIST EXPERIENCE

Coaching Behavior Change outlines the best practices in behavior-change science and provides opportunities for readers to apply and practice what they have learned. Readers interested in taking their skills and knowledge to the next level should consider pursuing the full Behavior Change Specialist experience.

Throughout this book, readers will notice a variety of icons highlighting additional educational opportunities, such as engaging in instructional interviews with renowned experts like psychologist Bill Miller, the founder of Motivational Interviewing, and Dan Goleman, author of the *The New York Times* bestsellers *Emotional Intelligence* and *Focus,* or listening to an interview with psychologist James Prochaska, the founder of the transtheoretical (stages of change) model of behavioral change. Each of these educational opportunities serves to enhance the learning experience and help coaches most effectively translate enhanced knowledge into improved skill in empowering people to change their behaviors.

Each of these supplemental materials is a component of the online, self-directed comprehensive Behavior Change Specialist training curriculum, of which this text serves as the foundation. In this training, learners will have the opportunity to engage with the content through completion of practical exercises and by listening to interviews with leading experts in coaching and behavior change, engaging with an online learning community, and taking advantage of the opportunity for real-time feedback on their coaching skills.

Those who pursue the expanded experience will engage in 25 hours of educational instruction and practice in coaching. Upon completion of the curriculum, eligible participants will earn a Behavior Change Specialty Certification. The course is approved to provide professional continuing education hours for professionals from a variety of disciplines. For more information and details about eligibility, contact ACE Educational Services at (800) 825-3636, ext. 782, or support@ACEfitness.org.

Introduction to Section I:

COACHING FUNDAMENTALS

Coaching is the art of communication with individuals or groups to help them achieve a goal. To be effective, a coach must have mastery of coaching fundamentals. In this section, coaches learn how to establish a client–coach relationship and coaching plan, increase competency in emotional intelligence, gain skills in structuring a program, and learn to approach coaching from a strength-based perspective through the use of positive psychology.

OVER THE COURSE OF THIS SECTION, COACHES WILL GAIN COMPETENCY IN THE FOLLOWING THREE PRINCIPLES:

- Establishing the client–coach relationship
- Emotional intelligence
- Positive psychology

The International Coach Federation (ICF) Core Competencies that are addressed in the three chapters in this section include: (1) Meeting ethical guidelines and professional standards; (2) Establishing the coaching agreement; (3) Establishing trust and intimacy with the client; and (4) Coaching presence.

▶ **For more information on the ICF Coaching Competencies, refer to the Introduction and Appendix A.**

CHAPTER 1

CHAPTER 1

THE CLIENT-COACH RELATIONSHIP

LEARNING OBJECTIVES

After reading this chapter, the coach will be able to:

- Outline the International Coach Federation Standards of Conduct and Ethical Guidelines
- Describe the role of a coach
- Distinguish the role of a coach from that of a psychologist, therapist, dietitian, exercise professional, and healthcare professional
- Establish clear coaching agreements
- Help increase clients' internal motivation for change
- Recognize and manage discord in the client–coach relationship

As a coach travels on the journey of behavioral change with a client, the client places a lot of trust in the coach. It is absolutely essential that throughout any coaching relationship—whether one is acting as a professional coach or integrating coaching techniques into a pre-existing relationship with a client (such as patient–provider, client–personal trainer or registered dietitian, executive client–consultant, or health advisor–community group)—establishing a positive working relationship based on mutual trust and understanding is fundamental. This requires that the coach always demonstrates the highest level of professional conduct and integrity from the first contact with the client to the last.

STANDARDS OF CONDUCT AND ETHICAL GUIDELINES

The American Council on Exercise supports the International Coach Federation's (ICF) Standards of Conduct and Ethical Guidelines and calls for ACE® trained professionals to apply the standards in all coaching encounters. While the ICF represents the voice of professional coaches, the standards and ethics are also applicable to those professionals from other disciplines that include coaching as a part of their services.

ACE SUPPORTS THE ICF CODE OF ETHICS

Part 1: Definition of Coaching

Definitions:

- *Coaching:* Coaching is partnering with clients in a thought-provoking and creative process that inspires them to maximize their personal and professional potential.
- *A professional coaching relationship:* A professional coaching relationship exists when coaching includes a business agreement or contract that defines the responsibilities of each party.
- *An ICF Professional Coach:* An ICF Professional Coach also agrees to practice the ICF Professional Core Competencies and pledges accountability to the ICF Code of Ethics.

In order to clarify roles in the coaching relationship, it is often necessary to distinguish between the client and the sponsor. In most cases, the client and sponsor are the same person and therefore are jointly referred to as the "client." For purposes of identification, however, the ICF defines these roles as follows:

- *Client:* The client is the person(s) being coached.
- *Sponsor:* The sponsor is the entity (including its representatives) paying for and/or arranging for coaching services to be provided.

In all cases, coaching engagement contracts or agreements should clearly establish the rights, roles, and responsibilities for both the client and sponsor if they are not the same persons.

Part 2: The ICF Standards of Ethical Conduct

Preamble: ICF Professional Coaches aspire to conduct themselves in a manner that reflects positively upon the coaching profession; are respectful of different approaches to coaching; and recognize that they are also bound by applicable laws and regulations.

Section 1: Professional Conduct At Large

As a coach:

1) I will not knowingly make any public statement that is untrue or misleading about what I offer as a coach or make false claims in any written documents relating to the coaching profession or my credentials or the ICF.
2) I will accurately identify my coaching qualifications, expertise, experience, certifications, and ICF Credentials when applicable.
3) I will recognize and honor the efforts and contributions of others and not misrepresent them as my own. I understand that violating this standard may leave me subject to legal remedy by a third party.
4) I will, at all times, strive to recognize personal issues that may impair, conflict, or interfere with my coaching performance or my professional coaching relationships. Whenever the facts and circumstances necessitate, I will promptly seek professional assistance and determine the action to be taken, including whether it is appropriate to suspend or terminate my coaching relationship(s).
5) I will conduct myself in accordance with the ICF Code of Ethics in all coach training, coach mentoring, and coach supervisory activities.
6) I will conduct and report research with competence, honesty, and within recognized scientific standards and applicable subject guidelines. My research will be carried out with the necessary consent and approval of those involved and with an approach that will protect participants from any potential harm. All research efforts will be performed in a manner that complies with all the applicable laws of the country in which the research is conducted.
7) I will maintain, store, and dispose of any records created during my coaching business in a manner that promotes confidentiality, security and privacy, and complies with any applicable laws and agreements.
8) I will use ICF Member contact information (email addresses, telephone numbers, etc.) only in the manner and to the extent authorized by the ICF. (*Note:* This is only relevant if the coach is a member of the ICF.)

Section 2: Conflicts of Interest

As a coach:

9) I will seek to avoid conflicts of interest and potential conflicts of interest and openly disclose any such conflicts. I will offer to remove myself when such a conflict arises.
10) I will disclose to my client and his or her sponsor all anticipated compensation from third parties that I may pay or receive for referrals of that client.
11) I will only barter for services, goods, or other non-monetary remuneration when it will not impair the coaching relationship.
12) I will not knowingly take any personal, professional, or monetary advantage or benefit of the coach–client relationship, except by a form of compensation as agreed in the agreement or contract.

Section 3: Professional Conduct with Clients

As a coach:

13) I will not knowingly mislead or make false claims about what my client or sponsor will receive from the coaching process or from me as the coach.
14) I will not give my prospective clients or sponsors information or advice I know or believe to be misleading or false.
15) I will have clear agreements or contracts with my clients and sponsor(s). I will honor all agreements or contracts made in the context of professional coaching relationships.
16) I will carefully explain and strive to ensure that, prior to or at the initial meeting, my coaching client and sponsor(s) understand the nature of coaching, the nature and limits of confidentiality, financial arrangements, and any other terms of the coaching agreement or contract.
17) I will be responsible for setting clear, appropriate, and culturally sensitive boundaries that govern any physical contact I may have with my clients or sponsors.
18) I will not become sexually intimate with any of my current clients or sponsors.
19) I will respect the client's right to terminate the coaching relationship at any point during the process, subject to the provisions of the agreement or contract. I will be alert to indications that the client is no longer benefiting from our coaching relationship.
20) I will encourage the client or sponsor to make a change if I believe the client or sponsor would be better served by another coach or by another resource.
21) I will suggest my client seek the services of other professionals when deemed necessary or appropriate.

Section 4: Confidentiality/Privacy

As a coach:

22) I will maintain the strictest levels of confidentiality with all client and sponsor information. I will have a clear agreement or contract before releasing information to another person, unless required by law.
23) I will have a clear agreement upon how coaching information will be exchanged among coach, client, and sponsor.
24) When acting as a trainer of student coaches, I will clarify confidentiality policies with the students.
25) I will have associated coaches and other persons whom I manage in service of my clients and their sponsors in a paid or volunteer capacity make clear agreements or contracts to adhere to the ICF Code of Ethics Part 2, Section 4: Confidentiality/Privacy standards and the entire ICF Code of Ethics to the extent applicable.

THE FOUR BROAD ETHICAL PRINCIPLES

Four broad ethical principles underlie not only the client–coach relationship, but all professional relationships: **nonmaleficence, beneficence, autonomy,** and **justice** (Beauchamp & Childress, 2001).

1 Nonmaleficence refers to the Hippocratic principle of "First, do no harm." Coaches should always consider whether an action, or lack of action, holds potential for harm to a client. The duty to avoid harm to a client is paramount.

2 Beneficence describes the aim to provide benefit to a client. Coaches should apply the best scientific evidence and information to optimize the likelihood of benefit to the client.

3 Autonomy, or the respect for an individual's capacity to make decisions for oneself, is a critical component of the client–coach relationship. It includes the recognition that the client is an expert on him- or herself and is the one best positioned to determine whether and how to pursue or not pursue a behavioral change.

4 Justice is the practice of fairness, with equal access for the client to the benefits of treatment as well as the protection from risk. Ideally, the availability and course of intervention is based solely on factors related to the likelihood of benefit or harm.

ACCOMPANYING VIDEO:
Hear experts discuss the coach's scope of practice using real-life case scenarios.

THE ROLE OF THE COACH

Coaching is an art in which a coach engages with a client to help increase the client's **internal motivation** for change. Coaching sessions are client-centered. That is, the coach does not tell the client what to do or how to do make a change, but rather helps the client identify opportunities and solutions. The coach provides information and advice sparingly and only with permission, unless specifically requested by the client. Coaching sessions are forward-looking, with discussion of the future rather than reflection on the past. Coaching sessions are strengths-based rather than deficit-driven. Ultimately, the coach's role is to help a client identify and mobilize his or her own strengths and motivations to change a behavior.

> Coaching sessions are client-centered

SCOPE OF PRACTICE

The field of coaching is diverse and relatively new. As such, there are few regulations or laws surrounding the **scope of practice** for coaches, other than by way of a clearly defined scope of practice of other professionals whose work may overlap with that of a coach, such as psychologists, therapists, dietitians and nutritionists, physical therapists, and fitness professionals. Despite the paucity of federal laws and regulations specifically defining the scope of practice of coaches, ACE advocates that ACE trained professionals adhere to the guidelines outlined on the following page.

> The field of coaching is diverse

ACE POSITION STATEMENT ON SCOPE OF PRACTICE FOR ACE CERTIFIED HEALTH COACHES AND ACE TRAINED BEHAVIOR CHANGE SPECIALISTS

Because research has clearly demonstrated the value of coaching in helping people improve health behaviors, and because the United States is currently facing an epidemic of obesity, diabetes, and other lifestyle-related diseases resulting from poor nutrition and physical inactivity, it is the position of the American Council on Exercise (ACE) that coaching services should be widely available in communities throughout the country, provided by both lay and professional coaches, and by healthcare providers with specialized training in coaching principles.

ACE believes that all professional coaches, who are primarily compensated in their role as a coach, should attain a nationally accredited professional certification such as the National Commission for Certifying Agencies (NCCA) accredited ACE Health Coach Certification or other health or wellness certification accredited by the NCCA or ICF. This is the highest standard of competence for a coaching professional and provides assurance to the general population that the coach has mastered foundational principles in coaching.

ACE recognizes that professional coaches, professionals from other disciplines who aim to integrate coaching into their work, and lay coaches will benefit from practical training and coaching skill development. The ACE Behavior Change Specialist curriculum prepares these individuals to greatly improve their communication skills and effectiveness in helping to coach individuals toward effective behavioral change. These skills may serve as an adjunct to another professional role, or they may help the professional or aspiring health coach to improve the quality of his or her work. The Behavior Change Specialist training is not intended to replace an accredited coaching credential, and an individual who has completed the Behavior Change Specialist training should not represent him- or herself as an ACE Certified Health Coach.

Ultimately, an individual coach's scope of practice is determined by state policies and regulations; credentials, education, and experience; and competencies and skills. With that said, all individuals who engage in coaching relationships are expected to:

- Apply effective communication skills such as use of open-ended questions, affirmations, reflective listening, and summarizing to help a client increase internal motivation and ownership to making a change
- Help clients develop achievable and measurable goals to monitor success and motivate ongoing behavioral change
- Help clients develop and exploit their strengths to support successful behavioral changes

The actions that are *outside* the scope of practice of the coach include:

- Counseling, therapy, and consulting
- Nutrition prescription and meal planning
- Exercise prescription
- Laboratory evaluation and assessment
- Diagnosis of medical or mental health ailments
- Recommendation, promotion, or sale of nutritional supplements
- Other practices or activities in which the coach does not have the requisite training or credentials required by professional standards or by law

» Engaging in these activities can place a client's health and safety at risk and possibly expose the coach to disciplinary action and litigation. To ensure maximal client safety and compliance with state policies and laws, it is essential that the coach recognize when it is necessary to refer clients to the appropriate professional such as a psychologist, physician, registered dietitian, exercise professional, or other credentialed or licensed professional.

A TEAM OF PROFESSIONALS, A COMMUNITY OF RESOURCES

Coaches acquire a large body of knowledge and a diversity of skills to help create an environment to foster positive behavioral change. Yet, coaches frequently rely on a broader team of professionals to help clients most effectively and safely achieve their goals. This team may include psychologists, physicians, dietitians, exercise professionals, or any of a number of other professionals who help a client to attain a given goal. It is very important that the coach be able to identify when a client is best served by consultation with another provider and when referral is advisable or necessary. On occasion, the process of coaching may reveal mental health problems that require the expertise of a mental health professional. Coaches are strongly advised to develop relationships with these professionals in an effort to best meet clients' needs. The American Psychological Association (APA) website provides a link to find a local psychologist (locator.apa.org).

Coaches acquire a large body of knowledge

Once a coach has determined that a client may be best served by consultation with another professional or access to a community resource, the coach can play a valuable role in helping to link the client with the needed resource. The processes of referral and accessing community resources may vary considerably depending on the community, the coach's work environment and role, and many other factors. Following are some suggestions to get started:

- Identify governmental resources and programs by visiting the local city and/or county websites.
- Dial 2-1-1. Many communities maintain a 2-1-1 webpage and/or call center to provide referral for food, housing, employment, healthcare, and counseling services.
- Identify potential professional referrals in the community through locator services of professional societies such as the APA for psychologist referral (locator.apa.org), the Academy of Nutrition and Dietetics for registered dietitians (www.eatright.org/programs/rdfinder), or the American Council on Exercise www.ACEfitness.org/acefit/locate-trainer) or the Coalition for the Registration of Exercise Professionals (www.usreps.org) for personal trainers and exercise professionals.
- Reach out to local nonprofits, businesses, and faith-based organizations such as YMCAs, churches, and universities.
- Network with other professionals by becoming involved in coalitions, attending business meetings and conferences, volunteering in the community, and engaging in online social networks and communities.

THE EDUCATIONAL REQUIREMENTS AND SCOPE OF PRACTICE FOR VARIOUS TEAM MEMBERS

Mental Health Professionals

- Psychiatrist: Medical doctor with post-graduate residency training in mental health care; the only mental health professional who can prescribe medication.
- Psychologist: Ph.D. or D.Psy. (doctor of psychology): Doctorate level degree in psychology. Psychologists receive specialized training in diagnosis, psychological assessment, psychotherapy, and research. Multiple subfields exist, including clinical, cognitive, community, counseling, developmental, educational, engineering, environmental, evolutionary, experimental, forensic, health, industrial/organizational, rehabilitation, school, and sports, among others. The scope of practice of a psychologist includes the diagnosis, prevention, treatment, and management of psychological problems and emotional and mental disorders of individuals and groups.

- Clinical Social Worker: M.S.W. (master's degree in social work) and L.C.S.W. (licensed clinical social worker) if psychotherapy is included within the scope of practice and state certification. Training programs require thousands of hours of direct clinical experience. Social workers help individuals and families in many capacities, including problem solving life situations and identifying community resources, as well as providing therapy for behavioral, emotional, and mental disorders such as anxiety and depression.
- L.P.C. (licensed professional counselor) or L.M.H.C. (licensed mental health counselor): Baccalaureate- or master's-level degree in counseling or a related field plus supervised clinical experience and a state certification, with variation by state. Therapy is included within scope of practice.
- M.F.T. (marriage and family therapist): Masters-level degree in most states, plus hundreds to thousands of hours of clinical experience, and licensure in some states. Trained to assess, diagnose, and treat individuals, couples, families, and groups. Therapy is included within scope of practice.

Physicians

- M.D. (doctor of medicine): Typically four years of post-baccalaureate medical school, at least three years of postgraduate training upon completion of the degree; able to prescribe medications and therapies; may have admitting privileges at hospitals.
- D.O. (doctor of osteopathy): Same academic and clinical training as M.D.s, but also have instruction and practicum in osteopathic manipulation, which is the use of the hands to diagnose, treat, and prevent illness or injury.

Nurses

- L.P.N. (licensed practical nurse): Typically an associate-level degree with clinical practicum.
- R.N. (registered nurse), B.S.N. (bachelor of science in nursing): A baccalaureate-level degree with clinical practicum and national certification testing.
- M.S.N.: Master of science in nursing.
- A.R.N.P. (advanced registered nurse practitioner): Graduate-level degree, typically requiring several years of practical clinical experience; able to prescribe some medications and practice somewhat independently, varying by state. Nurse practitioners blend clinical expertise in diagnosing health conditions with emphasis on disease prevention and health management (www.aanp.org).
- Ph.D.: Doctorate in nursing studies; typically a title used in an academic setting.

Medical Assistant

- Medical assistant: Requirements for education and experience vary by state; typically an associate-level degree with clinical practicum and national certification testing, though training can vary substantially and in some cases requires only a high school diploma and on-the-job training. Blends administrative with clinical roles, mainly in outpatient clinics and medical offices (www.aama-ntl.org).

Dietitian

- RD (registered dietitian) or RDN (registered dietitian/nutritionist): A registered dietitian is a food and nutrition expert who has met the minimum requirements to earn the "RD" or "RDN" credential. Requires a baccalaureate-level degree with clinical practicum and national certification testing. Most RDs work in the treatment and prevention of disease in hospitals, health maintenance organizations, private practice, or other healthcare facilities (www.eatright.org).

Exercise Professional

- Specially trained in designing effective exercise programs. This may include personal training, group fitness instruction, or small-group training. While a bachelor's degree is not required, many exercise professionals hold a degree in exercise science or a related discipline. The professional standard is certification from an organization accredited by the NCCA. Currently no states require licensure.

Physical Therapists

- P.T.A. (physical therapy aide/assistant): Aides are frequently trained on the job, while assistants have an associate-level degree; in some states, the latter is required to have licensure in order to practice.
- P.T. (physical therapist): A baccalaureate- or master's-level degree in a physical therapy course of study; P.T.s help injured people improve their movement and manage their pain, an important part of rehabilitation and treatment of individuals with chronic injury.
- D.P.T. (doctor of physical therapy): A doctorate-level degree with a dissertation defense in physical therapy.

Occupational Therapists

- C.O.T.A. (certified occupational therapy aide/assistant): Aides are frequently trained on the job, while assistants have an associate-level degree; in some states, the latter is required to have licensure in order to practice.
- O.T. (occupational therapist): Baccalaureate- or master's-level degree in an occupational therapy course of study; O.T.s treat injured or disabled individuals through the therapeutic use of everyday activities.
- Dr.O.T. (doctor of occupational therapy): A doctorate-level degree with a dissertation defense in occupational therapy.

Naturopathic Physicians

- N.D. (naturopathic doctor): A four-year, graduate-level naturopathic medical school with all of the same basic sciences as a medical doctor (M.D.), but also holistic approaches to therapy with a strong emphasis on disease prevention and optimizing wellness; in addition, the naturopathic physician is required to complete four years of training in clinical nutrition, acupuncture, homeopathic medicine, botanical medicine, psychology, and counseling; licensure is by a state or jurisdiction as a primary care general practice physician; scope of practice varies by state law.

Chiropractor

- D.C. (doctor of chiropractic): Post-baccalaureate degree program, typically four years in length; a variety of different chiropractic philosophies and practices exist; do not have prescription-writing or surgical privileges; however, depending upon the state, may prescribe and dispense nutritional and herbal supplements.

PRACTICAL APPLICATION

1. A client shares information that raises your concern for possible binge-eating disorder and depression. You share with your client that you are concerned for his or her health and believe that he or she will be best served by a mental health professional. Your client has limited resources.

   Describe the process you will take to help your client access needed services.

   List several organizations in your community that may be of help to this client. Describe the types of services provided.

   List at least three or four specific organizations or individuals in your community to whom you might refer clients who require mental health services.

THE COACHING AGREEMENT

As a coach and client embark on their partnership, having a clear coaching agreement in place to guide the process is important.

LOGISTICS AND COACHING DETAILS

At the onset of a coaching relationship, both coach and client should be clear about logistics, including fees, scheduling, location, and set-up of the coaching experience as well as an explanation of what will and will not be included or offered in the coaching program.
This information is generally best shared through a written coaching agreement that is signed by both parties. At minimum, the coaching agreement should include the following information (Figure 1-1):

- The parties whom the agreement is between: the client(s) and the coach
- A description of coaching services
- The role of the coach
- The required commitment of the client and the right of the client to terminate
- Coaching session procedures, including length of sessions and modality (e.g. is the coaching by phone, in person, video conferencing, email, a combination of multiple forms, or via some other means?)
- Cancellation and no-show policy
- Confidentiality statement
- Fee schedule and any required financial commitments
- Signatures

Figure 1-1

SAMPLE COACHING AGREEMENT

This agreement is made between ______________________ ("Coach") and ______________________ ("Client") on this _____ day of _____, 20__. Both parties agree to the following:

Coaching is a collaborative process with an ongoing relationship between the Client and the Coach. The coaching experience helps the Client to establish new behaviors and grow personally and/or professionally. The coaching relationship is strengths-based, forward-looking, and collaborative. The coaching agenda is developed and implemented in partnership between the Client and Coach. The role of the Coach is to help the Client progress toward achieving a goal.

- The Client and Coach agree to engage fully in the coaching experience.
- The Client recognizes that coaching is not therapy, counseling, consulting, or didactics.

Confidentiality

The Coach agrees to keep all conversations and information with the Client private and confidential, as allowable by law. No personal information will be shared with anyone without the Client's express permission. Exceptions may be made if there is an imminent threat of serious injury to oneself or someone else.

Coaching Commitment

By entering into this relationship, the Client and Coach acknowledge that the Client desires to make a behavioral change or some type of improvement in his or her life. Behavioral change often takes time to implement and sustain. The pace of change is uncertain and varies amongst individuals. As such,

- The Client and Coach agree to a minimum of a 3-month relationship

Coaching Session Procedures

Coaching sessions may occur in person, by phone, through video conference, or over email, depending on the venue that works best for the Client and what coaching package is selected.

- The Coach and Client agree to adhere to established appointment times.
- The Coach and Client agree to begin and finish all appointments on time. If the Client is more than 15 minutes late to an appointment, the Coach will assume that the appointment is canceled and the Client will be responsible for the full coaching fee. If the Coach is more than 15 minutes late to an appointment, the Client may assume that the session is canceled and the Client shall not be responsible for any payment for that session.
- The Client agrees to cancel or reschedule an appointment at least 24 hours in advance, without a change fee. Any changes or cancellations within 24 hours are subject to a 50% cancellation fee.

Coaching Fees

- Specific coaching fees and packages are outlined in Schedule 1. For each of these packages, the Coach requests a 3-month commitment from the Client. If the Client desires to terminate the relationship prior to 3 months, at least 30 days advance notice is required for a full refund of remaining sessions.

Fees are payable at the first of the month, and prior to the coaching services being provided each month. Payments may be made by cash, check, credit card, or EFT.

______________________	______	______________________	______
Coach	Date	Client	Date

Schedule 1: Coaching Fees

[Here the coach can insert various coaching packages, modalities, and prices.]

Note: This document has been prepared to serve as a guide to improve understanding. Coaches should not assume that this form will provide adequate protection in the event of a lawsuit. Please see an attorney before creating, distributing, and collecting any legal documents, including contracts, informed consent forms, and waivers.

PRACTICAL APPLICATION

2. You have a meeting scheduled with a new client. Prepare your own coaching agreement (see Figure 1-1). What listing of services and fees would you include in your Schedule 1?

SESSION SPECIFICS

The client and coach should also agree on the approach to the coaching sessions. To achieve optimal outcomes, each coaching session should begin with establishing a focus. Through **powerful questioning**, the coach can elicit from the client specific goals for each session as well as markers of success. During the coaching session, a seasoned coach will periodically check in with the client to ensure that the goals are being met. Importantly, the process of focusing is a collaborative process between client and coach to identify the best approach to facilitate forward movement toward change. Focusing and powerful questioning techniques are described in detail in Chapter 5.

Focus and powerful questioning

SUMMARY

Coaches are advised to take the time needed to establish the client–coach relationship on firm ground. Coaches should ensure that the coaching expectations, logistics, and early interactions set the stage for a successful coaching experience.

EXPANSION QUIZ
Multiple-choice quiz available if you expand to the full experience

Reference

Beauchamp, T.L. & Childress, J.F. (2001). *Principles of Biomedical Ethics* (5th ed.). New York: Oxford University Press.

CHAPTER 2

CHAPTER 2
EMOTIONAL INTELLIGENCE

LEARNING OBJECTIVES

After reading this chapter, the coach will be able to:

- Define the concept of "emotional intelligence" and its four domains
- Approach the client–coach relationship with competency in each of the areas of emotional intelligence
- Implement coaching strategies while practicing a high degree of emotional intelligence, with an emphasis on the expression of empathy

Emotional intelligence (EI), also known as emotional quotient (EQ) and emotional competence, is described as the ability to recognize, interpret, and manage emotions in oneself and in others. As a coach—a trusted companion to a person or a group making very personal and challenging behavioral changes—a high degree of emotional competence is important for career success and client outcomes. Unlike intelligence quotient (IQ), which tends to be somewhat predetermined, hardy, and resilient, EI can be boosted with training and practice. A coach is encouraged to spend the time and energy required to continuously improve his or her emotional competence. This chapter helps to engage the coach in that process.

THE SCIENCE OF EMOTIONAL INTELLIGENCE

Psychologists Peter Salovey and John Mayer first introduced the notion of emotional intelligence in 1990, though the concept of "social intelligence" roots back to the early 1900s (Salovey & Mayer, 1990). Salovey and Mayer (1990) defined EI as "the ability to monitor one's own and others' feelings and emotions, to discriminate among them, and to use this information to guide one's thinking and actions." Daniel Goleman's book *Emotional Intelligence* helped the concept gain widespread recognition in 1995 (Goleman, 1995). This book's popularity and the cottage industry that grew from it may have come too soon for EI as a scientific construct, as a clear definition and understanding of EI continues to be debated despite a growing body of literature on the topic spanning over 25 years. While the evidence to date is not adequate to prove a relationship between EI of a coach and health-behavior change, the concept is included in this text to help coaches increase awareness of, and skill in, effective communication. In the broadest sense, EI is a marker of how well a person is able to navigate the "softer" side of the human experience, including emotions, communication, and relationships.

ACCOMPANYING VIDEO:
The course interview with Dan Goleman further elaborates on the important role of focus in emotional intelligence.

THE FOUR DOMAINS OF EMOTIONAL INTELLIGENCE

Emotional Intelligence is divided into four domains, discussed in hierarchical order from the most fundamental to the most complex: **self-awareness, self-management, social awareness,** and **relationship management**. Within each domain, skills range from easy to complex (Mayer & Salovey, 1997).

Self-awareness

Self-awareness, or the "ability to perceive emotions in oneself and others accurately," is the most foundational of the EI skills (Mayer & Salovey, 1997). Individuals with a high degree of self-awareness are able to identify their own emotions and feelings as well as the emotions and feelings of others. The simplest task of self-awareness is to correctly identify one's own emotions, while a more complicated task may include correct identification of emotion in a client based on subtle body language.

Self-management

Self-management, or self-control, is the "ability to use emotions to facilitate thinking" (Mayer & Salovey, 1997). Goleman describes it as "the term for putting one's attention where one wants it and keeping it there in the face of temptation to wander" (Goleman, 2013). A person who scores high in this area may have a high degree of willpower and self-discipline. A high degree of self-management also helps one to hone focus and attention. Goleman (2013) describes focus, or the ability to concentrate on the task at hand and ignore distractions, as a powerful driver of performance and goal attainment. While improving focus may initially be a self-management strategy—after all, managing distractions is a huge feat of willpower for many—a sharp focus can also boost higher-level EI.

> The ability to use emotions to facilitate thinking

Social Awareness

Social awareness is described as the ability to "understand emotions, emotional language, and the signals conveyed by emotions" (Mayer & Salovey, 1997). A key attribute that is strongly tied to social awareness is **empathy,** which is broadly defined as being attuned to the needs and feelings of others and acting in a way that is sensitive to those needs. There are at least three types of empathy: cognitive empathy (understanding what the client knows and understands), emotional empathy (being attuned to understanding what the client is feeling), and empathic concern (the ability to sense what another person needs from you) (Goleman, 2013). As a coach develops and strengthens skills in emotional intelligence over time and with practice, he or she gains increasing effectiveness in communicating with empathic concern, which can be a potent facilitator of behavioral change.

> Being attuned to the needs and feelings of others

ASSESSING COACH EMPATHY

The most important quality a coach can express to a client is that of empathy, or an attempt to truly understand the client's experience. In any particular coaching session, coaches can range from "low" to "high" in their expression of empathy. Coaches who are low in empathy have nearly complete disregard for the client's feelings or experience, and lead from an expert mindset. These coaches may blame the client for the problem. On the other hand, coaches with a high degree of empathy are naturally curious about their clients and want to learn more about their experiences, thoughts, and ideas. This type of coach listens intently to the client. Tools to enhance empathy are provided in Chapter 5.

Table 2-1 presents a scoring system to help classify coach empathy into a 5-point scale ranging from "low" to "high."

Table 2-1
EMPATHY SCORING SYSTEM

Coach's Degree of Empathy	Description	Examples
(1) Low	No apparent interest in the client's point of view	Ask information-seeking questions only Probes only for factual information
(2) Low-moderate	Occasional effort in understanding the client's situation	Offers reflection, but frequent misinterpretations Only superficially interested in understanding the client
(3) Moderate	Actively attempting to understand the client's perspective, with errors	Offers few accurate reflections (a "best guess" at the meaning of what the client said) Attempts to understand the meaning of statements, but with limited success
(4) Moderate-high	Actively attempting to understand the client's perspective, mostly accurate	Shows interest in the client's situation Offers many accurate reflections Communicates an understanding of the client's situation
(5) High	Evidence of deep understanding of what the client has said and the underlying meaning of what the client has said	Communicates understanding of the client beyond what he or she has explicitly expressed Frequently encourages the client to elaborate Uses many accurate reflections that help to reveal underlying meanings for the client

Data from: Miller, W. & Rollnick, S. (2013). *Motivational Interviewing: Helping People Change* (3rd ed.). New York: Guilford Press; Hendrickson, S.M.L. et al. (2004). Assessing reliability of the Motivational Interviewing Treatment Integrity behavioral coding system under limited range. *Alcoholism: Clinical and Experimental Research,* 28, 5, 74A.

1. The following activities aim to help build skills in the four areas of emotional intelligence: self-awareness, self-management, social awareness, and relationship management.

Identify an important life experience of your own or of a close friend or family member, such as a marriage, birth of a child, a new job, a graduation, or a relocation. The experience can occur in real time, or you can think back to a previous experience.

› Write down all of the emotions that come to mind from your perspective.

› Write down how you believe a close friend or family member felt about that experience from his or her perspective.

› Optional: Ask the close friend or family member to share with you how he or she feels (or felt) about that experience. How aligned were your feelings?

Identify an area in your life where you are impulsive—where perhaps you tend to make rash decisions without fully considering the consequences. This could be in dietary choices, relationships with a partner or colleague, or shopping habits, for example. The next time you are in the situation, consciously choose not to act in the way that you normally would. Describe your experience.

Spend some time people-watching. This can occur on a city street, at a shopping mall, beach, playground, party, or any other social scene. As you people watch, try to put yourself in the shoes of the people you are watching. Continue watching until you notice that someone needs help with something. Then perform a "random act of kindness" to help that person.

› Describe your experience. What did you observe? How did it feel to you to perform the "random act of kindness"? How do you think that the person you helped felt?

Identify a person with whom you would like to have a stronger relationship. Make a concerted effort to engage with that person. This could be someone you have never met but whose work has intrigued you, or an old friend, a colleague, or a family member.

› Who did you reach out to? What happened? What did you learn from this experience?

Relationship Management

Relationship management is defined as the "ability to manage emotions so as to attain specific goals" (Mayer & Salovey, 1997). The most accomplished leaders often excel within all areas of EI, including the highest order, which is relationship management. This domain includes a variety of skills and attributes, such as influence, clear communication, conflict management, collaboration, and effective team building. A leader becomes effective in each of these areas due to highly developed self-awareness, self-management, and social awareness. As Goleman describes in a now-classic *Harvard Business Review* article: "People tend to be very effective at managing relationships when they can understand and control their own emotions and empathize with the feelings of others" (Goleman, 1998).

> The ability to manage emotions so as to attain specific goals

A CONSTRUCT FOR IMPROVING EMOTIONAL INTELLIGENCE

In an effort to integrate the various teachings of EI, psychologists have begun to discuss how one might improve and build this emotional competence. The construct of knowledge, abilities, and traits is used as a framework to help improve EI (Mikolajczak, 2009):

KNOWLEDGE: What one knows about emotions. This includes both what a person has learned from others as well as from personal experience.

»

ABILITIES: How one applies this knowledge in real-life situation

»

TRAITS: How one instinctively responds to emotional situations

Anyone whose job relies on communication with other people benefits from skill development in emotional intelligence. This is especially critical for a coach. Coaches can take steps to improve their own skill as well as that of their clients through attention and skill practice in each of these domains.

The process of improvement may simply begin with reading and learning more about the concept of EI. This helps improve knowledge. The next area of focused attention is on improving skills and abilities in identifying and managing emotions. The various skill-building activities contained within this chapter and the recommended resources can help to start that process of increased ability. Ultimately, the true learning ground is in real life with every client encounter. Here the coach can practice EI skills, most importantly that of empathy. Traits are the most difficult construct to permanently change. This is where a coach-the-coach model is helpful to provide feedback and direction to help change ingrained communication challenges.

THE CLIENT–COACH RELATIONSHIP

A coach will rely most heavily on his or her communication skills and emotional intelligence during key stages of the client–coach relationship, such as when building **rapport** and managing conflict and discord.

BUILDING RAPPORT

A thriving client–coach relationship sets the groundwork for a client to successfully implement a behavioral change. It begins with developing a strong rapport. In the *ACE Health Coach Manual*, building rapport is described as "a process that promotes open communication, develops trust, and fosters the client's desire to participate" in the coaching program (Galati, Merrill, & Comana, 2013).

Rapport should be developed early through open communication and initial positive experiences, and enhanced through coaching strategies that respect a client's **autonomy** while helping him or her strengthen **internal motivation** and **self-efficacy** for change. Development of key coaching skills to build rapport and nurture the client–coach relationship is the focus of the ensuing chapters. In addition to skill development, coaches also are advised to take notice of other factors that can affect rapport, including the physical environment and location of the coaching sessions, the way the coach presents him- or herself, and the total client experience.

A process that promotes open communication

MANAGING DISCORD

Despite the best of intentions, on occasion a coach and client will experience discord and conflict. Miller and Rollnick (2013) emphasize the importance of quickly identifying and addressing signs of discord in a collaborative relationship. The following are four signs of discord:

- *Defending:* This is when the client begins to deflect blame ("it's not my fault"), minimizes the situation ("it's no big deal"), or justifies decisions ("this just makes the most sense"). People defend when they feel threatened. If a client begins to defend actions, it is likely the person feels attacked or threatened by the coach.

- *Squaring off:* This is a signal that the client feels like he or she is in an adversarial relationship with the coach. Typically, squaring off statements come in the form of "you" statements—"you don't understand"; "you don't know what it's like to be me"; "you are wrong."

- *Interrupting:* When a client frequently interrupts a coach, it may be a sign that the client feels that the coach is talking too much, does not understand, or is not listening.

- *Disengagement:* Disengagement is marked by poor eye contact, distracted behaviors such as looking at a phone or text messaging, or not participating in the conversation.

Regardless of the specific type of discord, the most important step a coach can take is to recognize discord and respond to it immediately. Coaches can address discord with strategies such as reflective questioning (described in detail in Chapter 5), apologizing when appropriate ("I didn't mean to lecture you"; "I understand that I may have insulted you"; "I'm sorry, I misunderstood."), affirming the client's autonomy or positioning ("You are best positioned to make this assessment"; "I see how important this is to you"), and shifting focus away from a sensitive topic, when appropriate.

Discord commonly presents when making a difficult change. It is not an automatic sign of a failed client–coach partnership. However, in some cases discord may not be easily remedied, or may be ongoing across multiple sessions. In these cases, it may be worth exploring with the client if there is another professional who may be better able to support the client in the change. If this occurs, it is incumbent upon the coach to offer recommendations and attempt to facilitate the transition, if desired by the client.

PRACTICAL APPLICATIONS

2. Complete the UC Berkeley Greater Good Science Center facial expressions quiz at greatergood.berkeley.edu/ei_quiz.

   How many questions did you get right?

   Which questions did you miss?

   What did you learn?

3. Over the course of one day, focus on being present in every activity that you do. Every time you find your mind wandering, or you have the temptation to multitask, remind yourself to refocus. Describe your experience.

4. This activity addresses building rapport and managing discord.

   Describe a time during which you were able to build excellent rapport with a client. What do you think were the ingredients that helped to facilitate building such a strong rapport?

   Describe a time when you experienced discord with a client. What do you think triggered the discord? How did you manage the situation? If you could repeat the situation, what would you do the same? What would you do differently?

SUMMARY

In *Motivational Interviewing*, Miller and Rollnick (2013) describe the ideal relationship between client and coach as if the duo is doing a dance: "[the coaching session is] dancing rather than wrestling.... conversation looks as smooth as a ballroom waltz. Someone is still leading in the dance... without tripping or stepping on toes. Without partnership there is no dance."

A coach's competency in understanding and managing emotions in both oneself and others is crucial to success. While people have natural communication styles, within that style one's emotional intelligence can be honed and improved upon to support a client in making a successful behavioral change, in essence setting the stage for a successful waltz. This discussion of EI opens this guide to serve as a foundation for improving coaching skills.

EXPANSION QUIZ
Multiple-choice quiz available if you expand to the full experience

References

Galati, T., Merrill, S., & Comana, F. (2013) Exercise programming considerations and guidelines. In: *ACE Health Coach Manual.* San Diego, Calif.: American Council on Exercise.

Goleman, D. (2013). The focused leader. *Harvard Business Review*, December, 51–60.

Goleman, D. (1998). What makes a leader? *Harvard Business Review*, November-December, 93–102.

Goleman, D. (1995). *Emotional Intelligence: Why It Can Matter More Than IQ.* New York: Bantam Books.

Hendrickson, S.M.L. et al. (2004). Assessing reliability of the Motivational Interviewing Treatment Integrity behavioral coding system under limited range. *Alcoholism: Clinical and Experimental Research,* 28, 5, 74A.

Mayer, J.D. & Salovey, P. (1997). What is emotional intelligence? In: P. Salovey & D. Slayter (Eds.). *Emotional Development and Emotional Intelligence: Educational Implications* (pp 3–31). New York: Basic Books.

Mikolajczak, M. (2009). Going beyond the ability-trait debate: The three-level model of emotional intelligence. *Electronic Journal of Applied Psychology*, 5, 2, 25–31.

Miller, W. & Rollnick, S. (2013). *Motivational Interviewing: Helping People Change* (3rd ed.). New York: Guilford Press.

Salovey, P. & Mayer, J.D. (1990). Emotional intelligence. *Imagination, Cognition, and Personality,* 9, 185–211.

Additional Resources

The Emotional Intelligence Consortium: www.eiconsortium.org

- Includes research citations supporting the efficacy of EI. Also contains a list of assessments that measure EI, their uses, and pros and cons.

UC Berkeley: The Greater Good Science Center.
www.greatergood.berkeley.edu

- Link to an EI quiz as well as myriad resources on leading a more meaningful life

www.morethansound.net: Podcasts and DVD resources for translating knowledge of emotional intelligence and focus into action

www.danielgoleman.info

Bennett-Goleman, T. (2013). *Mind Whispering: A New Map to Freedom from Self-Defeating Emotional Habits.* New York: HarperOne.

Bennett-Goleman, T. (2002). *Emotional Alchemy: How the Mind Can Heal the Heart.* New York: Harmony.

Goleman, D. (2013). *Focus: The Hidden Driver of Excellence.* New York: Harper.

Goleman, D. (2005). *Emotional Intelligence: Why It Can Matter More Than IQ* (2nd ed.). New York: Bantam Books.

NOTES

Read:

Emotional Alchemy

Mind Whispering

by Tara Bennett-Goleman

Emotional Intelligence

Focus

by Daniel Goleman

CHAPTER 3

CHAPTER 3
POSITIVE PSYCHOLOGY

LEARNING OBJECTIVES

After reading this chapter, the coach will be able to:

- Define positive psychology and how it is foundational to the coaching relationship
- Approach the client–coach relationship from the perspective of exploring strengths
- Implement coaching strategies to improve happiness and flow

Taking a strengths-based approach to coaching through application of **positive psychology** elicits physical health benefits in addition to enhancements to mental health. For example, studies have shown that positive affect is associated with enhanced immune function, improved cardiovascular function, decreased pain, decreased use of healthcare, overall improved health, and increased longevity (reviewed in Biswas-Diener, Kashdan, & Minhas, 2011).

ACCOMPANYING VIDEO:
View an interview with Dr. Robert Biswas-Diener on positive psychology.

POSITIVE PSYCHOLOGY AS THE FOUNDATION FOR BEHAVIOR-CHANGE COACHING

Positive psychology is defined by Martin Seligman, the founder of positive psychology and Director of the Positive Psychology Center at the University of Pennsylvania, as the scientific study of "valued subjective experiences: well-being, contentment, and satisfaction (in the past); hope and optimism (for the future); and flow and happiness (in the present)" (Seligman & Csikszentmihalyi, 2000). As Seligman and Csikszentmihalyi articulate in their introduction to a 15-article series on positive psychology in the *American Psychologist,* "the aim of positive psychology is to begin to catalyze a change in the focus of psychology from preoccupation only with repairing the worst things in life to also building positive qualities." In fact, Seligman likens it to raising children: "Raising children, I realized, is vastly more than fixing what is wrong with them. It is about identifying and nurturing their strongest qualities, what they own and are best at, and helping them find niches in which they can best live out these strengths" (Seligman & Csikszentmihalyi, 2000). And so it is with coaching.

The concept that human behavioral change is most likely to occur in the context of a supportive, strengths-based, forward-looking environment is the foundation upon which coaching is built, and is the core priority for a coach. The objective of the client–coach relationship is to help clients identify and nurture the strengths that will help them successfully get from point A to point B. It is not so much about identifying and correcting deficits, and it is not about identifying and treating pathology. Rather, the role of the coach is to identify, nurture, and promote the many aspects of "health," which is not merely the absence of disease.

KEY NOTIONS IN POSITIVE PSYCHOLOGY

The field of positive psychology is shaped by the scientific study of key principles, among them happiness and flow.

Happiness or "Subjective Well-being"

Psychologists have extensively studied the notion of happiness—more often referred to as "subjective well-being" in the scientific literature. From this work, it is believed that people have what is referred to as a "happiness set point," or a genetic predisposition for a level of happiness that can fluctuate up and down based on life events. While this set point tends to be stable over short periods of time (1–2 years), with repeated life events, experiences, or interventions it can reset over time. That is, happiness can be increased sustainably. But it takes work. One might think of this in parallel to a weight set point, and the notion that with an effective intervention, weight can be lost and that weight loss can be sustained.

People generally state that they would like to be "happier." The practice of positive psychology helps to bring that desire into fruition. "Happiness" is more than merely a feeling of emotional contentment, though that is one aspect of happiness that Seligman refers to as the **pleasant life.** Seligman describes the notion of the **full life** as the end state when the three domains of happiness merge: the pleasant life, the **engaged life,** and the **meaningful life.** The engaged life is evident through connection in work, relationships, and hobbies. The meaningful life is living with a sense of purpose and value. Coaches may choose to help clients to improve their happiness by focusing on one or more of the three paths to happiness. Research supports the effectiveness of the use of positive psychology to improve happiness and well-being (reviewed in Biswas-Diener, Kashdan, & Minhas, 2011). In fact, an entire scientific journal, *The Journal of Positive Psychology,* is dedicated to advancing the scientific study of positive psychology and its applications.

Pleasant life.
Engaged life.
Meaningful life.

Each of the individual studies, as well as a meta-analysis assessing the effectiveness of 51 positive psychology interventions, has shown that they significantly enhance well-being and alleviate depression (Sin & Lyubomirsky, 2009). Positive psychologists hypothesize that these interventions are successful due to their influence on positive emotions, positive behaviors, positive thoughts, and need satisfaction (Lyubomirsky & Layous, 2013). Ongoing studies are underway to assess these hypotheses. One key finding that has come from this work is the key role of gratitude and the expression of gratitude on improving personal happiness. Of course, many of these studies have occurred in a laboratory setting without regard to context, such as a person's relationships, financial circumstances, employment, or personal health and social histories. Coaches should always take into consideration a client's unique and specific situation, and tailor the coaching intervention (as well as referrals to other professionals) accordingly.

A PATHWAY TO HAPPINESS

Seligman promotes an Authentic Happiness Coaching model. On his website www.authentichappiness.org, he has made available for free several assessments that coaches may find of interest when working with clients to improve any of the three domains of happiness—the pleasant life ("Emotion Questionnaires"), engaged life ("Engagement Questionnaires"), or the meaningful life ("Meaning Questionnaires"), as well as overall happiness and life satisfaction ("Life Satisfaction Questionnaires"). Of note, ethical codes for psychologists state that when training non-psychologists in the use of psychological techniques such as these, there is a requirement to ensure that the methods will be used properly and appropriately, and that the users understand the potential harms of inappropriate use. It is with this caveat that the resources and activities shown in Table 3-1 are shared.

Table 3-1

ACTIVITIES TO HELP CLIENTS INCREASE HAPPINESS

ACTIVITY	DESCRIPTION
	THE PLEASANT LIFE
Savoring a Beautiful Day	The client sets aside a period of time to devote to a favorite activity and is instructed to fully absorb the experience and note and address negative thoughts.
Three Blessings Exercise	Each evening, the client writes down three good things that happened that day and what the client *did* to make each thing happen.
Gratitude Visit	The client identifies someone who showed the client kindness but was never adequately thanked. The client writes a letter of gratitude explaining the specific reason for the letter and how the person's act of kindness affected the client's life. *Optional:* The client then makes an appointment to meet in person and reads the letter aloud.
Optimism Building	The client lists a past failure and a past success. When addressing the failure, clients are asked to search for circumstances that may have contributed to the failure. For the success, the client is asked to search for character strengths that may have contributed to the success.
Rapid-fire Disputation	The client is taught to dispute negative beliefs by identifying evidence that challenges his or her thoughts. For example, a client who believes that he or she is a "willpower failure" would be asked to identify specific situations in which the client effectively exerted willpower.
	THE ENGAGED LIFE
Engagement With Activity	The client chooses one of his or her top strengths, goes through a day and notes when the strength is already being used, then tries using the strength in a new way.
Strengths Date	After the client and a coworker, family member, or friend take the VIA Classification of Strengths to identify key strengths, they plan an activity that uses one or more of the key strengths of each person.
Relational Engagement	The client helps two people or a group of people work more effectively together by taking an active, constructive approach to providing immediate feedback to each other, rather than a passive or destructive approach.
	THE MEANINGFUL LIFE
Fun versus Philanthropy	The client is asked to plan two activities: one for personal fulfillment and the other to bring happiness to another person. After each activity, he or she fills out the "happiness rating scale" (available at www.authentichappiness.org) and notes which activity made him or her feel better.
Strengths Family Tree	The client asks his or her family members or coworkers to take the VIA Classification of Strengths and report the results. The client then creates a family tree (or organizational chart) identifying each family member's key strengths. The group then discusses the findings and notes anecdotes of how the strengths have been in use and how relationships change due to this activity.
Gift of Time/Positive Service	Using the client's key strengths, the client develops a plan for how the strengths could be put to use to benefit others.
The Life Summary	The client writes out an account of his or her life how he or she may want a great-grandchild to see it. The client notes the things that he or she feels are most meaningful. The aim is for the client to reflect on what aspects are most meaningful and what, if anything, is missing that could be done to provide more meaning.
	THE FULL LIFE
Diary Exercise	During a routine day, the client is asked to complete an hour-by-hour diary answering: What did I do? How enjoyable was it? To what degree was I in "flow"? To what degree was the activity meaningful? The client then reflects on the day.
Plan for Happiness	A client plans an activity to enhance each of the domains of happiness: pleasant, engaged, and meaningful.
The Best Possible Self	The client writes about his or her best possible life in the future (regarding family, friends, partner, career, health, and hobbies) and imagines that everything went as well as it possibly could.

Note: VIA = Values in Action (see page 35)

PRACTICAL APPLICATION

1. Choose two or three positive psychology activities shown in Table 3-1. Guide a different client, friend, colleague, or family member for each activity.

   Summarize your experience as a coach assigning these activities.

   Summarize the experience from the perspective of your clients who completed each of the activities.

   Which activity did you find to be most effective? Why?

   Do you think that you will integrate these or other positive psychology activities into your coaching practice? Why or why not?

Flow

Flow, also known as "being in the zone" or "one with the music," occurs when one becomes so engaged in an activity that "time flies." This is the state when performance peaks and a person feels a keen sense of accomplishment and well-being. While one may think of elite athletes or only a select few who ever experience this state, the work of Csikszentmihalyi (2004) demonstrated that even the "average" person can achieve this state when the conditions are right. Csikszentmihalyi transferred this concept into a Flow Chart (Figure 3-1), which demonstrates that flow is most likely to occur when the interaction of skill and challenge are matched. On the other hand, when skills and challenges are not matched, myriad unpleasant emotions can occur, as demonstrated in the Flow Chart. Note that flow is more likely to occur when both challenge and skill are at a relatively high level, but can also occur when both skill and challenge are relatively low, such as going for a walk in the woods. When working with clients aiming to achieve a **performance goal,** coaches can help the client to manage goals and daily activities through changes to help better match skill with challenge. This concept is further refined and described—especially in terms of addressing health behavior goals—in Chapter 9.

> One becomes so engaged in an activity that "time flies"

Figure 3-1

CSIKSZENTMIHALYI'S FLOW DIAGRAM

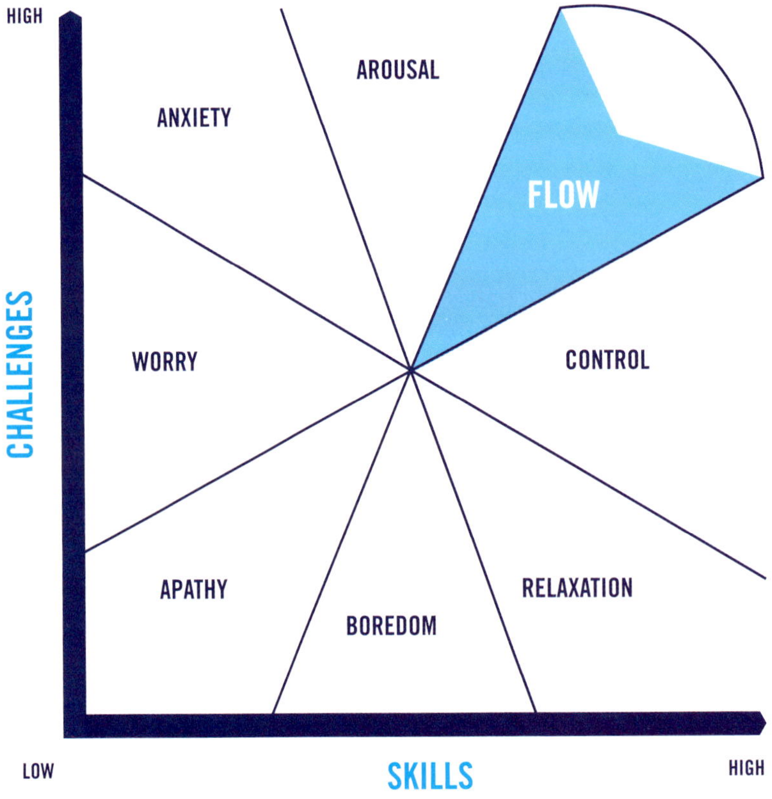

Reprinted with permission from Csikszentmihalyi, M. (2004). Flow, the secret to happiness. Ted Talk, Filmed Feb 2004. www.ted.com. Retrieved January 15, 2014: www.ted.com/talks/mihaly_csikszentmihalyi_on_flow.html

APPLYING POSITIVE PSYCHOLOGY TO THE COACHING EXPERIENCE

While it may be easy to "buy into" the notion that a focus on strengths should be a key driver of the client–coach relationship, the practice of coaching to strengths may prove challenging at first.

As Kaufman (2006) notes, "The clinician is trained to follow the trail of tears. If someone is dissatisfied with life, for example, a coach needs to resist the inclination to immediately hone in on client skill deficits or automatically search for signs of depression, anxiety, or emotional conflict as the true cause of the client's challenges." In fact, it would be outside the coach's **scope of practice** to do so. The coach needs to develop skill in reframing the deficit-based downward spiral of focusing on failures and what is wrong to help the client to see what has proved successful and what is right. Then, the coach must help the client hold onto that success to drive future success. Of course, this is not to say that there is never an occasion to assess weaknesses or aim to improve areas of deficit (see Chapter 7). Rather, the coach should spend vastly more time in the positive realm, while not neglecting an opportunity to undo negative thought processes or behaviors. Importantly, if a sign of a mental health disorder arises during the coaching experience, it is incumbent upon the coach to refer to a mental health professional and not engage in a therapeutic relationship with the client to address that issue, as this is outside the scope of practice of a coach who is not a licensed mental health professional.

ASSESSING WELL-BEING THROUGH THE SATISFACTION WITH LIFE SCALE

One tool that coaches may consider using is the Satisfaction With Life Scale (SWLS) (Pavot & Diener, 1993). This validated survey helps to assess a client's level of subjective well-being. The SWLS offers a global assessment of a client's perception of life satisfaction. For the coach, it offers a starting point for the coaching interaction and opportunity to discuss opportunities for improvement with the client.

SATISFACTION WITH LIFE SCALE

The SWLS is a five-item instrument designed to measure global cognitive judgments of satisfaction with one's life. The scale usually requires only about one minute of a respondent's time. It is available for professional use from Dr. Diener's website: internal.psychology.illinois.edu/~ediener/SWLS.html.

Below are five statements with which you may agree or disagree. Using the 1–7 scale, indicate your agreement with each item by placing the appropriate number on the line preceding that item. Please be open and honest when responding.

7 – Strongly agree

6 – Agree

5 – Slightly agree

4 – Neither agree nor disagree

3 – Slightly disagree

2 – Disagree

1 – Strongly disagree

____ In most ways my life is close to my ideal.

____ The conditions of my life are excellent.

____ I am satisfied with my life.

____ So far I have gotten the important things I want in life.

____ If I could live my life over, I would change almost nothing.

Data from: Diener, E. et al. (1985). The Satisfaction with Life Scale. *Journal of Personality Assessment*, 49, 71–75.

UNDERSTANDING SCORES ON THE SATISFACTION WITH LIFE SCALE

30–35 Very high score; highly satisfied

Respondents who score in this range love their lives and feel that things are going very well. Their lives are not perfect, but they feel that things are about as good as lives get. Furthermore, just because the person is satisfied does not mean he or she is complacent. In fact, growth and challenge might be part of the reason the respondent is satisfied. For most people in this high-scoring range, life is enjoyable, and the major domains of life are going well—work or school, family, friends, leisure, and personal development.

25–29 High score

Individuals who score in this range like their lives and feel that things are going well. Of course their lives are not perfect, but they feel that things are mostly good. Furthermore, just because the person is satisfied does not mean he or she is complacent. In fact, growth and challenge might be part of the reason the respondent is satisfied. For most people in this high-scoring range, life is enjoyable, and the major domains of life are going well—work or school, family, friends, leisure, and personal development. The person may draw motivation from the areas of dissatisfaction.

20–24 Average score

The average of life satisfaction in economically developed nations is in this range—the majority of people are generally satisfied, but have some areas where they very much would like some improvement. Some individuals score in this range because they are mostly satisfied with most areas of their lives but see the need for some improvement in each area. Other respondents score in this range because they are satisfied with most domains of their lives, but have one or two areas where they would like to see large improvements. People scoring in this range is normal in that they have areas of their lives that need improvement. However, an individual in this range would usually like to move to a higher level by making some life changes.

15–19 Slightly below average in life satisfaction

People who score in this range usually have small but significant problems in several areas of their lives, or have many areas that are doing fine but one area that represents a substantial problem for them. If a person has moved temporarily into this level of life satisfaction from a higher level because of some recent event, things will usually improve over time and satisfaction will generally move back up. On the other hand, if a person is chronically slightly dissatisfied with many areas of life, some changes might be in order. Sometimes the person is simply expecting too much, and sometimes life changes are needed. Thus, although temporary dissatisfaction is common and normal, a chronic level of dissatisfaction across a number of areas of life calls for reflection. Some people can gain motivation from a small level of dissatisfaction, but often dissatisfaction across a number of life domains is a distraction, and unpleasant as well. ▶

10–14 Dissatisfied

People who score in this range are substantially dissatisfied with their lives. People in this range may have a number of domains that are not going well, or one or two domains that are going very badly. If life dissatisfaction is a response to a recent event such as bereavement, divorce, or a significant problem at work, the person will probably return over time to his or her former level of higher satisfaction. However, if low levels of life satisfaction have been chronic for the person, some changes are in order—both in attitudes and patterns of thinking, and probably in life activities as well. Low levels of life satisfaction in this range, if they persist, can indicate that things are going badly and life alterations are needed. Furthermore, a person with low life satisfaction in this range is sometimes not functioning well because their unhappiness serves as a distraction. Talking to a friend, member of the clergy, counselor, or other specialist can often help the person get moving in the right direction, although positive change will be up to the person.

5–9 Extremely Dissatisfied

Individuals who score in this range are usually extremely unhappy with their current lives. In some cases this is in reaction to some recent bad event such as widowhood or unemployment. In other cases, it is a response to a chronic problem such as alcoholism or addiction. In yet other cases the extreme dissatisfaction is a reaction due to something bad in life such as recently having lost a loved one. However, dissatisfaction at this level is often due to dissatisfaction in multiple areas of life. Whatever the reason for the low level of life satisfaction, it may be that the help of others is needed—a friend or family member, counseling with a member of the clergy, or help from a psychologist or other counselor. If the dissatisfaction is chronic, the person needs to change, and often others can help.

Summary

To understand life satisfaction scores, it is helpful to understand some of the components that go into most people's experience of satisfaction. One of the most important influences on happiness is social relationships. People who score high on life satisfaction tend to have close and supportive family and friends, whereas those who do not have close friends and family are more likely to be dissatisfied. Of course, the loss of a close friend or family member can cause dissatisfaction with life, and it may take quite some time for the person to bounce back from the loss.

Another factor that influences the life satisfaction of most people is work or school, or performance in an important role such as homemaker or grandparent. When the person enjoys his or her work, whether it is paid or unpaid work, and feels that it is meaningful and important, this contributes to life satisfaction. When work is going poorly because of bad circumstances or a poor fit with the person's strengths, this can lower life satisfaction. When a person has important goals, and is failing to make adequate progress toward them, this too can lead to life dissatisfaction.

A third factor that influences the life satisfaction of most people is personal—satisfaction with the self, religious or spiritual life, learning and growth, and leisure. For many people, these are sources of satisfaction. However, when these sources of personal worth are frustrated, they can be powerful sources of dissatisfaction. Of course there are additional sources of satisfaction and dissatisfaction—some that are common to most people such as health, and others that are unique to each individual. Most people know the factors that lead to their satisfaction or dissatisfaction, although a person's temperament—a general tendency to be happy or unhappy—can color their responses.

There is no one key to life satisfaction, but rather a recipe that includes a number of ingredients. With time and persistent work, people's life satisfaction usually goes up when they are dissatisfied. People who have had a loss recover over time. People who have a dissatisfying relationship or work often make changes over time that will increase their satisfaction. One key ingredient to happiness, as mentioned above, is social relationships, and another key ingredient is to have important goals that derive from one's values, and to make progress toward those goals. For many people it is important to feel a connection to something larger than oneself. When a person tends to be chronically dissatisfied, they should look within themselves and ask whether they need to develop more positive attitudes to life and the world.

VALUES IN ACTION CLASSIFICATION OF STRENGTHS

Another practical tool to help clients focus on strengths is through use of the publicly available, validated, and heavily researched Values in Action (VIA) Classification of Strengths. Psychologists Peterson and Seligman (2004) developed this classification system to parallel psychiatry's diagnostic Bible of pathology—the *Diagnostic and Statistical Manual of Mental Disorders (DSM).* The VIA Classification of Strengths includes 24 character strengths (Table 3-2). Few individuals possess all 24 strengths.

Table 3-2

VIA CLASSIFICATION OF STRENGTHS

VIRTUES	Wisdom and Knowledge	Courage	Humanity	Justice	Temperance	Transcendence
CHARACTER STRENGTHS	Creativity	Bravery	Love	Citizenship	Forgiveness and mercy	Appreciation of beauty and excellence
	Curiosity	Persistence	Kindness	Fairness	Humility	Gratitude
	Open-mindedness	Integrity	Social intelligence	Leadership	Prudence	Hope and optimism
	Love of learning	Vitality			Self-regulation	Humor
	Perspective					Spirituality

After the client completes the 240-question survey (available to take free of charge at www.viame.org), he or she receives a report of strengths, highlighting those attributes that are most dominant (a preview of the survey is presented in Figure 3-2). From there, the client and coach can develop an action plan that will rely heavily on the client's most dominant strengths, which will help them with successful goal completion. The effectiveness of using this tool to help drive a coaching intervention is supported with scientific evidence. For example, in a randomized, controlled trial researchers asked clients to use their VIA-derived top strengths in new ways for one week. The result was increased measures of happiness and engagement and decreased feelings of depression compared to a control group. These differences persisted at follow-up six months later (Seligman et al., 2005).

Figure 3-2

A PREVIEW OF VIA CHARACTER STRENGTHS SURVEY

1. Being able to come up with new and different ideas is one of my strong points.
   ◯ Very much like me ◯ Like me ◯ Neutral ◯ Unlike me ◯ Very much unlike me

2. I have taken frequent stands in the face of strong opposition.
   ◯ Very much like me ◯ Like me ◯ Neutral ◯ Unlike me ◯ Very much unlike me

3. I never quit a task before it is done.
   ◯ Very much like me ◯ Like me ◯ Neutral ◯ Unlike me ◯ Very much unlike me

4. I always keep my promises.
   ◯ Very much like me ◯ Like me ◯ Neutral ◯ Unlike me ◯ Very much unlike me

5. I have no trouble eating healthy foods.
   ◯ Very much like me ◯ Like me ◯ Neutral ◯ Unlike me ◯ Very much unlike me

6. I always look on the bright side.
   ◯ Very much like me ◯ Like me ◯ Neutral ◯ Unlike me ◯ Very much unlike me

7. I am a spiritual person.
   ◯ Very much like me ◯ Like me ◯ Neutral ◯ Unlike me ◯ Very much unlike me

8. I know how to handle myself in different social situations.
   ◯ Very much like me ◯ Like me ◯ Neutral ◯ Unlike me ◯ Very much unlike me

9. I always finish what I start.
   ◯ Very much like me ◯ Like me ◯ Neutral ◯ Unlike me ◯ Very much unlike me

10. I really enjoy doing small favors for friends.
    ◯ Very much like me ◯ Like me ◯ Neutral ◯ Unlike me ◯ Very much unlike me

11. There are people in my life who care as much about my feelings and well-being as they do about their own.
    ◯ Very much like me ◯ Like me ◯ Neutral ◯ Unlike me ◯ Very much unlike me

12. As a leader, I treat everyone equally regardless of his or her experience.
    ◯ Very much like me ◯ Like me ◯ Neutral ◯ Unlike me ◯ Very much unlike me

PRACTICAL APPLICATION

2. Go to www.viame.org to register and complete your own free VIA Character Strengths survey.

What are your top three strengths?

How could knowledge of these strengths help you achieve a desired behavior-change goal?

USING STRENGTHS IN COACHING INTERVENTIONS

A growing body of research suggests substantial benefits from focusing on strengths, both on the individual level and on an organizational level. For instance, in one study, the use of strength-based curricula in school-aged children was associated with increased **internal motivation** and effort (Louis, 2009). Kids who were most skilled at using their strengths were better at engaging social supports and building upon prior success. In the workplace, those who consistently tap into their strengths have higher engagement, work satisfaction, goal attainment, and performance (reviewed in Biswas-Diener, 2011). Positive psychology is rooted in scientific evidence. The challenge for the coach is to apply strength-based interventions in a manner that parallels what the evidence supports.

In a compelling article, Biswas-Diener (2011) provides tools to help the coach do this effectively. Biswas-Diener conducted a survey of practitioners of positive psychology, mostly therapists and coaches. Nearly all practiced in a similar manner:

- Conduct a formal strengths assessment survey, such as the VIA assessment, to identify strengths. This assessment is typically done within the first three sessions of the client–coach relationship to help "set the stage" for the coaching intervention.
- Discuss and plan ways in which clients can use these strengths to achieve their goals.

Biswas-Diener (2011) refers to this as the "identify and use" approach to strengths assessment. While it is commonly practiced, Biswas-Diener advocates for a more sophisticated approach to positive psychology coaching, which he labels "strengths development." In contrast to "identify and use" approaches in which the intervention aims to encourage the client to use a strength more often, strengths development focuses on how to use one's strengths in an ideal way—either more or less—depending on the situation. Biswas-Diener advises coaches to apply the following principles with strengths assessment and intervention:

- Pay special attention to situational factors that may affect how strengths may be best utilized to achieve success.
- Ensure that clients understand that strengths are not necessarily "fixed" assets and can be enhanced and improved upon over time.
- Consider that strengths interact with values, personal interests, and other strengths. Individual strengths should not be assessed in isolation.
- Strengths-based coaching is not appropriate to every person in every circumstance. In some cases, a focus on strengths can decrease motivation or interfere with one's self-identity. Coaches should take individual client factors into consideration at all times.

In Chapter 8, an effective method of strengths-based coaching is presented based on the work of Dr. Biswas-Diener.

3. Identify a client, friend, colleague, or family member to take through a sample 20-minute positive psychology coaching session. For this session, proceed through the following steps:

Open the session with a request to the client to provide a 1–2 minute introduction of him- or herself, focusing on what the client perceives to be his or her strengths and successes. What were these strengths?

Reflect back to the client the most salient strengths that you heard him or her describe. Confirm your understanding. How did the client respond?

Ask the client to describe a situation in which these strengths are most salient or beneficial. Summarize the response.

Ask the client to describe how these strengths may help him or her to achieve the goal that he or she hired you to help with. Summarize the response.

Request that the client try to use one or more of these strengths in a new way over the next week. Follow up with the client to get a report of his or her experience. Summarize the client's experience.

PRACTICAL APPLICATION

4. You are working with the human resources director of a local nonprofit agency. She has been charged with implementing the organization's worksite wellness program. She read that implementing positive psychology in the workplace can help increase productivity, morale, and retention. She asks for your insights in helping her to develop a worksite wellness program rooted in positive psychology.

   What key characteristics should you include in helping to develop the intervention?

   Envision and describe what an ideal worksite wellness program rooted in positive psychology might look like.

   How would you help the human resources director position the initiative to get buy-in from the executive team and employees?

SUMMARY

Positive psychology provides a powerful framework upon which to build a coaching intervention to ultimately lead to sustained behavioral change. Developing competency in strengths-based coaching will help the behavior-change coach to effectively serve clients from broad backgrounds and with diverse goals.

EXPANSION QUIZ
Multiple-choice quiz available if you expand to the full experience

References

Biswas-Diener, R. (2011). Applied positive psychology: Progress and challenges. *The European Health Psychologist,* 13, 24–26.

Biswas-Diener, R., Kashdan, T.B., & Minhas, G. (2011). A dynamic approach to psychological strength development and intervention. *The Journal of Positive Psychology,* 6, 2, 106–118.

Csikszentmihalyi, M. (2004). Flow, the secret to happiness. Ted Talk, Filmed Feb 2004. www.ted.com. Retrieved January 15, 2014: www.ted.com/talks/mihaly_csikszentmihalyi_on_flow.html

Diener, E. et al. (1985). The Satisfaction with Life Scale. *Journal of Personality Assessment,* 49, 71–75.

Kauffman, C. (2006). Positive psychology: The science at the heart of coaching. In: Stober, D.S. & Grant, A.M. (Eds.). *Evidence-Based Coaching.* Hoboken, N.J.: John Wiley & Sons.

Louis, M.C. (2009). *A Summary and Critique of Existing Strengths-based Educational Research Utilizing the Clifton Strengths Finder.* Internal paper, The Gallup Organization.

Lyubomirsky, S. & Layous, K. (2013). How do simple positive activities increase well being? *Current Directions in Psychological Science,* 22, 1, 57–62.

Pavot, W. & Diener, E. (1993). Review of the Satisfaction with Life Scale. *Psychological Assessment,* 5, 164–172.

Peterson, C. & Seligman, E.P. (2004). *Character Strengths and Virtues: A Handbook and Classification.* Washington, D.C.: APA Press.

Seligman, M.E.P. & Csikszentmihalyi, M. (2000). Positive psychology: An introduction. *American Psychologist,* 55, 1, 5–14.

Seligman, M.E.P. et al. (2005). Positive psychology progress: Empirical validation of interventions. *American Psychologist,* 60, 410–421.

Sin, N.L. & Lyubomirsky, S. (2009). Enhancing well-being and alleviating depressive symptoms with positive psychology interventions. *American Psychologist,* 60, 410–421.

Additional Resources

Authentic Happiness: www.authentichappiness.sas.upenn.edu

The International Positive Psychology Association (IPPA): www.ippanetwork.org

Journal of Positive Psychology: www.psypress.com/journals

Dr. Ed Diener's lab and scales are available to use at no charge: internal.psychology.illinois.edu/~ediener/SWLS.html

Dr. Barbara Fredrickson's websites on positive emotions: www.unc.edu/peplab/news.html and www.positivityratio.com

Dr. Biswas-Diener's Positive Acorn Positive Psychology website: positiveacorn.com

Sonja Lyubomirsky's website on happiness: sonjalyubomirsky.com

University of Pennsylvania Positive Psychology Center website: www.ppc.sas.upenn.edu

Introduction to Section II:

AWARENESS

Through the course of behavioral change, clients go through a predictable, though nonlinear, cycle of change, herein referred to as the ACE cycle of change, which stands for awareness, choice, and execution (Stober & Grant, 2006). The first stage of awareness occurs as an individual begins to recognize and explore a gap between a current behavior and a desired behavior. Coaching a client through this phase of change includes the use of strategies and communication techniques to help the client better understand and explore his or her present state and future vision.

» The American Council on Exercise (ACE) is not to be confused with the ACE cycle of change referenced throughout this guide.

The coach's role in this process is to help identify a client's current stage of change, employ techniques to help the client continue to progress through the stages, explore a client's ambivalence about change, help the client come to his or her own recognition of whether and how a change should occur, and help a client more fully explore an overall vision of what life would be like once the change is complete.

OVER THE COURSE OF THIS SECTION, COACHES WILL GAIN COMPETENCY IN THE FOLLOWING THREE PRINCIPLES:

- Coaching to a client's stage of change
- Motivational interviewing
- Visioning

The International Coach Federation (ICF) Core Competencies that are addressed in the three chapters in this section include: (1) Meeting ethical guidelines and professional standards; (3) Establishing trust and intimacy with the client; (4) Coaching presence; (5) Active listening; (6) Powerful questioning; (7) Direct communication; and (8) Creating awareness

▶ **For more information on the ICF Coaching Competencies, refer to the Introduction and Appendix A.**

Reference: Stober, D.S. & Grant, A.M. (Eds.) (2006). *Evidence-Based Coaching.* Hoboken, N.J.: John Wiley & Sons.

CHAPTER 4

CHAPTER 4

STAGES OF CHANGE

LEARNING OBJECTIVES

After reading this chapter, the coach will be able to:

- ________ Define each of the stages of change: precontemplation, contemplation, preparation, action, and maintenance
- ________ Explain the concept of relapse and its role in the stages of change
- ________ Identify a client's stage of change and tailor the behavioral intervention accordingly

For most, behavioral change is a struggle. While a coach is poised to help a client be successful, the reality is that a lasting change will occur only once a client is psychologically ready to truly change his or her lifestyle. Even then, change is not guaranteed. An individual must have not only the motivation to change, but also the capability and opportunity (Michie, van Stralen, & West, 2011). **The transtheoretical model of behavioral change (TTM)** (also referred to as the **stages of change model**) acknowledges that behavioral change is a process that develops over time, with an individual progressing through several stages in the change process. Stages range from **precontemplation** ("I don't have a problem") to **maintenance** ("This is who I am and what I do"). Clients often travel through a nonlinear and convoluted path, frequently with multiple relapses along the way.

THE SCIENCE SUPPORTING THE STAGES OF CHANGE MODEL

Psychologist James Prochaska first described the stages of change in his work to increase the effectiveness of smoking-cessation programs (Prochaska, 1979). In the ensuing 35 years, more than 1,500 articles have been published on the stages of change in topics ranging from smoking cessation, exercise, eating patterns, radon testing, alcohol abuse, and weight control to condom use for HIV protection, organizational change, use of sunscreens to prevent skin cancer, drug abuse, medical compliance, mammography screening, and stress management (Prochaska & Norcross, 2010). A lack of uniformity and quality in study design precludes a strong statement of efficacy, though the framework appears to provide some benefit for many behavioral changes. A 2014 Cochrane Review concluded that the evidence to support the use of this model is limited due to risk of bias and imprecision in study design and that more high-quality randomized controlled trials are needed to prove its value. With that said, there is low-quality scientific evidence that use of the model may lead to improved nutrition behaviors, physical activity, and weight management (Mastellos et al., 2014). The model is particularly strong for smoking cessation, at least in young people (Stanton & Grimshaw, 2013).

Despite the lack of high-quality evidence supporting the role of the stages of change model in behavioral change, it serves an important purpose of helping action-oriented professionals who may be used to providing advice to gain skill in recognizing those individuals who may not yet be ready to change, and what to do to help them increase their readiness to change.

THE STAGES OF CHANGE MODEL AND ITS ROLE IN INCREASING AWARENESS

The stages of change model is useful in helping to recognize a client's readiness to change and to tailor the behavioral change intervention accordingly.

THE STAGES

As a client readies for a lasting behavioral change, he or she is likely to progress through five stages of change: precontemplation, **contemplation, preparation, action,** and maintenance. The client may progress linearly, waver between stages, or progress and then relapse. Each of the stages are described in subsequent sections, though the most important areas of focus in the **awareness** phase of the **ACE cycle of change** is for those in the precontemplation and contemplation stages of change.

Precontemplation

In the precontemplation stage, the individual is not considering change, does not believe change is right for him or her, is generally satisfied with the way things are, and does not have any intention of changing behavior in the foreseeable future, which ordinarily means six months. The individual very likely does not even have awareness that there is a need for change or that there is a problem behavior. Others around the individual may be aware of a need for change, so clients at this stage may often appear before a coach under duress. Clients at this stage likely have heard from doctors, spouses, family members, and friends that they "should" change. These individuals may be seen as being "in denial" or believe themselves to be "immune" to health problems, or simply have given up on change. The client is largely resistant to change, may fear failure (based on irrational thinking, including "I can't"), may lack accurate information, or may feel so overwhelmed by barriers to change that he or she sees no possibility of changing. Self-statements may involve things such as, "I don't have any problems that need changing," or "My family is just overweight and that's our genetics." People at this stage will avoid talking about, or even thinking about, changing their behavior and will appear unmotivated. They will not read or pay attention to outside influences or public information campaigns. Until these individuals see that their behaviors are in some way at odds with their own personal goals and strivings, they will not likely move past this stage.

The client is largely resistant to change

COACHING TIPS

The goals during the precontemplation stage incorporate encouraging exploration, identifying reasons for change, and validating the client's own thoughts, while leaving the relationship positive enough to revisit the idea of changing in the future. This involves some or all of the following techniques:

- *Validating:* "I get why you feel the way you do about not changing at this time."
- *Respecting the client's locus of control:* "You are the one who knows what's best for you in terms of whether or not you are ready to change your behavior."
- *Provision of information in an autonomy-supporting way:* "This may or may not interest you, but I do believe that performing more exercise would be a healthy and beneficial change to make for someone with your health risks."
- *Discussion of future concerns:* "What kind of difficulties does your weight/hypertension/anger/diabetes cause you now? What do you imagine it will be like if you don't adopt healthier behaviors?"
- *"Siding with the client" by recognizing the pressure the client must feel:* "I'm sure you get lots of input and people telling you that you 'should' change and it must be a real pain for you."
- *Respecting the client's lack of readiness to change and his or her autonomy:* "I get that you are not ready to change now, and that when it feels right for you, you'll do it in your own way and for the right reasons, just like everyone else does." **Empathy,** acceptance, reflection, and sharing are key elements of the developing relationship.

Zimmerman, Olsen, and Bosworth (2000) offer the following questions that coaches might ask a client in the precontemplation stage of change. These questions are designed to help "I won't..." turn into "I see the value..."

- What would have to happen for you to know that this is a problem?
- What warning signs would let you know that this is a problem?
- What have you tried to change in the past?
- You may not be ready now, which of course is your choice, but here's how we can stay connected if you change your mind in the future and want to discuss this some more.

Contemplation

This stage is characterized by those individuals who are actively considering making a change within the next six months. This stage is marked by **ambivalence** and weighing of the pros and cons of changing. Clients may be open to hearing about the value of making a change soon, and may be aware of the benefits of changing to a healthier behavior, but do not believe now is the right time. They may know why a change is necessary, but think the barriers outweigh the benefits of changing. This stage is best characterized by the belief, "I may." Coaches may witness ambivalence about change, hear beliefs that "it will be hard," uncover thoughts suggesting that the client cannot yet see him- or herself changing, and generally understand that the client is struggling with both the amount of effort involved in changing and the desire to do so. They may have self-talk that includes such statements as, "I have a problem and think I should work on it," or "I think if I stop smoking so much, maybe I'll stop coughing, but then again my diabetes might kick up if I eat instead of smoke." There is some ambivalence or "fence sitting." Clients in the contemplation stage may not necessarily be actively searching for answers, but are quite open to paying attention if information about change is brought to their attention. People at this stage can remain here for a long time, as they balance the costs and benefits of changing.

COACHING TIPS

The most effective tool coaches can use with clients in the contemplation stage is **motivational interviewing,** which is described in detail in Chapter 5. For clients who are not quite ready to explore their ambivalence about change, the coach may suggest to the client, "I understand that you are thinking about changing, but not in the near future, and that when you are ready, you will take the next step."

Zimmerman, Olsen, and Bosworth (2000) suggest asking:

- Why do you want to change at this time?
- What things, (people, programs, or behaviors) have helped you in the past?
- What would help you at this time?
- What do you think you need to learn about changing?

Here the coach is demonstrating active listening skills, evoking **change talk** (see Chapter 5), and using **positive psychology** to bring out the client's strengths and link them to the desired behavior changes.

THE READINESS TO CHANGE RULER

A useful tool for coaches to use in assessing a client's stage of change is the Readiness to Change Ruler (Miller & Rollnick, 1998). This involves the coach asking the client to simply self-report on a scale from 0 to 10, with 0 representing "Not considering change now" and 10 representing "Already changing." When working with clients who believe they are not ready to change, or are leaning on that side of the scale, ask the following questions:

- How will you know when it is time to think about changing?
- What signals will tell you to start thinking about changing?
- What qualities in yourself are important to you?
- What connection is there between those qualities and "not considering change now?"

For those who are in the middle range on this "ruler," the following questions will be helpful:

- Why did you put your mark there and not rate yourself lower in terms of readiness to change?
- What might make you put your mark a little higher on this scale?
- What are the good things about the way you are currently trying to change?
- What are the not-so-good things?
- What could be the positive results of changing now?
- What are the main barriers for you to change?

When working with clients who are closer to changing, but are not already doing so, have them do the following:

- Pick one of the barriers to change and together we can list some of the things that could help you overcome this barrier.
- Pick one of those things and together we can determine how you can do it by __________ (fill in a date).

When working with clients who are changing, ask the following:

- What made you decide to take this particular step in changing?
- What has worked in the past for you?
- What helped it work?
- What could help it work even better?
- What else could help?
- Can you break it down further to see what else could help?
- Let's pick one of those steps and do it by __________ (fill in the blank).

When working with clients who are changing and are in the maintenance stage, be sure to congratulate them and then ask:

- What's helping you stay in this stage?
- What else could help you?
- What are your high-risk temptations?

Ask clients who have relapsed the following questions:

- What worked for a while?
- Long-term change always involves a few steps forward and a couple backward in order to go forward again, so I'm wondering what you learned from this experience that will help you when you give it another try.

Preparation

Coaches with clients in the preparation stage of change understand that change is imminent, typically within the next month, though there is the likelihood that some unsuccessful efforts have been made within the past year. Perhaps the client has already joined a gym but does not go. The client is on the brink of change, actively planning and preparing for a specific change, and may have experimented with attempts in the past—in a sense, he or she is "testing the waters." These clients will appear more committed to change, are confident about their ability to create healthier behaviors, and understand the benefits of doing so. They may have gathered information, are motivated to accept support, and welcome offers to create new behaviors. Coaches may hear about their plans and previous actions, as well as self-talk such as, "I know I have to, and will do, something, so what should I do?" Think of this as a fact-gathering, research step. Clients require time, attention, and energy to move forward.

COACHING TIPS

Coaches with clients in the preparation stage are wise to encourage and commend the decision to explore avenues for behavioral change and assist in prioritizing the small steps necessary to take action and create the social support systems that can be harnessed, while identifying the barriers and obstacles that might get in the way.

Coaches may offer praise, such as, "I bet it feels great for you to know that you've decided to take steps toward a healthier lifestyle." They may also discuss priorities with clients—"I wonder what you might think would be a good next step."—and reinforce wise decisions and discuss further if the client is making poor choices.

Coaches can assist in overcoming barriers and obstacles by asking "What kinds of problems do you anticipate in getting to the gym/getting to your doctor/stocking your pantry with healthier foods, etc?"

The coach will use small-step thinking and planning: "So it sounds like you think buying avocados on the way home tonight is a great first step, and I totally agree. From what you said earlier, your wife/husband/partner may be able to meet you at the grocery store to help you decide what else would be good to keep in the pantry."

Clients in this stage need help in making their plans come to life and overcoming potential obstacles. Many find that writing plans down with dates attached will help turn their thoughts into action, and help them replace triggers with substitute behaviors such as not keeping alcohol in the home or bringing lunch to work. Tools such as brainstorming and listing many small steps that are SMART (i.e., specific, measurable, attainable, relevant, and time-bound) is helpful (see Chapter 9). Without telling clients what to do, wise coaches ask them to identify steps they can imagine taking to overcome barriers and resistances. Anticipating these feelings and real-life obstacles and discussing the client's remedies will go a long way to helping the client move to the next step, which is action.

COACHING TIPS

The preparation stage calls on the coach to help the client design action plans. Helping clients discover, create, and commit, rather than directing them is critically important. Effective goal setting is key in the preparation stage. Chapter 9 focuses exclusively on this skill.

Action

Individuals in the action stage have begun making observable changes in their lifestyle choices and behaviors, likely within the past three to six months. These clients are energetic and committed, and are searching for encouragement and incentives to continue engaging in their changes. This is a bridge to the next step, which is maintenance. During the action phase, clients rely on a great deal of willpower. A client may think, "I am really working at this!" The concern at this stage is relapse if the individual is not properly prepared and supported for behavioral change. This stage is a time to implement the plans made in the preparation stage and develop strategies to overcome anticipated obstacles. Clients will need help in remembering "why" they began the process of change.

These clients are energetic and committed

COACHING TIPS

Finding "early wins" for clients in the action stage is important to encourage continued behavioral change. In addition, helping clients see the bridge between their new chosen behaviors, perhaps their "ideal version of themselves," and their inner values and strengths, will strengthen the commitment to maintain the new behaviors. Helping clients celebrate even their smallest successes helps to build momentum for ongoing change.

Maintenance

Clients in the maintenance stage of behavioral change have sustained their change for more than six months. Being able to effectively avoid the lures of returning to old behavioral patterns is the essential challenge at this point. Clients will often remind themselves of how far they have come. Individuals at this stage are often more internally motivated for meaningful change, and are better able to rely on habit than willpower.

COACHING TIPS

Coaches find that clients in the maintenance stage benefit from continuing to set new "stretch goals" (i.e., difficult but attainable goals), always recalling their "why," developing new internal and external motivators, and actually serving as role models for others.

Relapse

Relapse is a normal part of behavioral change. In fact, most clients will progress through the stages of change up to the action stage multiple times prior to reaching the maintenance phase, due to repeated lapses into old behaviors. A critical part of coaching is to prepare clients for relapse.

COACHING TIPS

Coaches should always incorporate relapse-management activities into their sessions, such as rehearsing the management of difficult situations, strengthening coaching strategies, and purposefully avoiding situations that trigger the unwanted behavior.

In the awareness phase of the ACE cycle of change, attention is best focused on those in the precontemplation and contemplation stages of change. These are the stages during which effective behavioral change coaching can help a client progress to the **choice** phase of the ACE cycle of change. Those in preparation, action, and maintenance already have advanced to the choice and **execution** phases of the ACE cycle of change.

A summary of the stages of change and potential stage-specific coaching goals and strategies is presented in Table 4-1.

PODCAST
The founder of the stages of change model, Dr. James Prochaska discusses how to coach to a client's stage of change to help him or her ultimately achieve and maintain a behavioral change.

Table 4-1
THE STAGES OF BEHAVIORAL CHANGE

STAGE	TRAITS	GOALS	STRATEGIES
Precontemplation	Unaware or under-aware of the problem, or believe that it cannot be solved	Increase awareness of the risks of maintaining the status quo and of the benefits of making a change Focus on addressing something relevant to them Have them start thinking about change	Validate lack of readiness to change and clarify that this decision is theirs Encourage reevaluation of current behavior and self-exploration, while not taking action Explain and personalize the inherent risks Utilize general sources, including media, Internet, and brochures to increase awareness
Contemplation	Aware of the problem and weighing the benefits versus risks of change Have little understanding of how to go about changing	Inform them of available options Provide cues to action and some basic structured direction	Validate lack of readiness to change and clarify that this decision is theirs Encourage evaluation of the pros and cons of making change Identify and promote new, positive outcome expectations and boost self-confidence Offer invitations to become more active (e.g., free trials)
Preparation	Seeking opportunities to participate in activity (combine intent and behavior with activity)	Structured, regular programming with frequent positive feedback and reinforcements on their progress	Verify that the individual has the underlying skills for behavior change and encourage small steps toward building self-efficacy Identify and assist with problem-solving obstacles Help the client identify social support and establish goals
Action	Desire for opportunities to maintain activities Changing beliefs and attitudes High risk for lapses or returns to undesirable behavior	Establish the new behavior as a habit through motivation and adherence to the desired behavior	Behavior-modification strategies Focus on restructuring cues and social support toward building long-term change Increase awareness to inevitable lapses and bolster self-efficacy in coping with lapses Reiterate long-term benefits of adherence Require continual feedback on progress
Maintenance	Empowered, but desire a means to maintain adherence Good capability to deal with lapses	Maintain support systems Maintain interest and avoid boredom or burnout	Reevaluate strategies currently in effect Plan for contingencies with support systems, although this may no longer be needed Reinforce the need for a transition from external to internal rewards Plan for potential lapses Encourage program variety

PRACTICAL APPLICATION

1. With their permission, discuss behavioral change with three clients, friends, family members, or colleagues.

   Identify the stage of change for each individual.

   Develop a strategy to help each individual move the next stage of change.

   Describe your experience.

SELF-EFFICACY

Self-efficacy is the belief in one's own capabilities to successfully make a change. At least six types of experience inform a client's self-efficacy (Rogers & Mantell, 2013). Coaches can help support a client in building self-efficacy by creating program factors that will help create positive experiences in each of these six domains:

Past performance

Observation of someone else's performance

Persuasion from feedback and motivational statements

Perceptive of difficulty of change, both mental and physiological

Mood related to making the change. Excitement, happiness, and satisfaction improve self-efficacy, while fear, anxiety, and frustration decrease self-efficacy.

Imagined experiences of success or failure at making the change

2. A client shares that she would like to lose weight, but she does not think that she is capable of doing so.

Describe some potential reasons why the client may have low self-efficacy.

Outline several strategies a coach could use to help a client improve self-efficacy as it relates to weight management. Include one example from each of the six types of experiences that affect self-efficacy, as described in the chapter.

STRATEGIES FOR COACHES

Prochaska, Norcross, and DiClemente (2013) describe a number of "practice recommendations" in applying the stages of change model:

- *Assess the client's stage of change.* At the initial coaching session and subsequent visits, assess the client's current stage of change and adapt the coaching approach accordingly.
- *Recognize that not all clients are in the action stage.* Most coaching clients are not in the action stage. The tendency to jump to planning and action-oriented goal setting when working with clients does a disservice to most clients in facilitating long-term behavioral change. There is value in tailoring the approach to the client's current stage of change.
- *Assist clients in progressing through one stage at a time.* Focus on helping clients move from one stage to the next rather than on making monumental jumps. For example, an intervention for someone in the precontemplation stage may include efforts to increase awareness and recognition of the potential value of change. The goal should not be to start a new program tomorrow.
- *Conceptualize change as a process, not a technique.* Change occurs through a predictable process. While different tools and approaches can help facilitate changes, the techniques themselves are not the source of change.
- *Tailor the coaching approach to the client's stage of change.* A client's coaching needs and communication approach varies at different stages of change. Prochaska, Norcross, and DiClemente (2013) suggest the following:
    - ✔ A client in the precontemplation stage should receive coaching in a "nurturing parent" style.
    - ✔ A client in the contemplation stage should receive coaching in a "Socratic teacher" style (i.e., from someone who helps clients recognize their own strengths and insights—essentially, the process of motivational interviewing as described in Chapter 5).
    - ✔ A client in the preparation stage should receive coaching in an "expert coach" style—from a coach who has "been through many crucial matches" and can effectively work with the client to develop a top-notch action plan.
    - ✔ A client in the action or maintenance stage should receive coaching in more of a "consultant" approach in that—with the client's permission—the coach provides expert insights and tips when the plan starts to veer off course.

SUMMARY

The stages of change model is an important and useful theory of behavioral change with which every coach should be familiar. More, it is a framework for change that a coach can translate into action to help clients successfully progress through the stages to achieve long-lasting behavioral change.

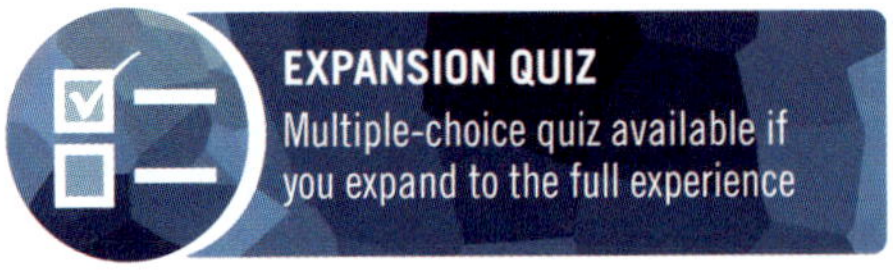

References

Mastellos, N. et al. (2014). Transtheoretical model stages of change for dietary and physical exercise modification in weight loss management for overweight and obese adults. *Cochrane Database of Systematic Reviews*, 2, CD008066.

Michie, S., van Stralen, M.M, & West, R. (2011). The behavior change wheel: A new method for characterizing and designing behavior change interventions. *Implementation Science*, 6, 42.

Miller, W.R. & Rollnick, W. (1998). *Motivational Interviewing: Preparing People to Change.* Professional training videotape series. Albuquerque, N.M.: University of New Mexico.

Prochaska, J.O. (1979). *Systems of Psychotherapy: A Transtheoretical Analysis.* Homewood, Ill.: Dorsey-Press.

Prochaska, J.O. & Norcross, J.C. (2010). *Systems of Psychotherapy: A Transtheoretical Analysis* (7th ed.). Pacific Grove, Calif.: Brooks-Cole.

Prochaska, J.O., Norcross, J.C. & DiClemente, C.C. (2013). Applying the stages of change. *Psychotherapy in Australia*, 19, 2, 10–15

Rogers, T. & Mantell, M. (2013). Health behavior sciences. In: American Council on Exercise. *ACE Health Coach Manual.* San Diego: American Council on Exercise.

Stanton, A. & Grimshaw, G. (2013). Tobacco cessation interventions for young people. *Cochrane Database of Systematic Reviews*, 8, CD003289, DOI: 10.1002/14651858.CD003289.pub5.

Zimmerman, G.L., Olsen, C.G. & Bosworth, M.F. (2000). A 'stages of change' approach to helping patients change behavior. *American Family Physician*, 61, 5, 1409–1416.

CHAPTER 5

CHAPTER 5

MOTIVATIONAL INTERVIEWING

LEARNING OBJECTIVES

After reading this chapter, the coach will be able to:

- Explain the concept of motivational interviewing, including what it *is* and what it *is not.*
- Use open-ended questions, affirming, reflective listening, and summarizing when communicating with clients
- Recognize when it is appropriate to use motivational interviewing
- Function at a beginner or higher level in using motivational interviewing

Motivational interviewing (MI) describes a communication strategy in which a coach partners with a client to explore **ambivalence** about a given behavioral change. The client takes center stage and the coach's role is to facilitate an evolution of a client's thought processes to help the client develop the internal desire to make a change.

Since 1983, when psychologists Bill Miller and Stephen Rollnick published their first paper on the efficacy of MI in the treatment of alcohol addiction, MI has revolutionized the field of behavioral change, including health behavior change. Over time, Drs. Miller and Rollnick have refined their teaching in response to findings from the massive amount of scientific literature accumulated on MI, including more than 25,000 citations and 200 randomized controlled trials (Miller & Rollnick, 2013). Importantly, however, the spirit of MI is unchanged. As the authors state in the 3rd edition of their text *Motivational Interviewing: Helping People Change:* "We continue to emphasize that MI involves a collaborative partnership with clients, a respectful evoking of their own motivation and wisdom, and a radical acceptance recognizing that ultimately whether change happens is each person's own choice, an **autonomy** that cannot be taken away no matter how much one might wish to at times" (Miller & Rollnick, 2013). This essence of MI underlies the concepts, definitions, and activities highlighted in this chapter. For a more complete education on MI, readers are strongly encouraged to review Miller and Rollnick's text.

ACCOMPANYING VIDEO: Interview and tutorial with Dr. Bill Miller, the founder of motivational interviewing

AMBIVALENCE

MI is a particularly effective approach to facilitate behavioral change among clients who experience a degree of ambivalence about the change—the person wants to change and sees the advantages but also feels some hesitancy to change and acknowledges its downsides. This is a well-recognized state on the path to change, in parallel with the **contemplation** stage of change described by Prochaska (1979) (see Chapter 4). The role of the coach is to help the client explore this ambivalence. If a client is not experiencing ambivalence—that is, the client has already bought in to the need to change—the strategy of MI is not necessary. The client may just be ready to get started! However, the fundamentals of effective communication upon which MI is built still apply.

ACCOMPANYING VIDEO: Master Coach Billie Frances helps coaches in training explore the concepts of ambivalence and empathy.

A COMMUNICATION STYLE

At the root of MI is a style of communication that may best be defined as a **guiding style** rather than directing or following styles. A guiding style of communication is one in which the coach helps to motivate, encourage, support, and assist a client in making a change; the coach is engaged, but the client is the main player. This is in contrast to a **directing style** in which the coach leads, tells, and decides (here the coach is "in charge" and the client is a passive player), and to a **following style** in which the coach allows, listens, and understands the client (where the coach is a passive player, and the client drives the agenda). While there are times to direct or follow, effective use of MI requires that the coach communicates in a guiding style the majority of the time.

Implementing a guiding style of communication is often challenging for health and fitness professionals who are used to directing and providing their expertise, advice, and recommendations. For example, a fitness professional working with an overweight client may feel compelled to direct the client to begin a walking program or resistance-training regimen. A registered dietitian may feel it is her duty to recommend five daily servings of fruits and vegetables to a client at risk for heart disease. Miller and Rollnick (2013) refer to this tendency to give advice, push recommendations, and offer solutions the **righting reflex.** While well meaning, the coach's eagerness to promote the positive change in a client ambivalent about change can invoke the ambivalent client's instinct to "defend" the status quo, making a sustained behavioral change less likely. As Miller and Rollnick (2013) suggest "if you are arguing for change and your client is arguing against it, you've got it exactly backward."

THE SPIRIT OF MI

Miller and Rollnick (2013) describe four key characteristics that make up the "spirit of MI": collaboration, acceptance, compassion, and evocation.

COLLABORATION

MI is inherently client-centered, with the fundamental belief that the client is the ultimate expert on his or her life. Miller and Rollnick (2013) describe the relationship between client and coach best: MI is "dancing rather than wrestling... a good MI conversation looks as smooth as a ballroom waltz. Someone is still leading in the dance...without tripping or stepping on toes. Without partnership there is no dance."

ACCEPTANCE

MI is rooted in an unwavering acceptance of the client, otherwise known as "unconditional positive regard." The client–coach relationship must be rooted in respect, trust, and **empathy,** as detailed in Chapters 1 and 2.

COMPASSION

Miller and Rollnick (2013) added compassion to their discussion of MI to emphasize that MI should be practiced in the best interest and for the ultimate welfare of the client, not for some secondary gain or benefit to the coach.

EVOCATION

While the coach may be able to quickly identify what the client "needs" to do to successfully change (e.g., eat less, exercise more, or stop smoking), it is the role of the coach to *evoke* this recognition from the client rather than *telling* the client what he or she needs to do (a clear-cut example of the righting reflex). It is the belief that the client already has the strengths, motivation, and desire that he or she needs, and together the coach and client will find them. Miller describes evocation as calling forth the strength and wisdom from within the client.

Calling forth the strength and wisdom from within the client

CORE SKILLS

MI focuses heavily on four key skill areas, which Miller and Rollnick (2013) refer to as OARS: open-ended questioning, affirming, reflecting, and summarizing. An additional skill of how to most effectively inform and advise is also discussed in this section. Mastery of these five skills is essential to be a highly effective coach.

OPEN-ENDED QUESTIONING

Open-ended questions cannot be answered simply with a "yes" or "no." For example, a nurse coaching a client with diabetes could ask the closed-ended question "are you checking your blood sugar?" or the open-ended version "What has been your experience with checking blood sugar this week?" The first question will get a yes or no response. The second will provide the client the opportunity to share more about the experience and provide the nurse with insights into the client's successes and challenges. This exploration strengthens the client–coach partnership and sets the foundation in evoking motivation to change.

PRACTICAL APPLICATION

1. Proceed through your day and keep tally of the times that you ask open-ended questions and closed-ended questions.

   What proportion of your questions were open-ended versus closed-ended?

   How were the quality of your conversations different based on the types of questions you asked?

   Summarize your experience.

AFFIRMING

Through the use of affirming statements that highlight a client's strengths, abilities, and positive efforts, the coach helps the client to gain **self-efficacy** and confidence—key attributes to drive **internal motivation** and desire to change. This is a focus on what is going right, rather than on what is going wrong. Affirming offers multiple benefits, including improved retention, decreased defensiveness, increased receptivity to constructive feedback, and progress toward a behavioral change.

The most productive **affirmations** are client-focused, with use of the word "you" much more than "I." For instance, instead of "I am proud of you," a coach might say "you did a great job of incorporating physical activity into your day today." Affirming statements also aim to reframe a "deficit" mentality ("I really screwed up my diet this week") to a "strengths" mentality ("You remembered to eat a fruit for breakfast! It wasn't long ago that you weren't eating any fruits or vegetables at all.") Coaches need not always be the source of the affirmations. Coaches can help clients learn to provide their own self affirmations and embrace their strengths. This is the essence of **positive psychology** (see Chapter 3) and strength-based coaching (see Chapter 8).

A coach helps the client to gain self-efficacy and confidence

REFLECTIVE LISTENING

Reflective listening describes a process by which the coach makes an informed guess about the meaning of what a client has shared. This process helps clients think more deeply about what they are saying, which ultimately helps them continue to move forward through their ambivalence to ultimately making a behavioral change. Mastery of reflective listening is critical not only in practicing MI, but also in any relationship or coaching encounter. Before describing in detail what reflective listening is, it is helpful to highlight what it is not, as first described by Thomas Gordon in 1970 and noted in Miller and Rollnick (2013).

WHAT REFLECTIVE LISTENING IS NOT

Thomas Gordon (1970) describes 12 listening mistakes that can sabotage a coaching effort:

- Ordering, directing, or commanding
- Warning, cautioning, or threatening
- Giving advice, making suggestions, or providing solutions
- Persuading with logic, arguing, or lecturing
- Telling people what they should do; moralizing
- Disagreeing, judging, criticizing, or blaming
- Agreeing, approving, or praising
- Shaming, ridiculing, or labeling
- Interpreting or analyzing
- Reassuring, sympathizing, or consoling
- Questioning or probing
- Withdrawing, distracting, humoring, or changing the subject

Reflective listening involves the coach taking a guess at the underlying meaning and intention behind a client's words. It is the translation of a question starting with "do you mean that" into a declarative statement. For instance, a question such as, "Do you mean that it will be hard to get the social support you need at home to change the food environment?" can be transformed to "It will be hard to get the support you need at home to change the food environment." From here, the client can agree or disagree with the statement. Reflective statements come in many forms. The most valuable reflections challenge a client to think deeply about what he or she is saying. A general rule of thumb is that there should be two or three reflections for every question asked.

- *Simple reflections:* Simple restatements of what the client has said. For example, "I heard you say that YOU are angry at your sister for failing to show up for the bike ride."
- *Complex reflections:* A guess at the underlying meaning of what the client has said. For example, "Is it right that you feel frustrated because you were counting on your sister's help to get a good workout?"
- *Straight reflection:* A simple or complex reflection in response to a client's **sustain talk.** For example, if a client says "I don't eat that much. I don't think changing the way I eat will affect my weight," a coach may respond with, "No matter how little you eat you cannot lose weight, so you feel that it is not worth it to make changes to your diet." Often, **change talk** follows after such a statement.
- *Amplified reflection:* An overstated reflection that challenges the client to think more about a statement he or she made (usually sustain talk). An example may be a client who states, "There's no reason to quit smoking. It makes me feel good." An amplified reflection might be, "Smoking feels healthy for you."
- *Double-sided reflection:* Integrates a client's sustain talk with the client's own previously stated change talk. The client's statements are restated joined by "and," with the sustain talk stated first, followed by the change talk. For example, "you don't have time to exercise and when you exercise you are more productive at work."

SUMMARIZING

Summarizing is the process of recapping to a client what the coach has heard him or her say. While reflective listening occurs in smaller bits throughout a conversation, summarizing often comes at the end of a session or a conversation about a particular topic. Summarizing a conversation in which the client expressed a great deal of ambivalence can be very powerful in helping him or her overcome ambivalence.

INFORMING AND ADVISING

While MI helps clients derive their own solutions, there still is a role for providing information and advice. However, this should only occur *with permission*—that is, if a client specifically asks for advice or if the coach explicitly requests permission to offer advice and permission is granted. Even then, the coach should be careful to make sure that the client recognizes that he or she is free to agree or disagree and that the information should be used in the context of the client's own plan for change. Miller and Rollnick (2013) advise an **elicit-provide-elicit** approach to providing information. The coach first asks for permission to provide information and asks open-ended questions to understand what the client already knows on the topic (elicit). Then the coach provides information of most relevance to the client in small doses (provide). The coach then checks back with the client to assess understanding and response to the information (elicit). A more detailed discussion of the best practices in providing information and education to adult learners is described in Detail in Chapter 12.

TIPS FOR PROVIDING ADVICE

Frequently, clients will ask a coach for advice. MI prescribes a very careful approach to providing advice. First, it should be provided infrequently and only after engagement with the client has occurred successfully. Coaches are advised to ask permission before providing advice and make clear that it is the client's personal choice whether or not to accept the advice. Finally, in providing advice, the coach should offer a "menu of options." That is, the coach should provide several possible scenarios that the client may select from or adapt.

While the five skills just discussed are essential to effectively practice MI, they do not define MI. Rather, MI is the "strategic use" of these skills to move people toward change (Miller and Rollnick, 2013).

PRACTICAL APPLICATION

2. Coaches who are new to MI may benefit from use of the following five open-ended questions when working with ambivalent clients. Miller & Rollnick (2013) have used these questions in their coaching around the world with a positive response from clients:

   ——— Why do you want to make this change?
   ——— How might you go about making this change?
   ——— What are the three best reasons for you to do it?
   ——— How important is it for you to make this change? Why?

   After the coach has received answers from the first four questions, he or she then reflects back and summarizes the responses to these questions before asking:

   ——— What do you think you'll do?

   Go through this process with three clients, friends, family members, or coworkers and summarize your experience here.

PRACTICING MI THROUGH THE FOUR PROCESSES OF CHANGE

MI consists of four broad processes: **engaging, focusing, evoking,** and **planning**. While a single MI session may not include all four components, or necessarily proceed in a linear fashion, this description of processes helps the student of MI see how a client–coach relationship rooted in MI may unfold.

ENGAGING

The first step of MI is engaging, which is "the process of establishing a mutually trusting and respectful helping relationship" (Miller and Rollnick, 2013). A component of engaging is building **rapport,** but it goes beyond that to establishing a deep trust and understanding so that the client feels comfortable and like an active participant in the coaching session. Chapter 2 outlines several strategies to help establish a strong client–coach foundation.

MILLER AND ROLLNICK'S SIX "TRAPS" THAT COMMONLY OCCUR IN THE ENGAGING PROCESS

- *Assessment trap:* The coach spends time asking the client a series of questions. This is one-directional and generally not that useful to the client. It shuts down the process of engaging from the start.
- *Expert trap:* Portraying oneself as the expert who has the answer of what the client should do does not help the client take ownership of the change. Activation of the righting reflex would fit here.
- *Premature focus trap:* This occurs when the coach tries to set the agenda and hone in on a specific needed behavioral change too quickly. It is important for the conversation to start with the client's concerns, not those of the coach.
- *Labeling trap:* The coach "names" the problem—e.g., smoking, obesity, or diabetes—that needs to be fixed. This can trigger in the client a feeling of alienation and stigma.
- *Blaming trap:* The client may feel guilty or feel that the coach will blame him or her for the problem. It is important from the start for the coach to disarm the client and acknowledge that the coach is not concerned with who is to blame for the problem but rather understanding better what the problem is and how the client may best address it.
- *Chat trap:* Spending too much time on "small talk" rather than moving the agenda forward with a sharp focus on the client's concerns and goals of the coaching experience.

FOCUSING

Once the coach and client have established a relationship, they can move on to setting to the agenda for the coaching, labeled as focusing. Miller and Rollnick (2013) describe focusing as "the process by which you develop and maintain a specific direction in the conversation about change." The client addresses what he or she hopes to accomplish from the coaching experience. Together, the coach and client come together to determine an agenda, or focus, of their time together. Miller and Rollnick (2013) describe three possible scenarios:

- *Clear direction:* This occurs when a client comes to the coach with a straightforward purpose such as to lose weight or stop smoking. The coach first confirms with the client that this is the intended focus of the training and then proceeds to ask permission to further explore the objective. From here, the relationship can progress to evoking or planning, depending on the client's extent of ambivalence about the behavioral change.

- *Choices in direction:* This occurs when there are several options from which to focus the coaching session. An approach to finding focus in this situation is referred to as "agenda mapping."

- *Unclear direction:* If a client comes with a vague concept of what he or she would like to attain from the coaching sessions, the coach can use his or her OARS skills to guide the client from broad concerns to specific area(s) of potential focus.

AGENDA MAPPING

- *Structuring:* This is when the coach asks the client's permission to step back from the conversation to explore potential options of discussion.

- *Considering options:* The client and coach explore possibilities for focus.

- *Zooming in:* This is when the coach and client choose an area of focus.

Using a visual aid known as a "bubble sheet" can be an effective tool for agenda mapping. A sample "bubble sheet" for a conversation about weight loss is shown in Figure 5-1.

Figure 5-1
BUBBLE SHEET FOR A CLIENT WHO DESIRES TO LOSE WEIGHT
"What should we focus on? Let's fill in some of these bubbles with possible areas of focus."

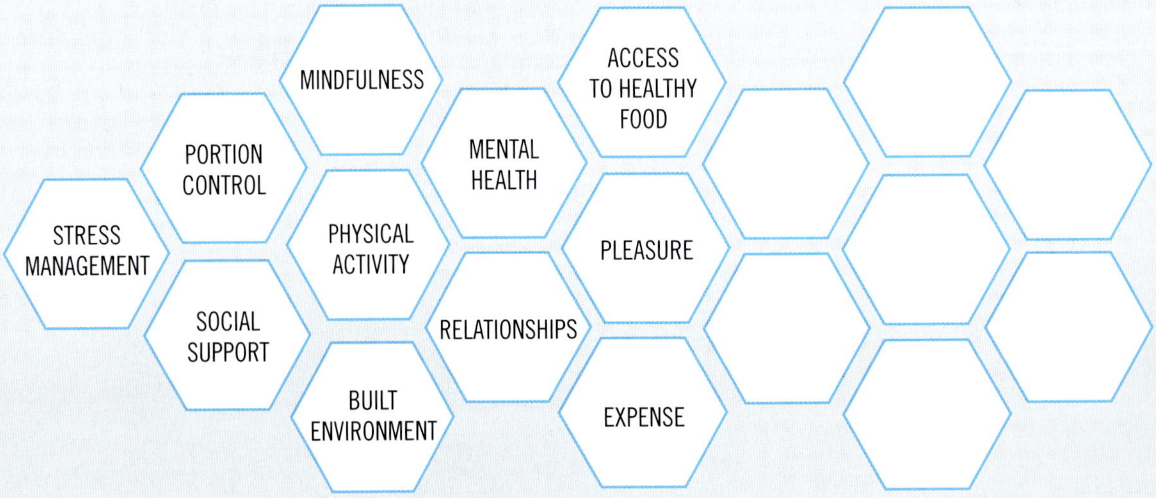

EVOKING

The process of evoking involves exploring the client's motivation to change. This is the opposite of the typical client–trainer, client–provider, or client–expert relationship in which the "expert" identifies the problem, tells the client what he or she is doing wrong, and then provides advice on how to fix it. Evoking guides the client to make his or her arguments for change by strategically responding to both sustain talk (statements reflecting a desire to maintain the status quo) and change talk (statements reflecting a desire to change).

Sustain Talk

Sustain talk includes the client's mention of barriers, challenges, and reasons that argue against a behavioral change. Miller and Rollnick (2013) advise that coaches use the reflection techniques described on page 63 and the strategies outlined below to respond to sustain talk:

- *Emphasizing autonomy:* The coach notes that it is up to the client whether or not a change occurs.
- *Reframing:* The coach suggests a different meaning or perspective on the client's statement.
- *Agreeing with a twist:* The coach first uses a reflective statement to agree with the client's statement but then follows with a reframing statement.
- *Running head start:* The coach requests that the client share reasons not to change first, followed by reasons to change. This is parallel to the concept of **decisional balance** in Prochaska's **transtheoretical model of behavioral change** (Prochaska, 1979), or listing of pros and cons. This should only be used when the client has volunteered little to no change talk.
- *Coming alongside:* In those cases when a client exhibits an abundance of sustain talk and little change talk, this method involves agreeing with the client's sustain talk, culminating in a comment such as, "For now, perhaps it is better to stay as you are."

Change Talk

Change talk refers to the words and phrases the client uses that express the desire to change and the benefits of doing so. Miller and Rollnick (2013) advise coaches to recognize change talk by picking up on "preparatory change talk" described by psycholinguist Paul Amrhein. It can be remembered through the pneumonic DARN: desire, ability, reasons, and need. Clients who are preparing to make a change will, over the course of a coaching session, make statements that talk about a change that they want to make (desire). They will make comments related to their perceived *ability* to make the change. This comes out in statements that begin with "I could" or "I am able to." Clients may also talk about reasons to change, including potential physical, mental, or social benefits. More, clients may also express a *need* to make the change, such as to avoid a feared illness or save a relationship. None of these statements indicate that the client *will* make a change, but rather that the client is articulating, in his or her ambivalence, the reasons for change.

As clients begin to express what Amrhein referred to as CAT statements—commitment, activation, and taking steps—also described as "mobilizing change talk," the coach should recognize that the client has worked through the ambivalence and is likely ready to begin planning for change. Commitment statements are versions of "I will change." Activation statements include "I am ready to" or "I am prepared to" change. Taking steps indicates that the client already has begun to make a change (this parallels with the **preparation** stage of change in Prochaska's transtheoretical model of behavioral change).

Mobilizing change talk

Miller and Rollnick (2013) offer several techniques for evoking change talk. These techniques include:

Using the importance ruler: As a client moves through ambivalence and develops increasing commitment to change, the "importance ruler" can help to gauge the client's perceived importance of the change. The coach may ask, "On a scale of 1–10, how important is it to you to make this change?" The key to this technique is in the follow-up question after the client provides a number: "Why are you a 6 and not a 5?" The answer will nearly always come as some formulation of change talk. (On the other hand, if the coach asks, "Why are you a 6 and not a 7?" sustain talk will ensue.)

The coach may follow up with a question, "On a scale of 1–10, how confident are you that you will be able to make this change?" The client's response and the coach's follow-up question (e.g. "Why are you a 7 and not a 6?") help to build self-efficacy for change.

Querying extremes: This method challenges the client to think about the best case scenario (if a change is made) and the worst case scenario (if a change is not made). Often, this positioning sparks change talk.

Looking back: The client remembers back to a time when he or she did not have the current problem behavior. This activity highlights the contrast between what life once was like and how it is today, and usually triggers a desire to change and change talk.

Looking forward: This process asks the client to envision what life will be like if the client successfully makes the change. Often, this leads to increased hope and motivation to change and consequently change talk.

Exploring goals and values: Asking clients to highlight those things that they hold most dearly in life and what they aspire to achieve can help to provide anchors for change and a source of motivation to begin the process of change.

As a coach hears change talk, the process of MI calls on the coach to engage OARS (open-ended questioning, affirming, reflecting, and summarizing) in responding specifically to the change statement. This is literally helping a client "talk him- or herself into" changing. This process helps move the dial to more change talk and less sustain talk, and ultimately helps the client to pass through ambivalence and commit to making a change.

PLANNING

Once a client has decided to make a change, he or she is ready to begin the planning stage, the time when the client is "thinking and talking more about when and how to change and less about whether and why" (Miller & Rollnick, 2013). Signs that a client is ready to progress to planning include increased frequency of change talk, decreased frequency of sustain talk, resolve (which is signaled by a calm and certainty in the value of moving forward), envisioning statements of what life might be like during or after the change, and increased questioning about what happens once the change begins. When the client signals a readiness to proceed with a change, the coach can progress beyond MI and help the client to begin planning and establishing goals. A suggested process of goal setting is described in detail in Chapter 9.

3. Reach out to other coaches who are working on improving their MI skills. Set up a schedule for practicing specific skills that are necessary to develop competency in the four processes of engaging, focusing, evoking, and planning. Specific skills may include use of complex reflections, affirmations, agenda setting, responding to change talk, developing a change plan, and evoking a commitment to change. In which skills are you strongest? Which skills do you find the most challenging? How will you continue to improve your skills?

4. Apply motivational interviewing in the work that you already doing.

   Is the spirit of MI consistent with the culture where you work? Why or why not?

   How have your colleagues and clients responded to the integration of MI into your work?

   What has been your most surprising experience?

   What has been your biggest challenge?

5. Review the "Is that Motivational Interviewing?" case example and commentary developed by Drs. Miller and Rollnick, available at www.guilford.com/add/miller2/is_that_mi.pdf, and record your thoughts here.

SUMMARY

MI is an extremely effective tool for coaching a person who initially is ambivalent about making a behavioral change. At the minimum, basic skill in MI—especially the use of OARS—is critical for all coaches. However, to become truly expert at the art of MI requires hours and often years of practice and ongoing skill refinement. This brief introduction and the activities and exercises that follow are only the beginning in developing a skill set that will continue to evolve over time.

EXPANSION QUIZ
Multiple-choice quiz available if you expand to the full experience

References

Gordon, T. (1970). *Parent Effectiveness Training.* New York: Wyden.

Miller, W. & Rollnick, S. (2013). *Motivational Interviewing: Helping People Change* (3rd ed.). New York: John Wiley & Sons.

Prochaska, J.O. (1979). *Systems of Psychotherapy: A Transtheoretical Analysis.* Pacific Grove, Calif.: Brooks-Cole.

Additional Resources

Rollnick, S., Miller, W., & Butler, C. (2007). *Motivational Interviewing in Health Care.* New York: The Guilford Press.

MINT: Excellence in Motivational Interviewing. www.motivationalinterviewing.org

CHAPTER 6

CHAPTER 6

EXPLORING VALUES AND ESTABLISHING A VISION FOR THE FUTURE

LEARNING OBJECTIVES

After reading this chapter, the coach will be able to:

- Identify a client's values and use them as a framework for future goal setting
- Help a client look to the future through the process of visioning
- Describe various tools and techniques coaches may use to support visioning

"Your beliefs become your thoughts. Your thoughts become your words. Your words become your actions. Your actions become your habits. Your habits become your values. Your values become your destiny." — Mahatma Gandhi

The process of awakening a person's own motivation for changing a behavior is best supported with an exploration of the individual's values and vision for what the future may hold. What does the client aspire to achieve? What drives and motivates this person? What does the client hope the future will hold in one year, five years, and even 10 years? Near the end of life and looking back, what will have made it a "good life"? Having a solid understanding of a client's values will help to engage the client in articulating a vision for the future and establish the groundwork for helping the client set goals to make progress toward achieving that vision.

A VALUES INTERVIEW

As coaches help clients increase awareness in their process of behavioral change, devoting a coaching session to exploring a client's values can go a long way to better understanding the client and also in evoking a client's own motivation and commitment to change. Miller and Rollnick (2013) recommend that coaches complete a **values interview** with their clients. This can include asking open-ended questions ranging from "What do you care most about in life?" to asking clients if they were to write a "mission statement" for their lives, how would they describe their goals and purpose in life? Importantly, coaches should use the **OARS model** (**open-ended questions, affirmations, reflections,** and **summarizing**) in exploring a client's values.

PRACTICAL APPLICATION

1. In one to three sentences, write your own personal "mission statement" describing your goals and purpose.

One structured way of helping explore a client's values is through a personal values card sort (Figure 6-1). The most important component of this activity is not the "ranking" of a client's values, but the discussion that follows.

In the values card sort, a client is given a list of 100 values, each on its own card, and the client sorts the cards into piles based on the degree of importance of each value to the client. The client may then identify five to 10 values that are of most importance. From here, the client and coach can further explore these values and use them as a foundation for articulating and planning for the client's vision for the future. The value card sort activity is available at www.guilford.com/add/miller2/values.pdf.

Figure 6-1
A VALUES CARD SORT

Acceptance	Duty	Inner peace	Practicality
Accuracy	Ecology	Integrity	Protect
Achievement	Excitement	Intelligence	Provide
Adventure	Faithfulness	Intimacy	Purpose
Art	Fame	Justice	Rationality
Attractiveness	Family	Knowledge	Realism
Authority	Fitness	Leadership	Responsibility
Autonomy	Flexibility	Leisure	Risk
Beauty	Forgiveness	Loved	Romance
Belonging	Freedom	Loving	Safety
Caring	Friendship	Mastery	Self-acceptance
Challenge	Fun	Mindfulness	Self-control
Comfort	Generosity	Moderation	Self-esteem
Commitment	Genuiness	Monogamy	Self-knowledge
Compassion	God's will	Music	Service
Complexity	Gratitude	Noncomformity	Sexuality
Compromise	Growth	Novelty	Simplicity
Contribution	Health	Nurturance	Solitude
Cooperation	Honesty	Openness	Spirituality
Courage	Hope	Order	Stability
Courtesy	Humility	Passion	Tolerance
Creativity	Humor	Patriotism	Tradition
Curiosity	Imagination	Pleasure	Virtue
Dependability	Independence	Popularity	Wealth
Diligence	Industry	Power	World peace

PRACTICAL APPLICATION

2. Complete the value card sort outlined in Figure 6-1 for yourself. What are your top five values? How do these values guide your personal and professional goals?

FROM VALUES TO VISION

An appreciation of a client's values, and the client's exploration of these values, sets the stage to establish a client's vision of what the future will be, or could be, if he or she makes a behavioral change. Some clients may come to the coaching session with a clear vision and hope to achieve clearly defined goals. Others may have more general intentions and choose to work with a coach to release what has not been working and establish new, healthy approaches and behaviors. Whether goals are clearly or vaguely defined, coaching can help clients envision what their experience will be like once they have made the behavioral change. The remainder of this chapter provides guidance, ideas, and activities to help guide a client through a process of visioning.

Of note, as with all coaching tools, a coach should seek permission from a client prior to engaging in visioning activities, especially the types of activities described here that extend beyond open-ended questions and simple reflections.

Do your clients wish to grow in awareness, develop a new skill, expand their knowledge, live a healthier lifestyle, master a sport, overcome a physical challenge, or create a support network? So often, people begin with action rather than contemplation. They want to get into motion, sow some wild oats, work by the sweat of the brow, and stir up some dust. They fill out planners and electronic calendars with unending tasks. They huff and puff and exhaust themselves in the belief that surely enough activity will give them what they want. Yet, people discover that activity disconnected from vision is short-lived. Vision is the life force that inspires transformation. Vision reveals the higher purpose served by labors and gives people stamina. Allow time to be still and know. Embrace inactivity in order to discover the grand plan that is right for fulfillment.

Excerpted with permission from Frances B. (2001). Mindful coaching: A process in fulfillment. Carness, F. (Ed.) *Wise Women Speak: 20 Ways to Turn Stumbling Blocks into Stepping Stones.* Portland, Ore.: Carness Health Management.

AFFIRMATIONS

Thoughts are powerful. Scientific evidence has shown that a person's beliefs impact outcomes (see Chapter 7). As clients endeavor to move from where they are to where they want to be, it is prudent to be mindful of ongoing thoughts that accompany the journey and influence the outcome. Affirmations are statements of intended results spoken or written in the first person and in present tense (Table 6-1). They are statements of intentions. While positive affirmations intuitively are beneficial and are a mainstay in many coaching programs, little scientific research has been published to test their effectiveness, especially when it comes to health-related behavioral change. Of note, there is some evidence that the use of affirmations may do more harm than good for people with low self-esteem (Wood, Perunovic, & Lee, 2009). They are included here to serve as a potential adjunct to a science-based coaching intervention, when appropriate.

Table 6-1
EFFECTIVE AFFIRMATIONS

THOUGHT	AFFIRMATION
I need to lose weight.	My body is at its perfect weight now.
I need to eat better.	I easily make healthy food choices.
I'm a couch potato!	I respond to my body's need to move.
I'm stressed out!	I live a life of health, joy, and ease.
It's hard to change.	I make daily choices for my highest good.

COACHING ACTIVITY

This activity can be done in groups, pairs, or individual coaching sessions. Ask the clients to think of three words that describe themselves as they would like to be, such as "healthy," "content," and "fit." Then ask each client to use the word in an affirmation sentence, such as "I am a healthy, content, and fit person." After each person makes his or her statement, the rest of the group responds with "Yes, you are!" Remind the clients that even though they may not yet think of themselves in this way, visualizing the future will be the first step in making progress to realize that vision.

JOURNALING

Clients may find it helpful to write out their thoughts, ideas, progress, questions, or answers to key questions. Journals are typically not shared. Journaling can include stream-of-thought writing, list-making, drawings, or responses to some key questions, such as:

- What do I want to create?
- What does my inner wisdom say?
- How can I best use my energy?
- If I were 5% healthier, I would...
- What will ground me when the going gets tough?
- What are the pros and cons of this situation?

COACHING ACTIVITY

During the exploration of a client's vision for the future, ask open-ended questions to help the client discover his or her best approach to considering how this future might look. When providing a menu of options, include journaling as one of the options. If a client chooses to journal, offer several prompts for the client to consider. Remind the client that the content of the journaling is entirely private. During a follow-up coaching session, ask the client if he or she gained any insights from the journaling process to share. This reflection may help the client solidify the learning and make progress toward changing the behavior.

MINDFULNESS AND MEDITATION

Quieting the mind—and developing increased **mindfulness**—is another practice that may inspire greater clarity. Mindfulness can be thought of as "the nonjudgmental awareness of the sensations, thoughts, and emotions of the present moment" (Marchand, 2013). This is in contrast to an "autopilot" mindset in which behaviors, responses, and reactions to events are "hard-wired," occur without much thought, and often interfere with implementing a behavioral change. Mindfulness practices such as Zen meditation, mindfulness-based stress reduction (combined meditation with elements of yoga and teaching on stress and coping strategies), and mindfulness-based cognitive therapy provide myriad mental and physical health benefits, including reduction in stress and anxiety (Marchand, 2013; Marchand 2012). *For many of these activities, further education and training is important to provide maximal benefit to the client and to ensure adherence to standard protocols.* However, a client may begin with simple meditation, such as sitting quietly with focus only on the breath. Meditation can also include anything that allows for a singular focus such as walking with awareness, listening to music, dancing, or being in nature. Coaches who are interested in improving their own mindfulness and meditation practice are encouraged to review the science-based resources mentioned in the Additional Resources section at the end of this chapter.

Sitting quietly with focus only on the breath

COACHING ACTIVITY

For clients who are interested in increasing mindfulness and stress relief, beginning a coaching session with a few minutes of focused deep breathing can be enough to calm the mind and set the stage for a successful coaching session. Clients should begin seated comfortably with their backs straight, with one hand on the chest and the other on the stomach. Next, the client should take a deep breath in through the nose; the hand on the stomach should rise. Then the client exhales, pushing as much air out of the lungs as possible. The hand on the stomach should move in, but the hand on the chest should move very little. Repeat.

MEDITATION ACTIVITY

Coaches can improve their own mindfulness through integration of meditation and other mindfulness activities into their daily practices. Billie Frances provides a mindfulness activity for coaches in the multimedia supplement.

CREATING A VISION BOARD

In addition to words of affirmation and contemplation, some clients find it helpful to create a pictorial representation of their desired future. Vision boards can answer in pictures what cannot readily be put into words alone and can include:

- Drawings
- Collages
- Collections of words or symbols

Possible subjects for a vision board include:

- What nurtures me?
- What do I love/value?
- My life in 10 years
- The ideal scene for a healthy life
- My home life, family life, love life, career life

COACHING ACTIVITY

For the interested client, assign the creation of a vision board as homework. The client should purchase a poster board, craft supplies (scissors, glue, stickers, colored paper, etc.), and a few magazines. Advise the client to ask him or herself "What is it that I really want?" before getting started. The client should then go through the magazines, selecting images, headlines, and words that resonate. The next stage of selecting, arranging, gluing, and decorating the images will pull together a visual representation of client's vision for the future.

Clients who are not inclined to complete a vision board, but who may be interested a similar visioning activity, may find value in completing the personal transformation worksheet shown in Figure 6-2.

Figure 6-2

A PERSONAL TRANSFORMATION WORKSHEET

The Old Me (a self-portrait)	The Current Me	The Future Me
Things I love about the old me that I do not want to change:	How I will integrate the things I do not want to change into my new lifestyle:	What the future me looks like with a new lifestyle, but having kept the things I do not want to change:
Things about the old me that I would like to change:	Things about the old me that I am working on changing or have changed:	What the future me looks like with these changes (words or pictures):

PRACTICAL APPLICATION

3. Complete the personal transformation worksheet in Figure 6-2, comparing your current self with your past self and your future self. What did you learn? How did this activity affect your motivation to make a behavioral change? Do you think this activity would be of value to your clients? Why or why not?

VISUALIZATION

Some clients may respond to a guided visualization where they are led through an experience to envision a positive future. The visualization process invites clients to tap into wisdom beyond their rational thinking. For some, the wisdom from the future generates a big picture perspective that can serve to inform or inspire choices. However, in other cases visualization may not be an appropriate technique. For example, some individuals who suffer progressive chronic disease such as heart failure or diabetes may not benefit from such an activity, or could even be harmed. Coaches should use discretion when applying this technique and make sure that clients are fully informed of the goals of the activity and what the activity entails. Coaches should also be prepared to respond to any signs of client distress developing from this activity. An example of a visualization activity is the "Wisdom from the Future" visualization.

Envision a positive future

"WISDOM FROM THE FUTURE" VISUALIZATION EXERCISE

This exercise is designed to expand your awareness of things you know yet may not consistently remember or apply. During the exercise, you will be guided through a five-minute visualization process and you will silently engage in a dialogue with yourself at a future time. This exercise does not require that you adopt different thoughts or actions (as in hypnosis). Rather, you will draw upon your own wisdom in order to help inform your present-day choices and achieve the results you desire.

Take a moment to ask yourself: Is this visualization exercise right for me? If not, you can pass on doing it or, if you become uneasy during the exercise, gently disengage from the visualization by breathing and slowly becoming reoriented to your physical surroundings as you gently open your eyes. If you wish, dedicate the next few minutes to this Wisdom from the Future exercise.

Begin by sitting comfortably and breathing naturally.

Gently close your eyes.

Allow yourself to be aware of any sounds and aromas. Notice the temperature of the air. Feel the chair that is supporting you. Feel your feet on the floor. Now, just allow these things to be in the background.

Notice if there are any areas in your body where you are holding tension. Begin to relax on your exhale and allow the breath to carry away any tightness or tension. As you inhale fresh oxygen, direct its renewing qualities to those areas.

Continue to focus your attention on your breath. Without changing it, just notice the quality of your breath today... where do you feel your breath in your body? What is the quality of your breath? How does the air feel entering and leaving your nose or mouth?

For a few minutes you will be guided on a journey into a positive future. And, although an aspect of you will travel through time and space, throughout this visualization, your body is safe and intact. You can reunite your mind and your emotions with your physical body whenever you wish.

For now, allow an aspect we'll call your "future self" to begin to venture out and travel ahead in time. Choose a point in time 10, 15, or 20 years into the future when you are fully enjoying the life of your dreams. You may be anywhere you choose.

Take all the time you need to locate your place. Which season you have chosen? What do you begin to notice about the surroundings?

When you are ready, find that you are on a pathway that leads to a building or home. This is where you live or work in the future. As you walk along the pathway, continue to be aware of details about how this place in the future looks and how it feels in this future where you are fulfilled and successful.

As you are ready, approach the building and knock on the door. As the door opens, you are greeted warmly by your "future self." As he or she invites you in, notice the surroundings on the inside of the building. Are there items or photos that tell some of the story of your journey?

Go with your future self to a comfortable area to sit together and begin your dialogue. Ask your future self: "What do I need to learn in order to be fulfilled and successful? What do I need to learn in order to have more love and peace in my life?"

Listen for answers, which may come in the form of words or impressions.

Continue to ask questions of your future self: "How can I fully live my potential and vision for my life? What do I need to let go of in order to be happy?"

Continue to allow yourself to receive wisdom from your future self as you simply breathe and receive.

Continue to ask questions and receive wisdom.

When you feel complete, thank your future self for the wisdom you have received. And, if it seems right, agree to meet again to continue your dialogue.

Slowly find your way back to the entrance and bid each other farewell.

Once you are outdoors, take a couple of deep breaths to help you integrate the experience.

Then imagine that you can gently lift off from this place and easily move back through time.

Allow yourself to gradually move into your town, your home or office, and your body.

Allow yourself a couple of deep breaths to integrate… and then gently open your eyes.

COACHING ACTIVITY

With the client's permission, and with the appropriate preparation from the coach, proceed through the sample "Wisdom from the Future" visualization.

ACCOMPANYING VIDEO:
In the video supplement, Billie Frances facilitates a sample "Wisdom from the Future" visualization exercise.

Begin to write or draw some impressions of your journey. Include what you noticed about the surroundings and any wise messages from the future.

If you wish, share your impressions with your coach.

4. How would you incorporate the visualization activity into your work?

5. What safeguards would you need to be aware of, and what would you do or say to:

   Take the lead from the client

   Ask permission to share tools that my help

   Remain unattached to whether or not the client opts to employ the tool

   Only use tools with which you are competent and experienced

   Be prepared to refer emotionally troubling issues to other professionals

6. Case Study: You begin working with a new client who wants to lose weight. She tells you she gained weight while pregnant and that her son is now 9 months old and she is still carrying 25 extra pounds. You decide to help her by suggesting a visualization technique. You ask her to close her eyes and you begin to guide her through the following:

   "Imagine that you are on a beach on a sunny day. You are there with your son enjoying the sounds of the surf and seagulls and the feel of the sun and warm sand. You are wearing a cute two-piece swimsuit and you feel great! Everyone around you is also smiling and happy. Now, open your eyes and tell me how you feel."

   After the visualization, your client tells you that she is very upset. She was reminded of a time as a teenager when she went to the beach with some girlfriends who were flirting with some older teenage boys. She felt awkward and embarrassed and her friends made fun of her for wanting to leave. Your client's voice begins to break as she describes the scene and she looks to you for help.

   In this example of a visualization that did not serve the client, several pieces "went wrong." Provide a statement that you might say to a client to address each of the following:

   The coach did not ask and receive permission to use a visualization technique.

   The coach did not adequately describe what would occur during the visualization.

   The coach did not let the client know that she could discontinue the process or how to do so.

The coach told the client what to visualize rather than allowing the client to imagine the details.

The visualization ended abruptly.

The coach was ill-prepared to deal with the client's reaction.

The experience undermined the client's safety and trust.

7. Consider each of the following scenarios. How could you invite your client to expand the possibilities without forcing your idea?

Example:
You Hear: I sometimes lose track of the big picture.
You Say: "You mentioned that you wished you could picture your desired result. Might it be helpful to explore some visioning tools?"
You Avoid: "You should create a vision board."

You Hear: I tell myself I can't do it, yet I know I should be more positive.

You Say:

You Avoid:

You Hear: For me, unless I see it in writing, it just isn't real.

You Say:

You Avoid:

PRACTICAL APPLICATIONS

You Hear: I think if I could find some time to be quiet I'd do less emotional eating.

You Say:

You Avoid:

You Hear: Some of my friends made up a collage with their wellness goals. Does that work?

You Say:

You Avoid:

SUMMARY

Guiding clients through the process of identifying their most important values and envisioning what their future may be serves as a critical link between increasing awareness of what is needed for change and beginning the planning process of achieving it. It is the link between the "awareness" and the "choice" phases of the ACE cycle of change, which serves as the foundation for much of what is covered in subsequent chapters.

EXPANSION QUIZ
Multiple-choice quiz available if you expand to the full experience

References

Frances B. (2001). Mindful coaching: A process in fulfillment. In: Carness, F. (Ed.) *Wise Women Speak: 20 Ways to Turn Stumbling Blocks into Stepping Stones.* Portland, Ore.: Carness Health Management.

Marchand, W.R. (2013). Mindfulness meditation practices as adjunctive treatments for psychiatric disorders. *Psychiatric Clinics of North America,* 36, 1, 141–152.

Marchand, W.R. (2012). Mindfulness-based stress reduction, mindfulness-based cognitive therapy, and Zen meditation for depression, anxiety, pain, and psychological distress. *Psychiatric Practice,* 18, 4, 233–252.

Miller, W. & Rollnick, S. (2013). *Motivational Interviewing: Helping People Change* (3rd ed.). New York: Guilford Press.

Wood, J., Perunovic, E., & Lee, J (2009). Positive self-statements: Power for some, peril for others. *Psychological Science,* 20, 7, 860–866.

Additional Resources

Kabat-Zinn, J. (2013). *Full Catastrophe Living, Revised Edition: How to Cope with Stress, Pain, and Illness Using Mindful Meditation.* New York: Bantam Books

Teasdale, J., Williams, M., & Segal, Z. (2014). *The Mindful Way Workbook: An 8-Week Program to Free Yourself from Depression and Emotional Distress.* New York: Guilford Press.

Williams, M. & Penman, D. (2012). *Mindfulness: An Eight-Week Plan for Finding Peace in a Frantic World.* New York: Rodale.

NOTES

Introduction to Section III:
CHOICE

Through the course of behavioral change, clients go through a predictable, though nonlinear, cycle of change, referred to here as the ACE cycle of change, which stands for awareness, choice, and execution (Stober & Grant, 2006). The choice stage occurs after an individual has come to recognize that a behavioral change is warranted. At this point, most clients will have an idea of what they hope the end outcome will be, whether that is quitting smoking, weight loss, attainment of a desired state of health, a successful relationship with a family member, or a job promotion. Coaching a client through this phase of change includes use of strategies and communication techniques to help the client set the stage for a successful change through goal setting, planning for successes and challenges, and establishing a positive mindset for approaching the change.

The coach's role in this process is to help clients set the best goals to fuel and inspire change, to help the clients recognize and rely on their own strengths and assets to be successful, and to help clients set and maintain a positive tone as they prepare to embark on the journey to a long-lasting behavioral change.

OVER THE COURSE OF THIS SECTION, COACHES WILL GAIN COMPETENCY IN THE FOLLOWING THREE PRINCIPLES:

- Cognitive behavioral coaching
- Identifying strengths, assets, and barriers
- Goal setting

The International Coach Federation (ICF) Core Competencies that are emphasized in the three chapters in this section include (3) establishing trust and intimacy with the client; (4) coaching presence; (5) active listening; (6) powerful questioning; (7) direct communication; (8) creating awareness; (9) designing actions; and (10) planning and goal setting.

▶ **For more information on the ICF Coaching Competencies, refer to the Introduction and Appendix A.**

Reference: Stober, D.S. & Grant, A.M. (Eds.) (2006). *Evidence-Based Coaching.* Hoboken, N.J.: John Wiley & Sons.

CHAPTER 7

CHAPTER 7
COGNITIVE BEHAVIORAL COACHING

LEARNING OBJECTIVES

After reading this chapter, the coach will be able to:

- Describe the principles of cognitive behavioral coaching
- Describe the A-B-C-D-E model of behavioral coaching
- Use cognitive behavioral coaching strategies to ask powerful questions that evoke insight and challenge the client's assumptions
- Coach a client to recognize and reframe cognitive distortions

When helping a person better his or her own health, well-being, happiness, and fitness, there is a wealth of knowledge and experience the behavioral change expert may bring to the relationship, from an understanding of complex medical information and disease processes to exercise physiology, nutrition, human performance, and a solid foundation in communication skills and strategies. With such an extensive list, it may be hard to imagine that something is missing, but indeed there is. Understanding the connection between thoughts, feelings, and behaviors, which is rooted in **cognitive behavioral therapy (CBT),** and how to apply it in helping clients help themselves in their quest for healthier, happier living, is important for effective coaching.

THE SCIENCE OF COGNITIVE BEHAVIORAL THERAPY

Among all of the behavioral change theories and practices, cognitive behavioral interventions are the most extensively researched form of psychological treatment (Butler et al., 2006). The expansive work initially began in the 1950s with the work of Albert Ellis (1961 & 1962), which was elaborated upon by Aaron Beck (1975), who developed the broad approach called cognitive behavioral therapy. There are now more than 500 published controlled outcome studies examining the effects of CBT for a wide range of mental and physical health-related problems (Norcross, Karpiak, & Santoro, 2005). The evidence is clear: CBT works for changing behaviors and improving disease outcomes.

THE BASIC PRINCIPLES OF COGNITIVE BEHAVIORAL INTERVENTIONS

While CBT is the domain of the licensed clinical psychologist, skilled coaches may borrow from CBT in non-clinical settings using a coaching strategy referred to as **cognitive behavioral coaching (CBC).** Research supports that this type of coaching improves emotional competencies, goal attainment, leadership skills, mental health, and overall quality of life (Green, Oades, & Grant, 2006; Grant, 2003; Conway, 2000; Laske, 1999).

CBC is based on the notion that the way people think about a given situation determines how they feel emotionally and physically, and this alters their behavior. By increasing a client's awareness of this connection and then helping him or her make the choice to change the way he or she responds to a given event, CBC facilitates lasting behavioral change.

Note, however, that working with an individual's thinking patterns should only be attempted if a coach discovers through the process of behavioral goal setting that the way a client thinks (or feels) may be getting in the way of what he or she wants to achieve. This occurs commonly when emotional factors present a barrier to change. With that said, coaches should use the techniques only to the extent to which they feel comfortable, and be ready to refer to a mental health professional when underlying mental health problems or concerns become apparent.

THE CONNECTION BETWEEN THOUGHTS, FEELINGS, AND BEHAVIORS

A straightforward way to understand this relationship between thought processes and behavior is outlined below:

1. **Event:** Something happens.
2. **Thoughts:** The person has a belief or thought(s) about the situation, event, circumstance, person, place, or thing.
3. **Feelings:** The person experiences feelings in response to the thoughts. Thus, the link between an event and the emotions or feelings that ensue is what one thinks.
4. **Reaction:** The person reacts, or practices a behavior in response to the feelings.

The 1-2-3-4 model provides a simplified model of considering how events affect behavior (Figure 7-1). An event triggers thoughts, then feelings, which lead to reactions. The aim of CBC is to undo the automaticity of this process and stop to evaluate the thought processes that impact behavior.

Figure 7-1

THE 1-2-3-4 MODEL

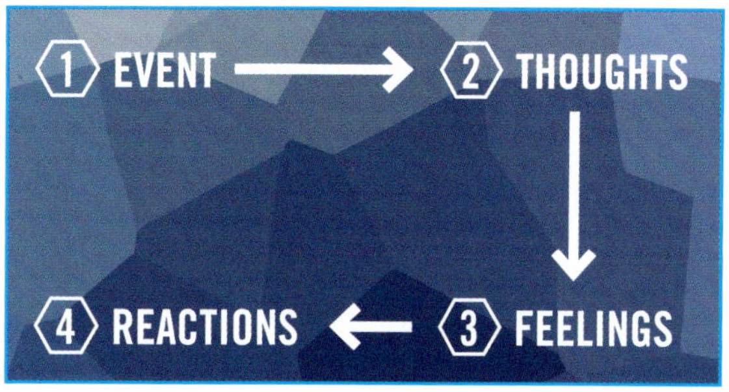

A-B-C-D-E MODEL

A well-described and parallel concept in psychology is the **A-B-C-D-E model,** where A is the activating event (the "1. Event" in the 1-2-3-4 model), B is the belief the client has about the event or situation (the "2. Thoughts"), and C is the emotional and behavioral consequence of the person's beliefs (the "3. Feelings" and "4. Reactions"). The intervention exists in the "D" and "E." This is when the coach helps the client dispute ("D"), challenge, and question the erroneous beliefs the client holds that lead to disruptive emotions and behaviors (Ellis, 1962; Ellis, 1961). The value of CBC is measured based on "E"—the effective reduction of the emotional output, whether that is sadness, anger, despair, or frustration. The goal is that "E" drives an effective behavioral change.

The goal is that "E" drives an effective behavioral change

Table 7-1 shows an example of a simple method a coach might use with a client to combat automatic negative thoughts using the A-B-C-D-E method:

- *Column A:* List the activating event (in the case of food, it might be a party or dinner).
- *Column B:* Write down any unproductive beliefs about the event, circumstance, person, or meal.
- *Column C:* Record the emotional consequences that result from the erroneous beliefs about the event (sadness, worry, anger, or guilt).
- *Column D:* Dispute the validity of the erroneous beliefs.
- *Column E:* Note the new, positive effects of substituting factual beliefs for the erroneous ones (healthier, positive, more resilient emotions that enable the client to get on with life in a more fulfilling way).

Table 7-1

SAMPLE A-B-C-D-E METHOD FOR COUNTERING AUTOMATIC NEGATIVE THOUGHTS

A	B	C	D	E
ACTIVATING EVENT	BELIEFS	EMOTIONAL CONSEQUENCES	DISPUTE THE VALIDITY	NEW, POSITIVE EFFECTS OF SUBSTITUTING FACTUAL BELIEFS FOR ERRONEOUS ONES
Friends outside smoking	"Wow, I need a cigarette. It is the only way that I can cope with this stress!"	Craving, distress, desire, and longing	"Sure, I want to smoke, but I don't need one. I've gone without one for a long time. I can do something else to cope with my stress. The desire will go away if I take a 5-minute walk instead."	Increased self-efficacy to quit smoking Recognition that replacing smoking with other stress-relieving activity will make it easier to quit

To help facilitate this process, a coach may ask clients the following questions:

- What is the evidence that your thought is true? What is the evidence that your thought is not true?
- What is an alternative explanation or viewpoint?
- What is the worst thing that could happen? How could you cope with that?
- What is the best that could happen? What is the most likely outcome?

COGNITIVE DISTORTIONS

The unproductive thought processes that can paralyze a client in making a positive and lasting behavioral change generally tend to fall into one of 10 categories, which are referred to as **cognitive distortions** in the psychological literature (Burns, 1999) (Table 7-2). These are the "thoughts," or the "2" in the 1-2-3-4 model described above, or the B (beliefs) in the A-B-C-D-E model. Recognition and diffusion of these thoughts are important targets for CBC.

Table 7-2

COGNITIVE DISTORTIONS

COGNITIVE DISTORTION	EXPLANATION	EXAMPLE
All-or-nothing thinking	A person looks at experiences in absolute, black-and-white categories.	"I already blew going 'cold turkey' when I smoked one cigarette today. I might as well just smoke the whole pack."
Overgeneralization	A person views a negative event as a never-ending pattern of defeat.	"Despite all my hard work to eat better and exercise more, my blood pressure is still too high! I'm never going to get off these meds!"
Mental filter	A person dwells on the negatives and ignores the positives.	"After all this work to improve my fitness, my body composition has barely budged." This person is ignoring the improvements in cardiorespiratory fitness, flexibility, and muscular endurance, and a decrease in waist circumference.
Discounting the positives	A person insists that his or her accomplishments or positive qualities "don't count."	"That's great that I have a lot of friends, am involved in my community, and got a promotion at work, but really none of that matters when I am 25 pounds overweight."
Jumping to conclusions:		
Mind reading	A person assumes that people are reacting negatively to him or her, even when there's no evidence for this.	"I am so stressed out at work because I know that everyone is thinking that I'm not the right fit for the job."
Fortune-telling	A person arbitrarily predicts that things will turn out badly.	"Nothing every works out right for me. Even if I get control of my blood sugar, I'm sure it will be short-lived."
Magnification or minimization	A person blows things out of proportion or shrinks their importance inappropriately.	"My doctor said my cholesterol is only slightly lower than it was last time. What am I going to do? This is terrible news and a huge setback for me." The client in the smoking scenario described in Table 7-1 exhibited magnification with his belief that smoking was the only way to reduce his stress.
Emotional reasoning	A person reasons from how he or she feels.	"I feel like an idiot, so I must really be one." Or "I don't feel like doing this, so I'll put it off."
"Should" statements	A person criticizes oneself or other people with "shoulds" or "shouldn'ts." "Musts," "oughts," and "have-tos" are similar offenders.	"I should have chosen the salad instead of the taco platter for lunch."
Labeling	A person identifies with his or her shortcomings.	Instead of saying "I made a mistake," he or she responds with "I'm a jerk," or "a fool," or "a loser."
Personalization and blame	A person blames himself or herself for something he or she was not entirely responsible for, or the person blames other people and overlooks ways that his or her own attitudes and behavior might contribute to a problem.	"I had a terrible day at work. My boss keeps hounding me to turn in my report that is late because he keeps wasting my time. It is stressing me out!"

THE PROCESS OF COGNITIVE BEHAVIORAL COACHING

CBC relies on a collaborative partnership with a client to explore his or her thought processes and the feelings and, subsequently, the behaviors that occur because of them. From there, the client–coach team work to develop action plans to neutralize and counter these thoughts and feelings, ultimately clearing the path to the desired behavioral change.

Cognitive behavioral interventions do not seek to provide people with answers to their problems or difficulties. Rather, much like the techniques of **motivational interviewing,** cognitive behavioral interventions rely on a collaborative process—referred to as "guided discovery" in cognitive behavioral interventions—to help clients arrive at their own solutions and insights into their thinking.

Coaches can facilitate "guided discovery" by walking clients through the six-step process presented in Figure 7-2. This process helps a client dissect a negative thought cycle and develop an action plan for change.

Figure 7-2

SIX STEPS TO DISSECTING A NEGATIVE THOUGHT CYCLE AND DEVELOPING A PLAN FOR CHANGE

1. Situation/Event:
2. What are my feelings/emotions?
3. What am I thinking that created these feelings/emotions?
4. What cognitive distortions are present?
5. What would be more accurate thoughts?
6. How will I respond differently next time this situation occurs?

Ultimately, the key in using Figure 7-2 is to help the client:

Catch the thoughts: Help the client catch "automatic thoughts."

Check the thoughts: How realistic are these thoughts?

Challenge the thoughts: Identify the cognitive distortions.

Change the thoughts: Replace any unrealistic, irrational, or inaccurate thoughts with more accurate thoughts.

An example of a common situation coaches may experience and how to put cognitive behavioral coaching into action using the model above is outlined below.

CASE STUDY: FEAR OF THE UNKNOWN

Overview: A client shares that she has an upcoming visit to the doctor. She states that "visiting the doctor makes me so anxious that I usually just fail to show up to the appointment. My dad died of high blood pressure and always had bad side effects from the medicines he had to take. I don't want to deal with that."

1. Situation/Event: Upcoming doctor's appointment.
2. What are the client's feelings/emotions?

> She expresses outright that she is anxious. One may assume that this is due to a fear of the unknown. The coach may ask open-ended questions and offer reflections to help understand better the client's feelings.
>
> These could include:
>
> - It sounds like you are worried that you will have a similar outcome to your dad.
> - You feel that not knowing is better than the doctor telling you that you may have to make some changes to control your blood pressure.
> - You feel scared of what the doctor might tell you.

3. What am I thinking that created these feelings/emotions?

> Use of OARS (open-ended questions, affirmations, reflections, and summarizing) can help the client articulate her underlying feelings. The coach may test the assumption that the client is thinking that she may have high blood pressure or that she is going to get sick like her dad.
>
> Potential questions may include:
>
> - What is the evidence for this thought? What makes you think that way?
> - What evidence argues against this thought?

4. What cognitive distortions are present? Explain.

There are a few potential cognitive distortions at play.

The client may be exhibiting "jumping to conclusions." The client seems to be fearful of hearing bad news, which would have activated thoughts and feelings associated with her father's illness, which she is motivated to avoid because it (a) might make her confront the reality that she could be heading down the same path, and/or (b) that she could not cope with the emotions associated with this.

Avoidance is a key issue in relation to avoidance of healthcare interactions, avoidance of monitoring behaviors (food diaries, glucose monitoring, and biometric assessments), or avoidance of negative thoughts or feelings in and of themselves. Helping clients recognize the avoidance and the underlying cognitive distortion triggering avoidance helps him or her take the first step on the path of positive behavioral change.

Additionally, the client may also be suffering from the distortion of "emotional reasoning," or thinking something along the lines of "because I feel scared, it must be that something bad is going to happen."

The coach might say:

- It sounds like you may be jumping to conclusions that it will be a bad experience.
- What would happen if you went to the doctor's appointment and you were told that you have high blood pressure?
- What is the worst case scenario? How would you handle that if it happened?

5. What would be more accurate thoughts?

A more accurate thought may be that there is a possibility, even a likelihood, that the client may be told she has high blood pressure. She may do well to be prepared with questions she will ask if that occurs. She might think that high blood pressure can be well controlled and that she is prepared to make healthy changes to accomplish that.

For instance, a client might state, "There is no reason that I should feel so scared. Millions of people have high blood pressure and handle it fine. I can too."

Of course, the coach cannot tell a client how to feel, but through the use of OARS, a coach can help a client to consider more logical thoughts that do not carry the emotional weight of the more reflexive emotional thoughts.

6. How will I respond differently next time this situation occurs?

> At this point, the coach may pose the question to this client, "How do you feel now about going to the doctor's appointment?"
>
> A successful cognitive coaching session will end with a client feeling empowered to not only attend the doctor's appointment, but also be prepared to respond rationally to the outcome of the visit.
>
> For example, the client might state, "Even if I receive news that I don't want to hear, I can handle it. It is better to know so I can make a change rather than to not know. I am going to make my appointment."

The A-B-C-D-E framework can also be applied to this scenario:

A	B	C	D	E
ACTIVATING EVENT	**BELIEFS**	**EMOTIONAL CONSEQUENCES**	**DISPUTE THE VALIDITY**	**NEW, POSITIVE EFFECTS OF SUBSTITUTING FACTUAL BELIEFS FOR ERRONEOUS ONES**
Doctor's appointment	The client may receive bad news	Anxiety and fear of the unknown	"There is no reason that I should feel so scared. Millions of people have high blood pressure and handle it fine. I can too."	"Even if I receive news that I don't want to hear, I can handle it. It is better to know so I can make a change rather than to not know. I am going to make my appointment."

PRACTICAL APPLICATIONS

1. Describe how knowledge of cognitive behavioral coaching strategies may or may not impact your approach to improving your own health behaviors.

2. Role play a cognitive behavioral coaching scenario with a friend or family member.
   Use the six steps outlined in Figure 7-2 to guide the coaching session.
   Complete the worksheet below to dissect the experience using the A-B-C-D-E model.

A	B	C	D	E
ACTIVATING EVENT	BELIEFS	EMOTIONAL CONSEQUENCES	DISPUTE THE VALIDITY	NEW, POSITIVE EFFECTS OF SUBSTITUTING FACTUAL BELIEFS FOR ERRONEOUS ONES

3. What came most naturally as you practiced cognitive behavioral coaching strategies? What was most challenging?

4. How might you adapt or improve your approach with future clients?

SUMMARY

The appropriate application of cognitive behavioral coaching can help increase a client's awareness of counterproductive thought processes, and also trigger in the client a choice to distance him- or herself from negative thoughts and cognitive distortions, and simply experience an event as it is. Ultimately, the client will gain skill in using cognitive behavioral strategies to support making positive behavioral changes. With this said, it is incredibly important to note that coaches who are not licensed therapists should not apply cognitive behavioral interventions when working with clients with mental health disorders, nor should coaches present themselves as therapists. It is incumbent upon the coach to recognize the defined scope of practice and engage a network of professionals, including psychologists and other mental health professionals, to refer to when warranted.

EXPANSION QUIZ
Multiple-choice quiz available if you expand to the full experience

References

Beck, A.T. (1975). *Cognitive Therapy and the Emotional Disorders.* Madison, Conn.: International Universities Press.

Burns, D.D. (1999). *Feeling Good: The New Mood Therapy* (revised edition). New York: Wm. Morrow and Co.

Butler, A.C. et al. (2006). The empirical status of cognitive-behavioral therapy: A review of meta-analyses. *Clinical Psychology Review,* 26, 17–31

Conway, R.L. (2000). *The Impact of Coaching Mid-level Managers Utilizing Multi-rater Feedback.* La Verne, Calif.: University of La Verne.

Ellis, A. (1962). *Reason and Emotion in Psychotherapy.* New York: Lyle Stuart.

Ellis, A. (1961) *A Guide to Rational Living.* Englewood Cliffs, N.J.: Prentice-Hall.

Grant, A.M. (2003). The impact of life coaching on goal attainment, metacognition and mental health. *Social Behaviour and Personality,* 31, 253–263.

Green, L.S., Oades, L.G., & Grant, A.M. (2006). Cognitive-behavioral, solution-focused life coaching: Enhancing goal striving, well-being, and hope. *Journal of Positive Psychology,* 1, 142–149.

Laske, O.E. (1999). Transformative effects of coaching on executives' professional agenda. *Dissertation Abstracts International: Section B: The Sciences & Engineering,* 60(5-B), 2386.

Norcross, J.C., Karpiak, C.P., & Santoro, S.O. (2005). Clinical psychologists across the years: The division of clinical psychology from 1960 to 2003. *Journal of Clinical Psychology,* 61, 1467–1483.

CHAPTER 8

CHAPTER 8
STRENGTHS-BASED COACHING

LEARNING OBJECTIVES

After reading this chapter, the coach will be able to:

- Apply the principles of positive psychology to a practical coaching session
- Conduct a strengths-based coaching session
- Explore barriers with clients and how to overcome them

As a person prepares to make a behavioral change and chooses what areas to focus on and what goals to pursue, highlighting strengths and assets, as well as planning for barriers and challenges, increases the opportunity for long-term success. When clients learn to recognize and circumvent obstacles, they save time, energy, and frustration.

STRENGTHS AND ASSETS

A focus on strengths and assets rather than weaknesses and deficits helps a person pursuing a behavioral change to achieve success.

APPLICATIONS OF POSITIVE PSYCHOLOGY

The foundation of coaching is **positive psychology.** The field of positive psychology and the evidence supporting its efficacy is discussed in detail in Chapter 3. Ultimately, positive psychology advocates that coaches help clients identify and utilize their strengths to successfully accomplish a goal and make a lasting behavioral change.

STRENGTHS-BASED COACHING APPLICATIONS

A demonstration of strengths-based coaching with psychologist and coach Dr. Robert Biswas-Diener is featured in the accompanying resources for this chapter. This practical application is intended to help guide coaches in implementing the principles of positive psychology in everyday coaching practice.

ACCOMPANYING VIDEO:
Dr. Robert Biswas-Diener offers a strengths-based coaching demonstration and debrief.

Ultimately, the overall objective is to help facilitate a client choosing to focus on strengths, assets, and possibilities for the future rather than weaknesses, deficits, and what went wrong in the past. For example, coaches can draw on client success by asking questions that allow clients to recall beliefs, behaviors, or attitudes they used in previous circumstances:

- What worked in the past that could help you now?
- What did you learn about in that previous circumstance that could save you time now?
- How did you successfully handle a similar situation?
- What do you know about yourself that could help you stay on track?
- How could remembering past successes help you in your current situation?

Working from strengths also requires that the coach assumes his or her clients' resourcefulness. The coaching relationship is based on the premise that clients are experts in their own lives. Effective coaches know that answers are within the client and that coaching is a process to uncover those solutions. When coaches regard their clients as resourceful, they create an atmosphere for clients to reflect on apparent strengths and reveal habits, patterns, attributes, or values that they may not have recognized as assets.

Answers are within the client

Coaches can use the following strategies to assess the belief that clients have their own best answers.

- Ask open-ended, unbiased questions.
  - "Where might you start?" vs. "Have you considered working with a personal trainer?"
  - "When would be a good time to learn more about that?" vs. "Can you set a goal to complete that by next week?"
  - "What would help you stay on track?" vs. "Have you thought about keeping a food log?"
- Be patient as clients ponder their options. After asking a clear, open-ended and unbiased question, simply practice silence.
- Consider yourself a "guide on the side" rather than an expert. Coaches are advised to relinquish the belief that they know what is best for each client, including what, when, and how they need to achieve their goals. Exceptional coaches become increasingly comfortable with not knowing. Coaches can monitor their own inclination to rush in with helpful suggestions during and between sessions by asking themselves the following questions:
  - What can I do or think when I'm tempted to prod my clients?
  - How can I become more comfortable with pauses as my client considers a response?
  - What clues is my body giving me about my level of presence or anxiety?
  - How can I best prepare myself for coaching to minimize my need to give advice?
  - What do I need to remember about each client's resourcefulness?
- Ask clients to consider what unique talents they could bring to the situation.

BARRIERS

The best plans do not guarantee a simple progression from point A to point B. More commonly, clients encounter many barriers along the way to lasting behavioral change. Coaches play an important role in helping clients plan ahead for obstacles that could impede success. It is important to note that inquiries about barriers are best made without judgment.

One useful framework from which to consider barriers and then develop strategies to prevent or overcome them is the **socio-ecological model.** This model shows that behaviors need to be considered in the context of multiple layers of influence (Figure 8-1). In this framework, coaching interventions extend well beyond providing traditional education to individuals and families about healthy choices, and can help build skills, reshape the environment, and reestablish social norms to facilitate individuals' healthy choices. Additionally, coaches have an opportunity to influence a client's response to challenges in each of these domains and advocate for changes to make the healthy choice the easy choice.

Make the healthy choice the easy choice

Figure 8-1
SOCIO-ECOLOGICAL MODEL

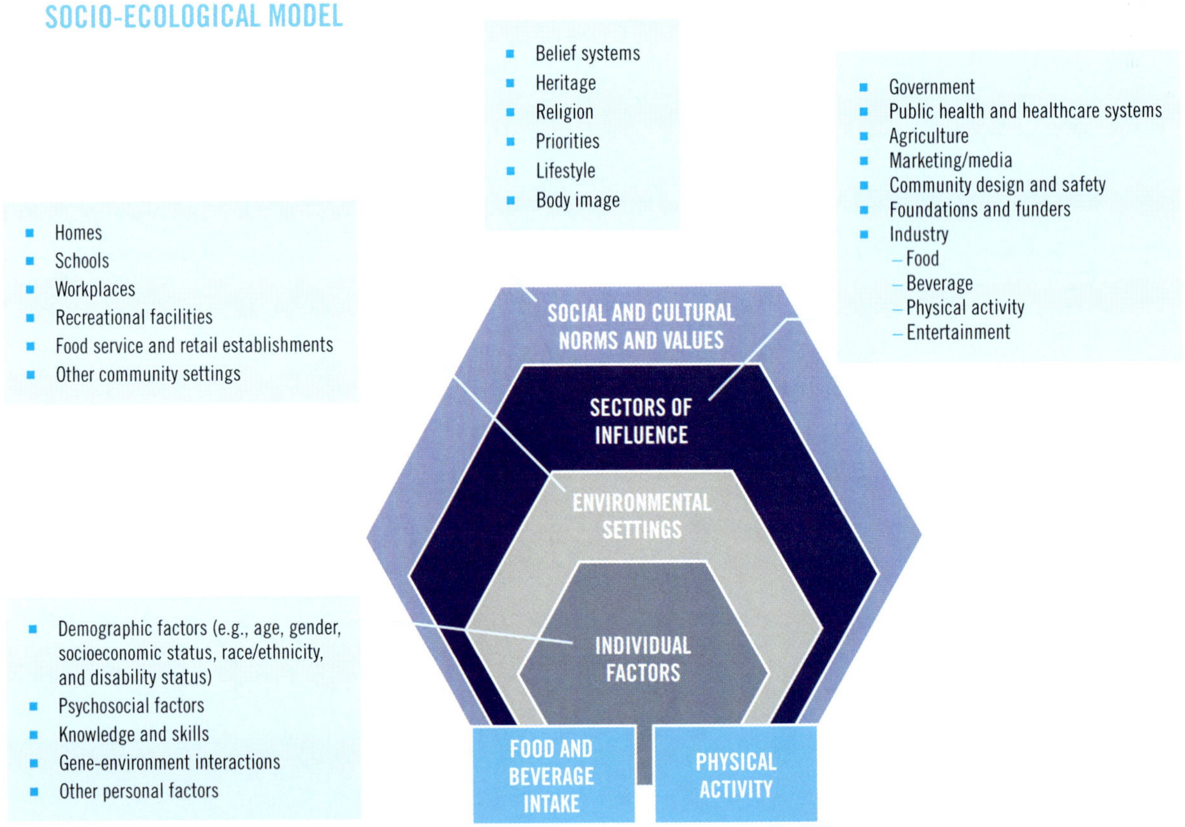

Consider the following example: A client living in Minnesota is planning a road trip to California. He hired a coach one month ago to help him make changes to his lifestyle to help manage his hypertension. One area that he has focused on is decreasing sodium intake. He is very excited about the trip, but anxious about how he will continue his new eating patterns while on the road. The client might save some time, energy, and frustration by exploring potential roadblocks he might encounter and developing a plan to address them. The coach might ask the following questions:

- What steps could you take before you leave to help support your behavioral change once you are on the road?
- What could you do while you are on the road to help maintain your new eating patterns?
- Are there resources you could utilize before you go to help making eating healthy easier while you're gone?
- What might you do if your only option is a fast food restaurant?
- What might you do if you revert back to your old eating habits?
- How else might you prepare for your trip?

Similarly, when clients begin a wellness program, coach them about potential obstacles that could interfere with success. Clients who have considered strategies to meet challenges will more likely circumvent roadblocks rather than be surprised and stalled by them. Coaches can use the following questions to lead this discussion:

What patterns of thinking could get in your way? [Coaches may consider the application of **cognitive behavioral coaching** strategies (see Chapter 7) in helping clients uncover ways to reduce the impact of unhelpful thought patterns.]

What patterns of behavior could get in your way?

How will you persevere when you hit a turn-around point or obstacle?

How likely is it that you will follow through with your action plan?

How could you best be supported when you encounter an obstacle?

PRACTICAL APPLICATIONS

1. Send an email survey to coworkers, friends, and family members asking for feedback about your strengths and assets. You may wish to include the following questions:

   In your opinion, what are my strengths?

   In general, how would you describe my gifts or talents?

   What do I do particularly well?

   In what ways can you count on me?

   How well do I take responsibility for my choices?

   What did you learn from this experience?

2. Have a client complete a survey of his or her assets and strengths (see Chapter 3 for examples of available surveys).

   How can you avoid leading your client to conclusions rather than allowing his or her interpretations to be valid?

   As you continue to coach, when might it be useful to remind a client about the survey results? What would you say to your client?

   What would you hope to accomplish?

PRACTICAL APPLICATIONS

3. Consider a personal behavioral change that you would like to make. Explore this change in the context of the socio-ecological model (see Figure 8-1). For each level of influence, discuss at least one strength or asset that will support your change and one barrier that could interfere with your change.

SUMMARY

Coaching is a profession based on client-centeredness, forward-looking orientation, and utilization of strengths. Practicing strengths-based coaching and working with clients to engage their strengths to anticipate and overcome barriers sets the stage for a positive and lasting behavioral change.

EXPANSION QUIZ
Multiple-choice quiz available if you expand to the full experience

CHAPTER 9

CHAPTER 9

GOAL SETTING

LEARNING OBJECTIVES

After reading this chapter, the coach will be able to:

- Describe the four mechanisms and five moderators of the role of goals in behavioral change
- Develop a coaching plan that incorporates specific, measurable, attainable, relevant, and time-bound goals and make revisions and updates to goals and the coaching plan when indicated
- Use the GROW model when developing goals with clients

The power of goal setting in helping to achieve meaningful change is well established. Individuals who have specific and challenging goals perform better than those with nonspecific and/or easy goals, or no goals at all. In order for a client to optimize success at actually attaining a desired outcome—to achieve one's vision of what life will be like after a behavioral change has been made—strategic goal setting is important.

GOAL-SETTING THEORY

Edwin Locke of the University of Maryland and Gary Latham of the University of Toronto are industrial/organizational psychologists who have pioneered the scientific investigation of goal setting, especially when used within worksites to drive employee performance. Their 40-plus years of studying goal setting and their integration of more than 400 studies has informed a general model of goal-setting theory.

This theory posits that a person's values drive his or her emotions and desires (or, in the case of behavioral change, a person's vision for oneself). The image of how a person envisions him- or herself informs his or her intentions, or goals. Goals then inspire behavioral change, or affect performance, through four mechanisms (Locke & Latham, 2002):

Directed attention: Goals direct attention and effort toward goal-relevant activities.

Mobilized effort: Difficult-to-attain goals inspire increased effort.

Persistence: Difficult-to-attain goals prolong the amount of time someone invests in a task.

Strategy: Goals compel people to employ familiar strategies and develop new strategies to achieve the goal.

How well a goal incites a change in behavior or performance is determined by five goal moderators (Locke & Latham, 2006):

- *Goal commitment:* A higher degree of goal commitment is more likely to lead to a change in behavior. Commitment is increased when attaining a goal is very important to the individual. Activities such as a public commitment to a goal or signing a behavioral contract help to increase importance (Figure 9-1). Commitment is also increased when a client has a high degree of **self-efficacy.** Coaches can help a client increase self-efficacy by helping to ensure that he or she has the necessary resources to achieve the goal, by identifying others with whom the client identifies who have been successful, and by providing support and encouragement.
- *Feedback:* Clients benefit from intermittent feedback on their progress toward attaining a specified goal. A coach can help a client establish a feedback mechanism, whether it is through goal check-ins during coaching sessions or via daily monitoring of goal progress through journaling, devices, or apps.
- *Task complexity:* Highly complex tasks (such as the need to lose a substantial amount of weight) may interfere with goal attainment. However, when **learning goals** (also known as process goals) are established—as opposed to **performance goals** (also known as outcome goals)—novices are more likely to be successful. In addition, in these cases, short-term goals are more helpful than long-term goals. However, once proficiency is developed, challenging performance goals are most effective.
- *Situational constraints:* A client is most likely to attain a goal if the necessary resources are available to be successful.
- *Goal framing:* A client is most likely to be successful if a goal is positioned as a challenge rather than as a threat. In the case of behavioral change, establishing a goal of adopting a new habit (e.g., eat vegetables and fruits during snacks) rather than breaking an old habit (e.g., stop eating cookies for snacks) may be more successful.

Figure 9-1

A BEHAVIORAL CONTRACT

I Will: (Do what) ____

____

(When) ____

(How often) ____

(How much) ____

How confident am I that I will do this? _______ (on a scale of 0 to 10, with 0 being not at all confident and 10 being completely confident)

If I successfully make this positive lifestyle change by ________, I will reward myself with ______________________

____

____.

If I fail to successfully make this positive lifestyle change, I will forfeit this reward.

I, ____, have reviewed this contract and I agree to discuss

(Client)

the experience involved in accomplishing or not accomplishing this health behavior improvement with

____ on ______________________________.

(Coach) (Date)

Signed (Client): ____

Signed (Coach): ____

PRACTICAL APPLICATION

1. Complete a goal-setting session with a client, colleague, family member, or friend. As part of this session, complete a behavioral contract such as the one shown in Figure 9-1 with the person.

   Describe your experience. What went well? What was difficult? What would you do the same in goal setting with a client in the future? What would you do differently?

   How do you think signing the behavioral contract affected the individual's goal commitment?

SMART GOALS

These principles of goal-setting theory have given rise to the concept of **SMART goals**—which stands for specific, measurable, attainable, relevant, and time-bound.

S

SPECIFIC

Broad-based goals such as "do your best" lead to only marginal success when compared to a specific high-performance goal. Specific goals provide a focused target, which in turn triggers directed attention, one of the four key mechanisms for a goal to facilitate a successful behavioral change.

M

MEASURABLE

A measurable goal provides a client with the feedback needed to assess how well he or she is doing in accomplishing the goal. This is a key moderator of goal attainment.

A

ATTAINABLE

While the best goals are difficult to achieve, a client must feel that the goal is within reach. A major driver of whether or not a client perceives a goal as attainable is his or her self-efficacy, which also impacts goal commitment. For the most complex or difficult tasks, short-term, process-centered goals are more likely to be achieved than long-term, outcome-centered goals.

R

RELEVANT

For a goal to drive a behavioral change, a client must feel that the goal is important. The degree of importance influences goal commitment, a major moderator of how effective a goal is at driving behavioral change.

T

TIME-BOUND

Deadlines increase the motivational impact of goals. In addition, progress toward goals is best evaluated regularly with goal modification and advancement of goals when indicated.

The process of attaining a desired outcome starts with a client's values. These values should inform the client's vision for him- or herself. The five moderators (goal commitment, feedback, task complexity, situational constraints, and goal framing) are key components of SMART goals. SMART goals help to improve performance/change behavior via the four mechanisms (directed attention, mobilized effort, persistence, and strategy). Once a client has successfully accomplished a goal, the experience readies the client to set and attain the next goal. As the cycle continues, the cumulative process of goal attainment leads to an outcome, which is the real-life manifestation of the vision. A visual representation of goal-setting theory is shown in Figure 9-2.

Figure 9-2

A GENERAL MODEL OF GOAL-SETTING THEORY

Data from: Lunenburg, F.C. (2011). Goal-setting theory of motivation. *International Journal of Management, Business, and Administration.* 15, 1, 1–6; Locke, E.A. & Latham, G.P. (2002). Building a practically useful theory of goal setting and task motivation. *American Psychologist,* 57, 9, 705–717.

THE GROW MODEL: A COACH'S GUIDE TO GOAL SETTING

Coaches are well-advised to consider goal-setting theory and the best practices when helping clients establish behavior-change goals. One way to do this is through implementation of the **GROW model**—"Goal, Reality, Options (or Obstacles), and Will (or Way Forward)"—when goal setting with clients (Whitmore, 2009). The GROW model assumes the coach is not an expert in the client's situation. Rather, the coach acknowledges that the client is his or her own best expert. The coach's role is simply to facilitate the client's goal-setting experience through use of the **OARS model**—**open-ended questions, reflections, affirmations,** and **summarizing.**

THE GROW MODEL IN PRACTICE

Goal: Ask open-ended questions, which help the client to establish a SMART goal. Questions may include:

- What do you want to achieve?
- What is important about this for you?
- How will you know that you achieved this goal?
- What is a reasonable timeframe to achieve this goal?

Reality: Ask open-ended questions to examine the current situation and context. Questions may include:

- What is happening now?
- What is the effect of your current situation?
- What steps have you taken toward your goal?
- How does this goal conflict with your other goals?

Options: Ask open-ended questions to explore all of the possible options for achieving the goal. Questions may include:

- What are possible obstacles in achieving this goal? How will you respond?
- What are the advantages and disadvantages of each option?
- What have you done in the past that has worked?
- What do you need to stop doing to achieve this goal?
- What do you need to start doing to achieve this goal?

Will: Ask open-ended questions to help the client commit to the stated goal. Questions may include:

- What will you do now?
- How will you move forward?
- What will help to increase your success?
- How often will you review your progress?

PRACTICAL APPLICATION

2. Take a client, colleague, family member, or friend through the GROW model of behavioral change.

What was his or her SMART goal?

How did the individual describe his or her current reality?

What were obstacles and options for proceeding?

How did the individual increase his or her will and commitment?

How do you feel that the goal-setting session went? What worked well? What could be improved?

Once the client has proceeded through the GROW process and developed a plan, the coach can help solidify the client's commitment to the goal by summarizing the conversation, including the SMART goal, the current situation and any foreseeable obstacles, the client's plan for the way forward, and the timeframe for a check-in to review progress and make adjustments if needed.

» Consider the following example of the goal-setting process used in a family coaching session to help six-year-old Johnny, who is at an unhealthy weight.

Help the family establish a SMART goal	Coach: "We have been talking about SMART goals. Can you think of a SMART goal you'd like to pursue to help Johnny achieve a healthier weight?"	Mom: "Ok. I think I understand. How's this: We would like to help Johnny achieve a healthier weight by eliminating juice and soda from the house for the next month until our next visit."
Assess the current reality	Coach: "How much juice or soda does Johnny drink now?"	Mom: "Currently Johnny drinks about 2 cups of juice per day and a soda 2 or 3 times per week."
	"What, if anything, have you done in the past to cut back on juice and soda?"	"We tried to cut back on Johnny's soda in the past, but since his older brother still drank juice, we had it in the house and that made it really hard. This time, we are all going to stop with the sugary drinks together. This is going to be hard because Johnny really likes juice and doesn't like water, but we can do it for the next month and then see how it goes. Right, Johnny?"
Explore options	Coach: "What are some options as you consider on how to cut back on the sugary drinks?"	Mom: "To us, the choice is simple: We either keep the sugary drinks and Johnny continues to struggle with his weight, or we get rid of them. We are going to get rid of them. To get started, we need to have a family meeting and let everyone know that we are no longer going to have these drinks in the house. They aren't 'off limits' completely. Sometimes when we go out the kids can have them. But we are no longer going to have them in the house."
	"What do you need to stop doing to achieve this goal?"	"We are going to stop drinking juice and soda. We need to stop buying them. And we need to stop bringing them into the house!"
	"What do you need to start doing?"	"What do we need to start? Well, we need to start learning to like water!"
Will	Coach: "Wow, it sounds like you are really motivated to change. What will you do today to get started"	Mom: "Johnny, what do you think? Are you ready for this? I'm ready for this." Mom: "Johnny, today when we get home we are going to dump the juice and soda. This is going to help us be healthier as a family. Ok?" Johnny: "Ok, mom. Ok."
	"When should we check in?"	"We set this goal for the next month. So let's try it out and we will check back with you in a month."

3. Using this worksheet, articulate three highly effective goals for yourself based on SMART goal setting and the GROW model.

SMART goal	Write your specific, measurable, attainable, relevant, and time-bound goal	
Reality	What is your present situation in relation to this goal? What steps have you taken toward your goal? What other goals conflict with this goal, if any?	
Options	What are possible options in pursuing this goal? What has worked for you in the past? What do you need to start doing to achieve this goal? What do you need to stop doing?	
Will	How ready are you to pursue your goal? What will you start doing now? How will you assess your progress?	

SUMMARY

Goal setting is a key driver of a client's success with a behavioral change. Coaches provide clients a great service by helping them develop effective goals and continually monitoring, reevaluating, and advancing goals as needed. With implementation of tools such as SMART goal setting and the GROW model, coaches can help clients to translate a vision of the future into reality.

EXPANSION QUIZ
Multiple-choice quiz available if you expand to the full experience

References

Locke, E.A. & Latham, G.P. (2006). New directions in goal-setting theory. *Current Directions in Psychological Science,* 15, 5, 265–268.

Locke, E.A. & Latham, G.P. (2002). Building a practically useful theory of goal setting and task motivation. *American Psychologist,* 57, 9, 705–717.

Lunenburg, F.C. (2011). Goal-setting theory of motivation. *International Journal of Management, Business, and Administration,* 15, 1, 1–6.

Whitmore, Sir J. (2009). *Coaching for Performance* (4th ed.). London: Nicholas Brealey.

Introduction to Section IV:

EXECUTION

This text is rooted in the ACE cycle of change, which stands for awareness, choice, and execution. Through the course of behavioral change, clients go through a predictable, though nonlinear, cycle. The stage of execution occurs when the client is ready to make the behavioral change. At this point, most clients will have an idea of what they hope the end outcome will be, they have developed a plan to achieve this outcome, and now they are ready to begin the challenging, yet rewarding task of making the changes necessary to achieve their goals. Coaching a client through this phase of change includes the use of strategies and communication techniques to help the client develop and implement action plans, hold the client accountable, increase the client's knowledge and skills to enhance likelihood of success, and evaluate how well the actual changes align with the desired changes.

The coach's role in this process is to help develop and implement action plans, set up a system for accountability, use adult learning techniques to fill knowledge gaps, and evaluate (and adapt) the plan.

OVER THE COURSE OF THIS SECTION, COACHES WILL GAIN COMPETENCY IN THE FOLLOWING FOUR AREAS:

Actions plans   Accountability   Adult learning   Evaluation

The International Coach Federation (ICF) Core Competencies that are emphasized in the four chapters in this section include: (3) Establishing trust and intimacy with the client; (4) Coaching presence; (5) Active listening; (6) Powerful questioning; (7) Direct communication; (9) Designing actions; and (11) Managing progress and accountability.

▶ **For more information on the ICF Coaching Competencies, refer to the Introduction and Appendix A.**

CHAPTER 10

CHAPTER 10

ACTION PLANS AND GROWING NEW HABITS

LEARNING OBJECTIVES

After reading this chapter, the coach will be able to:

- Describe several considerations when developing action plans
- Use brainstorming to help a client identify key actions
- Translate goals into action plans

Coaching is first and foremost about moving action forward in the direction of the client's goals. Whether a client's goal is simple or quite ambitious, he or she needs a plan of action to move the goal from idea to implementation, and ultimately to successful attainment. Just as businesses participate in strategic planning outlining their values, vision, mission, objectives, goals, and action plans, an individual striving to make a significant lifestyle change benefits from engaging in a similar process. The final step in the process of planning for change is outlining the necessary actions—and then doing them! An effective coach creates a supportive environment in which to do this, and also works with the client to create new small steps that eventually add up to big changes.

PREPARING FOR ACTION

An effective coach considers several factors when supporting clients to develop and implement a plan of action, including the client's readiness, support system, preferred terms, clarity about the client and coach's perspectives, how the plan is designed, and the need to access resources.

READINESS

It is often said that "timing is everything." This certainly applies to coaching someone in their process of change. Coaches can assess a client's level of motivation with direct questions:

- Are you ready to move the action forward?
- By when would you want to take the first step?
- What do you need in order to make this a priority?

SUPPORT SYSTEM

People who support a client's intentions are assets; people who do not support their intentions are liabilities. Understanding a client's support system (or lack thereof) provides critical information in planning for change, including developing strategies to enhance a client's support network. Some useful questions include:

- Who could support you as you take steps toward your goal?
- How can you respond to those who discourage you?
- Is there anything you can delegate?

PREFERRED TERMS

Coaches take the lead from their clients and allow clients to determine what they want to change or improve. One way coaches yield to their clients is to listen and reflect terms or phrases the client prefers to use. Coaches can support clients by using terms clients prefer rather than ones the coach may prefer.

- As clients take steps to move forward, some like to refer to "goals," "intentions," "action steps," or some other term. What term do you prefer?
- You mentioned that you like to set intentions rather than goals. So, would you like to set up a plan to fulfill your intentions?
- I noticed that you talk about fulfilling your potential. Are you ready to move forward with your fulfillment plan?

PERSPECTIVES: CLIENT AND COACH

Coaching involves deep, reflective, and critical listening. Effective coaches believe that their clients are experts in their own lives and are therefore capable of generating goals and action plans that are unique and attainable.

Coaches have the advantage of being unbiased

On the other hand, coaches have the advantage of being unbiased, outside observers who are not distracted by the details in their clients' lives, and can therefore hold the big picture per their clients' agendas. This larger view is at the heart of effective action strategy plans. Therefore, from time to time, a coach may check in with his or her clients about how their action plan may or may not be aligned with their larger life plan.

- How does this action contribute to the big picture for your life?
- You mentioned that your main objective is to stay active into your 50s and beyond. How does this step contribute to that long-range goal?
- What might keep you from completing this plan?

ACCESS TO RESOURCES

Action plans include work done between coaching sessions to gather information. Often, thoughtful preparation for action is a key to success. Clients may need to investigate outside resources or spend some time to self-reflect to gain information and insight regarding their next steps. Consequently, effective coaches are willing to coach clients about preparation as well as action.

Preparation for action is a key to success

- How could you get more information about that?
- You mentioned that you wanted to "think about it this week." How could you go about setting up the time to reflect?
- So, would talking to your friends who are already successfully walking at work be something you want to do?

THE COACH'S PERSONAL EXPERIENCES

The role of a coach is to support clients in fulfilling their own agendas. There may be many instances when clients discuss topics with which a coach has had personal experience or perhaps even professional expertise. The temptation to share a helpful comment may be very close to the surface. However, remember that a coach has knowledge of his or her own experiences and reactions but limited knowledge of what it is like to be the client. While there is a place for expertise, sharing personal opinions, experience, suggestions, warnings, or expertise should be done only sparingly during coaching. Several challenges exist related to giving advice or suggestions:

- A client may succumb to the coach's opinion and relinquish his or her best ideas.
- The client may become dependent on the coach for answers.
- The client's ability to discover, discern, and decide may be diminished.

Miller and Rollnick (2013) suggest that coaches think carefully about whether sharing a piece of information is likely to be helpful. A few occasions when self-disclosure may be helpful include the following:

- To promote trust
- To model openness and encourage reciprocity of disclosure from the client
- To answer a client's question
- To affirm the client's experience

Unless the disclosure fits into one of these categories, the coach is typically better off not sharing personal experiences.

CASE STUDY

You have been coaching with George for several weeks. He wants to better manage his stress at work and at home. George has successfully implemented some new strategies and has been happy with his progress. During today's session, he tells you that he is very upset about his teenager's recent behavior. George is so distraught that he is losing sleep and is at his wit's end. You like George and are impacted by his story. You have also experienced a lot of stress recently and opted to manage your stress with yoga and meditation. Knowing what has worked for you, you say to George, "Have you thought about trying out yoga? It really worked for me." George, replies, "Yoga? How could I sit through the calm of yoga when I am worrying about my son? This is really serious. "

- In what ways did you overstep your role as a coach?
- How could you have responded to George to empower rather than disempower him?
- What consequences might there be for the coaching relationship?

As you embrace the role of a coach, you will need to continuously monitor your thoughts, attitudes, beliefs, and actions by asking yourself the following questions:

- How can I resist the temptation to implement my action plan, as opposed to the client's action plan?
- What do I need to know or remember to allow my clients to discover their own answers?
- What strategies can I implement when I want to give advice?

PLAN DESIGN

An action plan, designed by clients with the support of their coach, involves a series of steps that lead the client in the direction of fulfillment (Miller & Rollnick, 2013).

- Confirm the goals. Review the client's overarching goals and confirm that these are in fact where the client would like to focus.
- Generate possible options, steps, or plans. This could be done through brainstorming in which the client generates a large number of possible actions to achieve the goal. During the brainstorming phase of generating ideas, it is important for the client to refrain from evaluating them.
- After all of the ideas have been captured, the client then chooses which actions to pursue. From these, the client and coach can generate the action plan, breaking the activities into small, doable steps.

TRANSLATING GOALS INTO ACTIONS THROUGH THE POWER OF HABIT

The end goal of working with a client who is trying to change a behavior is to establish a new, healthier behavior as a normal part of the client's everyday life. Essentially, it is to help the client acquire a new habit, or a routine behavior that is repeated regularly without much conscious thought involved. When addressing behavioral change, consideration of habits comes primarily in two forms:

- **CREATING NEW GOOD HABITS**
- **BREAKING OLD BAD HABITS**

Action plans may consist of a series of small steps established to create new healthy habits and replace unwanted or "bad" habits. The science of how habits form—and thus the best way to "plan" for creating new permanent ones and getting rid of old unwanted ones—is constantly evolving. Psychologist and innovation expert BJ Fogg of Stanford University has developed a promising model of how to form new healthy habits that stick. In the following feature, Fogg describes his journey to uncovering the Tiny Habits® method that can set the stage for meaningful and lasting behavior change.

ACCOMPANYING VIDEO:
In the multimedia supplement, leading behavior-change psychologist and founder of the Tiny Habits method of growing new habits BJ Fogg and his business partner and sister, professional coach Linda Fogg-Phillips, offer insights into the process of developing new habits, breaking bad habits, and coaching for successful behavioral change.

HOW I CRACKED THE CODE FOR CREATING HABITS

BJ FOGG, PHD
Stanford University

I began playing around with new ways to change my behavior in early 2011. And that led to a breakthrough now called Tiny Habits.

It all started one day when I had this insight:

"Hey, BJ, you already know how to floss all your teeth. What you haven't mastered is how to floss every day, automatically."

So I set out to find a solution.

SIMPLICITY MATTERS MORE THAN MOTIVATION

My background in studying human behavior made it clear that simplicity mattered; I knew that simplicity could mean the difference between doing a behavior and not doing it.

So I scaled flossing back to the simplest form: floss just one tooth. At the time, this sounded ridiculous to me, but I reminded myself: I didn't need to learn to floss all my teeth. Instead, I needed to focus on making flossing automatic.

As I was looking for my solution, I'd already developed the Fogg Behavior Model. That framework clearly shows that if a behavior is really easy, you don't need much motivation to do it. However, if the behavior is hard, you need a lot of motivation.

My research showed that motivation could be unreliable, going up and down moment by moment. I was wary about relying on motivation. It was natural for me to make simplicity a big part of my solution. The simpler, the better. I knew that.

EMOTIONS CREATE HABITS

The next insight—the role of emotions—was something of an accident.

Somehow I knew that if I felt good about flossing one tooth, I'd keep doing it. So each day as I flossed, I thought this to myself: "If everything ends up awful today, at least I did one thing right: I flossed one tooth. Good for me—Victory!"

I look back now and see that I got lucky. At the time I didn't fully realize that emotions create habits. In other words, if you feel a positive emotion while you're doing a new behavior or immediately after, the new behavior will become more automatic. Your brain will want to do it again. Here's how it works: **The speed of habit formation is directly related to the immediacy and intensity of emotions you feel.**

Back then, I used "Victory!" a lot. That was my goofy celebration. Today I have many ways to celebrate my Tiny Habits (dancing anyone?). But even my rudimentary "Victory!" worked well, because it made me feel good, like I was succeeding. As a result, I kept flossing. Soon flossing became a solid habit.

After a few weeks, I was flossing all my teeth daily, not just one. The habit didn't feel like a chore. Instead, I would look forward to the next opportunity. (I'd floss morning and night; I still do.) And when I couldn't floss, I felt like I was missing out. ▶

HACKING MORE OF MY BEHAVIORS

I then started applying this behavior hack—make it simple and celebrate it—to other behaviors I wanted: drink more water, eat veggie snacks during the day, and so on. I knew that making the behavior tiny was a good thing. If it was small, I had no excuse not to do it. And I didn't need much motivation.

And I also knew that saying "Victory!" after doing the behavior worked. It made me want to do the behavior again.

I look back now and see I'd solved two important pieces of the puzzle:

- Make the new behavior you want really small.
- Celebrate doing the behavior immediately.

These two things mattered, of course, but I hadn't figured out the entire solution.

PUT NEW BEHAVIOR "AFTER" AN EXISTING ROUTINE

I knew there was still a piece missing: How do I remind myself to do the tiny behavior?

I didn't try using reminder notes, because I knew that approach wouldn't scale. And besides, it was ugly. If I used notes, then I would probably end up with dozens, if not hundreds, of little notes plastered around my house and office. Did I want that? No.

The answer wasn't obvious to me, until one day . . .

I was getting out of the shower and drying off. I went into my bedroom to dress. I was doing a typical sequence of behaviors—my routines. And then it happened. I opened my sock drawer and this word struck me: after.

I recognized this as my answer. The final piece of the habit puzzle had five letters: A-F-T-E-R.

After!

I said to myself: "You won't be able to form habits quickly until you know what the new behavior comes *after*."

I got chills. It was a big moment.

You figure out where the new tiny behavior fits into your life

Today this is a key part of the Tiny Habits method. You figure out where the new tiny behavior fits into your life—What routine does it come after? In other words, you use an existing routine (brushing) to remind you to do the new tiny behavior (floss one tooth).

I call the existing routine an "anchor." In the Tiny Habits method, you pair the new tiny behavior with an anchor. If you pair it well, the tiny behavior flows easily after the anchor. Sometimes it feels like magic.

THE RECIPE FOR TINY HABITS

I call this a Tiny Habit "recipe," and you write it up like this:

"After I ___________, I will ____________."

Below are some examples of Tiny Habit recipes:

After I brush my teeth, **I will** floss one tooth.

After I start the coffee, **I will** open my "to do" list.

After I empty my spam folder, **I will** meditate for three breaths.

After I empty my water glass, **I will** refill it.

After I pee, **I will** do two push-ups.

After I walk in the door, **I will** hang my keys on the hook.

After I turn off the TV at night, **I will** set out my gym clothes.

ANATOMY OF TINY HABITS
1. Anchor Moment
An existing routine (like brushing your teeth) or an event that happens (like a phone ringing). The Anchor Moment reminds you to do the new Tiny Behavior.
2. New Tiny Behavior
A super simple version of the new behavior you want, such as flossing one tooth or doing two push-ups. You do the Tiny Behavior immediately after the Anchor Moment.
3. Instant Celebration
Something you do to create positive emotions, such as saying "Nicely done!" You celebrate immediately after doing the New Tiny Behavior.

REMARKABLE RESULTS

Once I figured out all the pieces to the puzzle, I started using my method to change lots of things in my life. One month I mapped out 16 Tiny Habit recipes. I practiced these habits, and I was successful at 15 of them. (What didn't work? Meditating for three breaths. I couldn't figure out where this fit naturally in my day.)

I thought 15 out of 16 was a striking result. So I posted it to Twitter. Right away, I saw that some people didn't believe me. They thought it was impossible. They tweeted back these misguided assumptions: *"You can only create one habit at a time"* and *"It takes 21 days to create a habit."*

I was happy to prove those old assumptions wrong—at least for me.

Change behavior without relying on willpower

I kept going with my Tiny Habits method, creating many new habits in my life. Over time, I dropped 10% of my body weight, and my blood pressure went down. All the while I felt more confident about everything I was doing. Why? I knew I could change my behavior quickly and easily.

With the Tiny Habits method, I cracked the code for adding new habits to my life. I was sure about that. I saw evidence that I could change my behavior without relying on willpower. I was pretty sure if I could teach other people the method, they would also be able to change quickly and easily.

SHARING TINY HABITS WITH OTHERS

I decided to teach a few friends my Tiny Habits method. I posted a question to Facebook to see if people were interested. A few people said "yes." So I wrote up the instructions and shared it with them in December 2011, nicely timed before the New Year.

That first week about 60 people joined me. It worked well for many of them. A few people didn't understand my instructions. So I revised and tried again. The next week about 150 joined in. People then told their friends, and it just kept growing.

The original Tiny Habits program runs for 5 days, Monday through Friday. It takes about 45 minutes from start to finish—about 20 minutes to get started and then about 5 minutes a day. Usually, I interact with people through email.

As the months went by, I coached a few hundred new people each week in the Tiny Habits method. At the time I knew my method worked, but I didn't fully understand why. Today I have more insight into the secret sauce of Tiny Habits.

WHY THE TINY HABITS METHOD WORKS

For a long time I've asked myself this question: Why hasn't anyone discovered this method before? As a Stanford-trained experimental psychologist, I have studied human behavior for almost 20 years. And I have never found anyone or any method that pulled all the right pieces together.

The Tiny Habits method seems obvious to me now. I suppose it's something like a riddle. When you don't know the answer, it seems like a hard problem, maybe impossible to solve. But once you see the answer, it seems obvious: "Aha! Of course that's the answer."

I don't have space here to explain all the ingredients in the secret sauce, but below are some of the vital elements:

- Pick new behaviors you want (not things you "should" do).
- Make it really easy to do the behaviors.
- Make sure there's something that prompts you to do the behavior.
- Find a way to feel good immediately after doing the behavior. ▶

If you do any one of these things, you are on the right path to creating habits. If you do all of them together—the Tiny Habits method—you will be on the express train to a better life.

Note what's not on my list above: willpower or motivation. I've learned that creating new habits is not a matter of willpower. It's a matter of design. To be clear, motivation is not the key to habit formation. Yes, you have to pick new behaviors you want (the method doesn't magically give you habits you don't want). But motivation isn't the critical factor if you make the behavior easy enough.

SUCCESS MAKES TINY HABITS GROW

Some people ask this question: Well, what's the use of flossing just one tooth? Or doing just two push-ups? I need to floss all my teeth. I want to do 20 push-ups so I can get strong.

I explain: What you're doing at the early stage is building automaticity. If you make the new behavior painful or hard in any way, your brain will find ways to stop you from doing it. You will conveniently "forget," or you'll find some excuse. So you need to start very small.

Tiny habits grow naturally to their expected size.

On days when you really want to do more push-ups, then do more. That's fine. But it's never a requirement. When you go beyond the tiny behavior, you should view it as "extra credit"—and you need to feel extra good about it. That way you can continue to strengthen the habit.

The more you do a behavior, the easier it gets

The more you do a behavior, the easier it gets. For example, when I got really good at flossing one tooth, then flossing all my teeth was also easier than ever before. You need to trust in this fact: Success leads to success.

In the Tiny Habits method, you allow the tiny behavior to grow naturally. You don't force it. It's a lot like growing a small plant: You can't force it to grow. Just keep nurturing it and making sure the environment is conducive to growth.

I believe this metaphor is perfect for how habits form:

"If you plant the right seed in the right spot, it will grow without coaxing."

The "right seed" is the tiny behavior that you want. The "right spot" is the sequencing—what it comes after. The "coaxing" part is amping up motivation, which I think has nothing to do with creating habits. In fact, focusing on motivation as the means to habits is exactly wrong.

Let me be more explicit: If you pick the right small behavior and sequence it right, then you won't need to motivate yourself to have it grow. It will just happen naturally, like a good seed planted in a good spot. (Unfortunately, this is also the process for bad habits—they start tiny, and they wedge themselves in a fertile spot.)

With time, Tiny Habits will grow to their natural size. You will go from flossing one tooth to flossing all your teeth. You'll expand from two push-ups to 15. You'll grow tiny exercise behaviors into longer sessions.

THREE TYPES OF TINY HABITS: BLADE, SHRUB, TREE

1 I classify Tiny Habits into three types. I call one "blade," like a blade of grass. It starts tiny. It won't grow big. And that's okay. It's pretty easy to create a lot of "blade" behaviors (metaphorically, think of it as a big lawn or meadow). Many blade-size behaviors can have a big impact on your life.

2 The next category, I call "shrub." The habit starts small and it grows a little bit. But it never gets huge. And that's okay. Flossing one tooth grows to flossing all your teeth. Pouring a glass of water becomes drinking water throughout the day. You start tiny and you allow the behavior to naturally grow.

3 The final category is what I call "tree." It starts small, and you hope it grows very large. Tree habits are things like exercising for an hour a day and radically changing your diet. These habits take a lot of time and nurturing. You have to be patient. If you artificially amp up the new behavior to a size or intensity that is painful, you are weakening the habit. You are going backward.

I'm a fan of blades and shrubs. It's so easy to form these habits. When you create many habits that are the size of blades and shrubs, your life will change in a big way. And when one habit breaks, they don't all break. In other words, changing many small behaviors seems to be more robust—a better investment—than trying to create one big change. ▶

TINY HABITS AND UNWANTED BEHAVIORS

You may be wondering how to use the Tiny Habits method to get rid of unwanted behaviors. My answer is this: I don't know for sure. To be clear, Tiny Habits is a method for bringing new behaviors into your life, not for getting rid of unwanted behaviors.

People have told me they've used my method to stop bad habits. So yes, I think it's possible. However, I haven't studied how this works. And I don't want to speculate. As it stands, I can vouch for all the insights in this section of the chapter. I don't want to put guesses next to what I know are facts.

HELP PEOPLE FEEL SUCCESSFUL

After personally coaching more than 25,000 people in Tiny Habits, I have a strong point of view about how to help people improve their lives. As coaches, we need to set people up for success, not for failure. When you put people on a program and they fail, you damage them. You make them less likely to succeed in the future.

> We need to set people up for success, not failure

So above all else, no matter what approach you take, help people feel like they are succeeding. I deeply believe that's the key to achieving long-term change in challenging areas like nutrition, stress, and physical activity.

I've seen this clearly: When people feel successful, they keep going. They start to change other behaviors in their life, both big and small. It's a natural process. But it only happens if people feel successful.

I believe the easiest, fastest way to show people they can change their lives is through the Tiny Habits method. In just five days, most people see evidence they are learning to change. They prove it each morning as they see themselves in the mirror, flossing one tooth. They see someone who is learning to change.

And with this new mindset—yes, I can improve my life—people are ready to take on bigger challenges.

Resources for Learning More

- For more information, see www.bjfogg.org/ace
- To check out Tiny Habits for yourself, see www.tinyhabits.com

PRACTICAL APPLICATIONS

1. Identify a personal goal and complete the process of developing an action plan.

   Write down the goal.

   Generate a list with as many actions as you can think of that would help you to achieve the goal. Refrain from judging your ideas as you jot them down.

   Go through the list of ideas and choose two or three that seem most promising or acceptable, and explain why.

   Break these two ideas into the smallest possible action plan.

2. Go to www.tinyhabits.com and sign up to complete a five-day "Tiny Habits" coaching session. Describe your experience. How will this experience influence your coaching?

3. Go to www.behaviorwizard.org. Identify at least one habit that you or a client would like to start or increase and one habit that you or a client would like to decrease or stop.

Where does the behavior you selected fit on the Fogg Behavior Grid?

On what path on the Fogg Behavior Grid did your old habit fall?

Describe the difference between Green, Blue, Purple, Gray, and Black behaviors.

Describe the difference between "Dot," "Span," and "Path" behaviors.

How might knowledge of the Fogg Behavior Grid and Behavior Wizard affect your coaching?

SUMMARY

Action plans are the critical final step in preparing to translate a vision of change into reality. Careful attention to the method and process of working with clients to develop action plans can set the stage for success as behavioral change begins. Then, the process of taking very small steps to grow new habits is the critical first step to make the change stick indefinitely.

EXPANSION QUIZ
Multiple-choice quiz available if you expand to the full experience

Reference

Miller, W. & Rollnick. S (2013). *Motivational Interviewing: Helping People Change* (3rd ed.). New York: Guilford Press.

Additional Resources

www.tinyhabits.com
www.behaviorgrid.org
www.behaviormodel.org

NOTES

CHAPTER 11

CHAPTER 11
COACHING ACCOUNTABILITY: FOSTERING CONNECTION, OWNERSHIP, AND RESULTS

LEARNING OBJECTIVES

After reading this chapter, the coach will be able to:

- Define and refine the art of effective accountability
- Review and practice methods to clarify, categorize, and prioritize client action steps in order to improve accountability success
- Practice accountability techniques to respectfully and appropriately respond to reluctance, acknowledge progress, and celebrate success

The coaching process is based on the creation of a powerful and synergistic partnership between client and coach. As emphasized in previous chapters, effective coaches focus on clients' strengths, facilitate ownership, and refrain from imposing their own agendas. Effective coaches also learn and employ proven coaching methods to help clients clarify their goals and objectives and design strategies to attain them. When clients have agreed on an action plan, it is through the effective use of accountability that the coach supports the client in achieving the intended results.

WHAT IS ACCOUNTABILITY IN COACHING?

Accountability is a clear and specific method to assess the client's progress or verify that a request has been completed. Accountability can be provided via various means, including a check-in at a future visit, an email follow-up, a quick phone call, entering data into a smartphone or app, or using social media. The coach and client agree early on in the relationship on the most helpful approach to ensure accountability. The important factor is not how accountability is provided, but that it is built into the coaching relationship from the outset, such as through the development of **SMART goals** and action plans.

Of course, the mere act of holding a client accountable does not mean that the client is expected to follow through 100% on all action plans or goals. As much as accountability can help in tracking progress, it is just as important to reassess intentions and goals. Accountability should focus on helping clients make progress toward a goal, while also giving clients the time, space, and permission to determine if the goal is in alignment with their overall plan for success.

It is by way of accountability that clients can evaluate their commitment to the original plan. For example, consider a client who sets a goal without careful consideration of relevance, significance, or interest. In this case, the client is unlikely to follow through with the goal. If accountability is a normal part of the coaching process, this will become apparent with a coach's nonbiased, nonjudgmental follow-up protocol. This time of reflection and recommitment provides an opportunity to set goals grounded in intrinsic values and mindful consideration rather than what a client believes he or she "should" do or become.

An environment of accountability also allows the client to explore the obstacles to completing a goal. Through this exploration, clients may discover that they face the same obstacles with a variety of endeavors. Perhaps time management is a constant concern; perhaps lack of focus prevents success; perhaps overcommitting is a pattern. Coaching can help the client unveil and overcome counterproductive habits that are interfering with attaining his or her goals and personal vision.

Incorporating accountability into the coaching session provides a built-in opportunity to celebrate clients' efforts and progress. When clients are genuinely pleased with their outcomes, and when coaches take the time to highlight that achievement, the client–coach relationship strengthens and the client makes progress toward achieving a lasting change. However, to empower clients and avoid dependency, coaches may endeavor to join the clients in their enthusiasm rather than lead the celebration. For example, a coach may say: "You seem happy to have gained that awareness" or "You seem pleased with your results," rather than "I think it's great that you figured that out" or "I'm glad you got that done." In the first two examples, the coach allows the client to "toot their own horn," while in the third and fourth options, the coach takes on the role of task master or cheerleader. Note that clients are seeking ways to improve their wellness, not to gain their coach's approval. Additionally, when clients receive their coach's endorsement for some results and not others, they may interpret silence as disapproval.

HOW TO BUILD ACCOUNTABILITY INTO THE COACHING SESSION

Accountability may come in a variety of forms. The best means of accountability is the one that the client chooses. A coach may ask: "How would you like to be accountable?" then allow clients to structure an accountability process they believe will work for them. Clients may be accountable to their coach, or they may set up ways to be accountable to friends, associates, family members, or an online app or written chart.

If it is agreed that a subsequent coaching session is the place for accountability, coaches may ask clients about the status of the goal ("Last session you set an intention to bring a healthy lunch to work each day. How's that going?"), rather than asking whether their goals were successfully completed ("Last session you set an intention to bring a healthy lunch to work each day. Did you complete that?").

When clients need more information in order to move forward, they may agree to take action outside of the session to explore their inner wisdom or outside resources. The purpose of the inquiry is to gain awareness, perspective, wisdom, ideas, or data and to move the action forward. In order to be accountable, clients agree to update their coach during a subsequent session or submit information to their coach by a specific date and in a specified manner. The coach's role is to receive the information, not to grade or evaluate the content of the information.

Gain awareness, perspective, wisdom, ideas, or data

Coaches can help establish client accountability through several methods, including:

- *Task completion:* Clients often establish a goal at the end of a coaching session and then commit to a "homework" assignment to move in the direction of that goal. For example, a client may choose to write down his or her food intake, commit to an exercise schedule, take daily stretch breaks at work, or throw out one item of clutter daily. In these scenarios, the client generally verbally updates the coach in a subsequent session regarding action that has or has not been taken. Apps or written charts to track completion of action steps are also helpful and serve to provide the client with more self-directed accountability.
- *Surveys:* Not every client is ready to take "action" to achieve a behavioral change. In some cases, the act of gaining more information to help set a goal or move toward being ready to change is more powerful than agreeing to a behavioral change. One way a client can gain more information is through the use of a survey. Surveys generally are used to collate opinions about an idea, product, program, or person. For example, clients may wonder about a product or program to improve their fitness or nutrition ("I want to get a fitness tracker, but I'm not sure which one would be best for me.") The client may opt to informally or formally survey friends, coworkers, or family members to learn more about a particular area of change. After clients agree to use a survey, the coach may ask "What would support you in conducting the survey before the specified date as agreed?" Some accountability options include:
    - ✔ Verbally updating the coach during a subsequent session regarding action that has or has not been taken
    - ✔ Submitting a draft of the survey to the coach
    - ✔ Submitting a plan and timeline to conduct the survey to the coach
    - ✔ Submitting the results of the survey to the coach

- *Interviews:* While coaches refrain from giving advice, clients nonetheless can benefit from learning from others. During coaching, clients may see value in talking with experts, mentors, or leaders to gain information and perspective. As clients agree to conduct interviews, the coach may ask "What would support you in speaking with that person by the specified date as agreed?" Some accountability options include:
    - ✔ Verbally updating the coach in a subsequent session regarding action that has or has not been taken
    - ✔ Submitting strategies for contacting experts, mentors, and supervisors
    - ✔ Submitting interview questions
    - ✔ Submitting the results of the interviews
- *Research:* In modern society, there are endless ways to acquire new knowledge. The resources that clients have access to and are willing to use may be revealed in the coaching process. For example, a coach may ask: "Where might you get more information about how many vegetables and fruits you should eat per day?" If the client replies, "I could go online," then the coach can follow with, "How would you go about your online search?" "When might you work on that?" and "How would you like to be accountable for doing this research?" Some accountability options include:
    - ✔ Verbally updating the coach in a subsequent session regarding action that has or has not been taken
    - ✔ Submitting action plans to collect information, attend classes, search the Internet, etc.
    - ✔ Submitting the research results
- *Networking:* Face-to-face meetings and online discussions are additional means to gather information and receive support. A client may find it helpful to learn about a weight-management program by attending a meeting or joining an online support network. As clients opt to network, coaches can ask, "What do you need in order to get started?" and "How would you like to be accountable for that action step?" Some accountability options include:
    - ✔ Verbally updating the coach in a subsequent session regarding action that has or has not been taken
    - ✔ Emailing plans for joining an online discussion or attending classes, groups, or meetings
    - ✔ Submitting plans for ongoing support

ROADBLOCKS TO EFFECTIVE ACCOUNTABILITY

While the value of accountability to the coaching relationship cannot be overstated, coaches and clients often face a series of roadblocks to establishing effective accountability. These generally tend to occur in the following situations:

A coach has not supported the client to establish clear, timely, and measurable action steps.

A coach is unaware of his or her own perspectives, biases, moods, or beliefs.

A coach has not invited the client to explore a variety of accountability options (e.g., the coach, a coworker or family member, or a written or electronic reminder).

The client feels attacked, scolded, or in any way uncomfortable.

When a client falls short of a goal, the coach does not recognize that it is the coach's responsibility to ask a different question, explore the coach's own motivation or intentions, or be more mindful and/or creative in order to serve the best interests of the client.

Coaches can overcome these accountability roadblocks by nurturing the client–coach relationship and maintaining open communication and discussion of expectations from the coaching relationship.

PRACTICAL APPLICATIONS

1. Develop your own goals and action plan, if you have not done so already. Include in your action plan specific checkpoints or deadlines for each action. Then, identify for each action how you will be held accountable to ensure that you complete your intended actions.

2. With a client, colleague, friend, or family member, complete a coaching session during which you focus on the client's accountability plan. Ask questions such as:

   What do you think is the best way for you to be held accountable for doing these planned actions?

   How might you hold yourself accountable?

   How could you build accountability into your action plan?

   How did the coaching session go? How can you improve upon this experience?

3. In what ways do you plan to hold your clients accountable for their actions?

SUMMARY

A key feature of an effective coaching relationship is a systematic way of following up and ensuring accountability. Whether that comes from a client's own self-driven accountability methods or from strategic and ongoing follow-up from a coach, it is a component of the coaching session that must not be overlooked in the effort to support a client in his or her journey to lasting behavioral change.

EXPANSION QUIZ
Multiple-choice quiz available if you expand to the full experience

CHAPTER 12

CHAPTER 12
ADULT LEARNING

LEARNING OBJECTIVES

After reading this chapter, the coach will be able to:

- Define and apply the six core adult learning principles
- Identify client cognitive and learning styles and provide information in a manner that facilitates optimal learning
- Implement "elicit-provide-elicit" when providing information
- List six considerations when providing client-centered advice
- Describe the use of a learning contract as a method to guide self-directed learning and increase accountability

While coaches generally provide expert advice and information only with permission, frequently a client not only will provide permission to share information, but will outright ask for it. In fact, many clients who are in the action stage of change—that is, they are in the midst of making behavioral changes and moving toward achieving a behavioral goal—benefit greatly from the provision of information to help them make better choices. A coach who is able to apply effective adult learning techniques to coaching interactions will be successful in sharing information that will ultimately inspire or inform a lasting behavioral change. The late Malcolm Knowles pioneered the field of adult learning, or **andragogy.** His insights and recommendations are highlighted throughout this chapter, based on largely on his text *The Adult Learner,* co-written with and updated by Elwood F. Holton and Richard A. Swanson (Knowles, Holton, & Swanson, 2011). The aim is to help coaches develop educational sessions and workshops that are best suited to meet the attending adult learners' needs.

SIX CORE ADULT LEARNING PRINCIPLES

For adult learners, the most effective health education does not come from lectures, slide presentations, or study guides—the standard teaching fare in elementary, high school, and college classrooms. While a child might memorize or learn something esoteric because the information is necessary to pass a test written by an authority figure, adult learners retain new information when they deem it to be important. A growing body of research suggests that adult learners benefit most when the learning is aligned with six core adult learning principles (Knowles, Holton, & Swanson, 2011).

1. **The need to know:** Adult learners are driven to acquire new information that they deem to be important in their everyday lives. The coach's role may be to help increase a client's awareness of why a certain piece of information is worth knowing. For instance, a coach providing a nutrition lesson about carbohydrates, proteins, and fats will be most impactful if the discussion is linked to actual foods and how they impact health.

2. **Self-concept:** This is the notion that an adult must feel some sense of **autonomy** and self-directedness in the process of learning. Respect for a client's autonomy is a fundamental principle in coaching as well as in providing information or advice. One way a coach respects client autonomy is by asking what the client would like to know about, or where there may be knowledge gaps in carrying out an action plan.

3. **Prior experiences:** Adults are more willing and able to learn new information when it builds upon prior experiences or knowledge. In many cases, adults at least in part define themselves based on their experiences. Building from a client's previous understanding and knowledge of a concept is likely to encourage the translation from information to action. For instance, a client who has successfully lost weight in the past, but then regained it, may benefit from exploring that previous experience and what went right and what went wrong. From there, the client and coach can identify knowledge gaps that when closed will help to set the stage for success this time.

4. **Readiness to learn:** Just as clients experience different stages in their readiness to change a behavior, they also experience different stages in readiness to learn new information. Coaches should be careful to time the sharing of information with the client's readiness to learn it. In many cases, asking a client for permission before sharing information and checking in with the client on how he or she may use the information can help identify a client's readiness to learn.

5. **Orientation to learning:** Adults are problem-centered in their learning. That is, they learn new information to solve a life situation or problem. A client who has been diagnosed with type 2 diabetes may be compelled to learn about lifestyle changes needed to help manage the disease, though he may have had little interest in learning about nutrition or physical activity prior to the diagnosis.

6. **Motivation to learn:** Most adults are primarily driven by **internal motivations** to learn, such as increased quality of life, job satisfaction, and self-esteem. Tapping into this internal motivation is a priority for the entire coaching relationship, including in deciding when and what information to share.

Table 12-1 provides a brief overview of each of these six principles as well as possible coaching applications of the principles when providing adults with information.

Table 12-1

COACHING APPLICATION OF THE SIX PRINCIPLES OF ADULT LEARNING

Core Principle	Coaching Objective	Possible Coaching Activities
Adults need to know why they need to learn something before learning it.	Help a client identify the gap between current reality and information that is needed to achieve a goal.	The client completes a worksheet with goals and prompts to identify learning gaps.
The self-concept of adults is heavily dependent upon autonomy and self-directedness of learning.	Engage a client in the process of identifying a plan for closing learning gaps, with reliance on the client to implement the plan.	The client implements a learning contract.
Prior experiences of the learner provide a rich resource for learning.	Elicit a client's prior experiences and knowledge before providing "education."	Ask the client to complete a brief survey and "pre-test" before a health education session or workshop. Adapt the session to the client's needs.
Adults are most likely to retain and act upon new information when they are in a stage of readiness to learn.	Link learning to successful pursuit of a client's vision, goals, and/or action plans; acknowledge when a client may not be ready to learn a given piece of information.	Query a client's interest in exploring a given topic before providing information.
Adults typically become ready to learn when they experience a need to cope with a life situation or perform a task.	Apply all or nearly all pieces of information, education, or advice shared to relevant problem-centered scenarios.	Role play several possible experiences as a client pursues change and troubleshoot areas where increased learning is needed.
The motivation of adult learners is internal rather than external.	Create and identify learning opportunities that may serve to provide increased personal satisfaction, well-being, and happiness.	Together with the client, plan experiential-based learning activities that serve to increase a client's self-efficacy and confidence to make a change. For instance, a client trying to improve nutrition behaviors may value a grocery store tour or pantry makeover.

Data from: Knowles, M.S., Holton, E.F., & Swanson, R.A. (2011). *The Adult Learner: The Definitive Classic in Adult Education and Human Resource Development* (7th ed.). New York: Taylor & Francis.

PRACTICAL APPLICATION

1. Describe how you might incorporate each of the six core adult learning principles in your coaching relationships. Be sure to include specific examples.

Need to know

Self-concept

Prior experiences

Readiness to learn

Orientation to learning

Motivation

INDIVIDUAL DIFFERENCES IN ADULT LEARNERS

Several individual-level factors influence how people learn new information. As such, coaches may adapt the way they share information with clients based on these factors to help increase learning outcomes—in this case, a change in behavior. These individual differences can be divided into the following four categories (Jonassen & Grabowski, 1993):

- *Cognitive ability:* **Cognitive ability** is typically referred to as an individual's degree of intelligence, or intelligence quotient (IQ). However, many experts advocate that it expand beyond IQ to include multiple other intelligences such as linguistic, logical-mathematical, spatial, musical, bodily kinesthetic, understanding oneself, and understanding others (Gardner, 1983). An awareness of a client's strongest intelligences can help tailor how information is shared.

- *Cognitive controls:* **Cognitive controls** refer to patterns of thinking about information. The best studied of the cognitive controls is an individual preference for "field-dependent" versus "field-independent" learning. People who tended to be more **field dependent** rely on cues in the external environment when learning new information, whereas people who are more **field independent** learn without regard for environmental cues. Table 12-2 highlights key difference between field-dependent and field-independent learners. This difference plays a particularly important role in self-directed learning. Field independents tend to be more successful in self-directed learning experiences, whereas field dependents may benefit from activities like forming study groups or engaging in a group coaching environment.

- *Cognitive styles:* **Cognitive styles** refer to the ways in which an individual processes information. Though most cognitive psychologists consider three **learning styles** (i.e., visual, verbal, and tactile/psychomotor), others have expanded the list considerably, including, among others, print, listening, interactive, visual, touch, kinesthetic/movement, and smell. Various ways coaches can take advantage of these learning styles are offered in Table 12-3. Additionally, in processing information, learners tend to take one of two approaches: global or analytical. People who prefer a global approach to processing information are "big picture" thinkers—they prefer to consider the whole picture and then the details. Those who prefer an analytical approach prefer to learn in a step-by-step approach. To accommodate both types of learners, experts advise presenting information in a **whole-part-whole** approach in which learners are introduced to the "big picture," learn the individual components, and then the parts are linked back together to form the "big picture" (Knowles, Holton, & Swanson, 2011).

Experts advise presenting information in a whole-part-whole approach

- *Learning styles:* Learning styles may be broadly defined as the range of preferred manners and methods of learning. This refers to how a person prefers to process information. Multiple assessments addressing a range of learning styles are available, but there is no scientific consensus of which is best (Knowles, Holton, & Swanson, 2011). The main take-away is the realization that people learn in different ways, and a modality that may be effective for one person may be wholly ineffective for another, lending support to the notion that coaching sessions and styles of providing information must be tailored to the individual. The Personal Adult Learning Style Inventory included in Appendix B serves as an excellent assessment to evaluate a coach's own learning style, as well as to best understand the learning styles of clients.

Table 12-2

FIELD-DEPENDENT VERSUS FIELD-INDEPENDENT LEARNERS

Field-dependent Learners Prefer:	Field-independent Learners Prefer:
Group-oriented and collaborative learning	Problem-solving
Clear structure and organization of information	Transferring knowledge to novel situations
A social environment	Independent, contract-oriented learning
External reinforcement	Inquiry and discovery learning
External guidance	

Data from: Knowles, M.S., Holton, E.F., & Swanson, R.A. (2011). *The Adult Learner: The Definitive Classic in Adult Education and Human Resource Development* (7th ed.). New York: Taylor & Francis.

Table 12-3

TAILORING COACHING TO HOW PEOPLE LEARN: LINKING CONTENT WITH COGNITIVE STYLE

Dominant Cognitive Style	Types of Learning Activities	Coaching Application
Print	Read a newspaper article or blog	The client follows a credible and popular health blog such as *The New York Times* "Well" blog
Verbal	Teach others	The client teaches a partner or friend about newly learned strategies to manage stress
Listening	Listen to a podcast; attend a lecture or a talk	The client listens each week to the ACE Fit Well podcast series
Interactive	Participate on a panel or engage in a debate	Group coaching session with hands-on nutrition activities
Visual	Watch a video or documentary	Group viewing of films such as *Weight of the Nation, Food, Inc., Fed Up*, or *Forks Over Knives,* with discussion to follow
Touch	Touch to increase bodily awareness or solidify learning, such as through visiting a children's museum or interactive museum exhibit	With permission, the coach cues clients through touch to increase awareness of proper form for physical exercise or weight training
Kinesthetic/movement	Do a physical activity related to learning topic	The client participates in group fitness class and shares with the coach what he or she learned
Smell	Attend a cooking class	The coach leads a cooking class or demonstration

COACHING APPLICATIONS

An understanding and recognition of how clients learn can turn a great coach into a transformational one. A coach who understands the essentials of adult learning will experience increased success in helping clients learn, retain, and apply new information to their everyday lives. Following are several specific techniques and strategies coaches may consider when designing optimal learning experiences for those clients who have given permission or expressed interest in learning new information to help support them in their behavioral change.

12 KEY PRINCIPLES OF LEARNING APPLIED TO COACHING

Goodwin Watson (1960 & 1961), an early pioneer in learning research, offered 12 key "principles of learning" that are easily translated to coaching (Table 12-4).

Table 12-4

LEARNING PRINCIPLES AND ASSOCIATED COACHING APPLICATIONS

LEARNING PRINCIPLE	COACHING APPLICATION
Behavior that is rewarded is more likely to recur.	Help clients celebrate and reward themselves when they successfully engage in a goal behavior.
Repetition without reward is a poor way to learn.	Help clients plan to celebrate when they have practiced a new skill, even if it is not yet mastered.
Threats and punishments commonly lead to avoidant behavior.	Fear tactics of what will happen if a client does not change are unlikely to be helpful in inspiring lasting change. Coaches should refrain from using them.
How ready a person is to learn something depends on past experiences, relevance, freedom from discouragement, and fear of failure.	Before providing any information, learn about a client's history and feelings about a particular topic to be most effective.
If a learner perceives something as impossible to learn, he or she will not learn it.	In goal planning, focus on making small changes rather than planning for big, overwhelming, hard-to-reach changes.
Novelty is rewarding.	Create opportunities for clients to try new things.
We learn best what we participate in selecting and planning ourselves.	Respect a client's autonomy and engage in client-centered coaching. This is more likely to lead to behavioral change than simply "teaching" or "educating" someone.
Genuine participation intensifies motivation, flexibility, and rate of learning.	Engage a client in an information exchange, rather than lecturing to the client.
A directive leader or teacher, or an autocratic atmosphere, increases dependence on the "authority."	Practice client-centered coaching rather than coach-centered coaching.
Closed, authoritarian environments condemn most learners to discouragement, failure, and destruction of self-confidence and a healthy self-concept.	People do not learn well when they are simply told what to do. Avoid this.
The best time to learn anything is when the learning is immediately useful.	Make every piece of information practical. If it is not practical, carefully consider whether it is worth sharing.
Open, non-authoritarian environments are conducive to learner initiative and creativity, originality, self-reliance, and independence.	Create a warm, safe environment where coach and client are equal partners.

BEST PRACTICES IN PROVIDING INFORMATION: BORROWING FROM MOTIVATIONAL INTERVIEWING

Miller and Rollnick (2013) recommend adherence to the following philosophical beliefs (which closely mirror the six principles of adult learning) when sharing information with clients:

- *"I have some expertise and the clients are the experts on themselves."* Here the coach learns what the client already knows, asks permission to provide information, and builds upon the client's previous knowledge. The client and coach are exchanging information in a shared mission of helping the client achieve sustainable behavioral change.
- *"I find out what information clients want and need."* The basis of providing information is to help fill a client's informational needs, building upon what a client already knows.
- *"I match information to clients' needs and strengths."* A coach tailors the approach to information delivery and content to each client's individual needs and learning style.
- *"Clients can tell me what kind of information is helpful."* The coach responds to the client's signals to understand the most appropriate and useful information to provide.
- *"Advice that champions client needs and autonomy is helpful."* Providing advice to a client can be beneficial as long as it is provided in the context of filling a need for a client while also respecting his or her autonomy, and being particularly careful not to fall into the "expert trap" in which a coach argues for change while the client argues against it. Miller and Rollnick (2013) suggest providing advice with the following precautions: engage with the client first, ensuring that there is good **rapport;** use sparingly; ask permission; emphasize personal choice; and offer a menu of options to choose from rather than telling the client just one way in which it should be done.

Be careful not to fall into the "expert trap"

ELICIT-PROVIDE-ELICIT

These best practices are most effectively implemented with an **elicit-provide-elicit** approach to information exchange described in *Motivational Interviewing* (Miller & Rollnick, 2013).

Elicit

First, the coach asks permission to provide information with questions such as:

- May I…? or Would you like to know about…?
- What do you know about...?
- Is there any information I can help you with?
- What have you been wondering about that I may able to help clarify for you?

This helps the coach to ask permission, explore the client's prior knowledge, and understand the client's interest in the information to be shared.

Provide

Next, the coach shares information in the context of the six core principles of adult learning outlined earlier in the chapter, thoughtfully providing information in a clear, jargon-free manner that builds upon a client's previous knowledge and respects the client's autonomy.

Elicit

The coach ends with asking the client for his or her interpretation or understanding of the information that was shared through the use of open-ended questions and reflections.

LEARNING CONTRACTS

In some situations, coaches may find value in asking a client to complete a **learning contract.** Learning contracts offer a way for the client to take ownership of the learning and report back to the coach. Research supports that adults learn more deeply and permanently when they engage in self-directed learning as compared to when they are passively taught something (Knowles, Holton, & Swanson, 2011). Coaches can use the following eight-step process for developing a learning contract (Knowles, Holton, & Swanson, 2011):

- *Identify learning needs:* A client may consider the gap in a personal vision and the current reality, looking to behavior-change goals and action plans to identify areas where increased knowledge is needed to effectively make the behavioral change.
- *Specify learning objectives:* Each learning need should be translated into a learning objective, stated in a way that carries the most meaning and significance to the client. For example, a client who identifies that he or she needs to learn more about the calories in foods might have a learning objective of "being able to approximate the number of calories in the six foods that I eat most often."
- *Specify learning resources and strategies:* The client identifies what tools and resources he or she will use to be able to accomplish the learning objective.
- *Specify evidence of accomplishment:* The client identifies how he or she will know that the learning objective has been achieved.
- *Specify how the evidence will be validated:* The client identifies the criteria from which the evidence will be judged. It can include measures of knowledge, understanding, skills, attitudes, or values.
- *Review the contract with others:* The client may ask the coach, colleagues, or family members to review the contract and provide additional ideas and suggestions.
- *Carry out the contract:* The client implements the contract, making revisions or adjustments as needed.
- *Evaluate learning:* Once the client has completed the terms of the contract, the coach, colleagues, or family members who initially reviewed the contract may again review the evidence and validation data and provide their input on the quality and strength of the measures.

PRACTICAL APPLICATION

2. Identify a personal learning interest and complete the details of the learning contract below. Describe your experience. Is a learning contract something you might use with your clients? Why or why not?

Name ______________________

Activity ______________________

Learning Objectives	Learning Resources and Strategies	Evidence of Accomplishment of Learning Objectives	Criteria and Means for Validating Evidence

AN EVALUATION OF THE LEARNING EXPERIENCE

One way coaches may evaluate a client's learning experience is by asking the client to rate on a scale of 1–10 how true each of the following statements is to him or her:

- This learning experience motivated me to give my best effort.
- I felt my prior life and work experiences helped my learning.
- It was clear to me why I needed to participate in this learning experience.
- This learning experience was just what I needed given the changes in my life/work.
- I felt I had control over my learning in this learning experience.

The longer version of this evaluation [referred to as the Andragogy in Practice Inventory (API)] has been validated in its ability to assess each of five core learning principles (Holton et al., 2009).

3. Engage in a learning activity with a client. Then ask the client to rate each of the following items below on a scale of 1–10:

- This learning experience motivated me to give my best effort. _____
- I felt my prior life and work experiences helped my learning. _____
- It was clear to me why I needed to participate in this learning experience. _____
- This learning experience was just what I needed given the changes in my life/work. _____
- I felt I had control over my learning in this learning experience. _____

What area was the strongest? Where was the most room for improvement?

What did you learn?

How could you improve for the future?

What went well that you want to continue to do?

SUMMARY

The six core principles of how adults learn are closely aligned with the core competencies in coaching, in that they both emphasize the importance of client-centeredness. Coaches who are carefully attuned to clients' learning needs and motivations are more likely to have clients who attain the knowledge and skills needed for successful behavioral change.

EXPANSION QUIZ

Multiple-choice quiz available if you expand to the full experience

References

Gardner, H. (1983). *Frames of Mind.* New York: Basic Books.

Holton, E. et al. (2009). Toward development of a generalized instrument to measure andragogy. *Human Resource Development Quarterly,* 20, 2, 169–193.

Jonassen, D.H. & Grabowski, B.L. (1993). *Handbook of Individual Differences, Learning, and Instruction.* Hillsdale, N.J.: Erlbaum.

Knowles, M.S., Holton, E.F., & Swanson, R.A. (2011). *The Adult Learner: The Definitive Classic in Adult Education and Human Resource Development* (7th ed.). New York: Taylor & Francis.

Miller, W. & Rollnick, S. (2013). *Motivational Interviewing: Helping People Change* (3rd ed.).New York: Guilford Press.

Watson, G. (1960 & 1961). "What do we know about learning?" *Teachers College Record,* 253–257.

CHAPTER 13

CHAPTER 13
EVALUATION

LEARNING OBJECTIVES

After reading this chapter, the coach will be able to:

- Define the current and ideal role of evaluation in the coaching process
- List several methods a coach could use to evaluate the effectiveness of a coaching intervention
- Describe best practices in data collection, including attaining informed consent and maintaining privacy and confidentiality

Coaching is a young profession with a limited number of peer-reviewed research studies demonstrating its efficacy. However, certain methodologies upon which coaching is built and in which this text is rooted, such as **motivational interviewing, cognitive behavioral coaching,** and **positive psychology,** have a very strong evidence base (see Chapters 2, 5, and 7). Coaches who employ these evidence-based methodologies are very likely to be successful in their coaching. Still, there is great value in systematic evaluation of each coaching relationship for the professional development of the coach, improvement of the coaching process, sharing of outcomes with others, and strengthening the credibility of coaching and the likelihood of third-party payment. While resources may be limited for an individual coach to implement a comprehensive evaluation process, every coach can engage in some degree of evaluation of his or her services and programs.

KIRKPATRICK'S FOUR LEVELS OF EVALUATION

Program evaluation can range from an informal query to a client to a randomized controlled trial, the gold standard in research design. While a gold standard research study is out of reach for most coaches, a systematic process of evaluation is attainable with advanced planning and application of the scientific method.

The industry standard for evaluating training and coaching programs is the Kirkpatrick Model, which was first described more than 50 years ago (Kirkpatrick, 1959) and since updated to the New World Kirkpatrick Model (Kirkpatrick & Kirkpatrick, 2010). This model suggests that a comprehensive evaluation plan include each of four levels of assessment:

LEVEL 1

Reaction: These methods evaluate a client's reaction to the coaching experience, including how much the client enjoyed the experience as well as the degree of engagement and relevance to the client. Information gleaned from a level 1 assessment is limited to a client's perception of the experience and does not assess degree of learning or change in behavior. For many independent coaches, level 1 evaluation may be all that is practical to attain.

LEVEL 2

Learning: Level 2 evaluations assess the knowledge, skills, attitudes, confidence, and commitment resulting from the coaching experience, based on the client's initial learning objectives. A learning evaluation includes a pre-test and post-test to determine what and how much was learned during the coaching experience. An informal level 2 evaluation may include use and review of a **learning contract** (see Chapter 12).

LEVEL 3

Behavior: These methods measure behavioral change resulting from the coaching experience, based on initial coaching objectives. A level 3 evaluation might measure how well a client applied learning to real-life situations, such as making healthy choices at a buffet or incorporating regular physical activity into a travel-heavy month. Coaches may informally use a self-reported level 3 evaluation either anecdotally with clients or through use of an online survey.

LEVEL 4

Results: These methods measure hard results, including progress toward a client's vision, and broader objectives, such as impact on the client's health, family, workplace, or community. In essence, it assesses the return on investment.

Ideally, coaching evaluations will include assessment of all four levels. In reality, the majority of coaches engage in evaluation methods in level 1 only—if they do any evaluation at all—though broadening into the other levels of evaluation is within reach for some coaches. For the most credible and unbiased results, development of evaluation tools and especially analysis of the data should be done by a third party, if possible. A more detailed description of the levels of evaluation as well as tools coaches can use are presented in Table 13-1.

Table 13-1

KIRKPATRICK'S FOUR LEVELS OF EVALUATION

Level	Key Evaluation Question	Description	How to Develop	Tools
1: Reaction	Did the client like it?	Measures how favorably a client reacts to the coaching experience, engagement, and relevance	Identify what you want to know Design a form to collect/quantify Complete immediately following intervention Follow up as needed	Questionnaire Survey Real-time poll Quiz
2: Knowledge	Did the client learn anything? Did the client develop any new skills? Did the client change his or her attitude?	Assessment of knowledge, skills, and attitudes (KSAs), confidence, and commitment	Identify key learning objectives Design tools to collect/quantify Compare to a control group, if possible Evaluate KSAs, confidence, and commitment before and after Aim for 100% completion Follow up as needed	Interviews Learning contract Self-assessment Pre- and post-test Observations
3: Behavior	Did the client change a behavior?	Transfer of KSAs to the real world	Identify key behaviors intended to change Observe behaviors in the real world Compare to a control group, if possible Evaluate before and after coaching Survey key people (e.g., partner or employer) Repeat evaluations at appropriate intervals	Observation of performance 360-degree survey Checklists and interviews
4: Results	Was it worth it?	Measures final results compared to the goal	Measure hard outcomes such as weight, control of disease, work productivity, etc. Use a control group Allow time for results to be realized Measure before and after the program	Correlation of life satisfaction/work performance/health/weight with assessment results

Data from: Kirkpatrick Partners (www.kirkpatrickpartners.com)

PRACTICAL APPLICATIONS

1. Develop a level 1 evaluation tool for your coaching program.

   What type of tool did you select?

   How will you implement this tool in your coaching practice?

   How will you assess, use, and share the information you obtain?

2. Develop a level 2 evaluation tool for your coaching program.

   What type of tool did you select?

   What are the advantages and disadvantages of employing this type of tool?

MAINTAINING PRIVACY AND CONFIDENTIALITY

When collecting client data, whether for an evaluation of a program or for information to help inform program design, it is very important to follow several best practices to ensure the privacy and confidentiality of the client's personal information. In fact, even though coaches are not expressly mandated to follow the **Health Insurance Portability and Accountability Act (HIPAA)** of 1996, making a concerted effort to comply with these regulations goes a long way in ensuring that clients' personal information is protected, while the coach can still gain needed information to design and evaluate coaching programs. Coaches who work within a healthcare setting or are paid for or reimbursed by a health plan are required to adhere to HIPAA.

HIPAA PRIVACY RULE HIGHLIGHTS

- Health information protected by the law (i.e., "protected health information") includes all individually identifiable health information in any form, whether electronic, paper, or oral. Health information includes the individual's past, present, or future physical or mental health condition; the provision of healthcare to the individual; and the past, present, or future payment for the provision of healthcare to the individual.
- The Privacy Rule applies to any healthcare provider, including all "providers of medical or health services" as defined by Medicare, and any other person or organization that furnishes, bills, or is paid for healthcare.
- The Privacy Rule permits a covered entity to use and disclose protected health information for research purposes without an individual's authorization, provided the covered entity obtains necessary documentation of approval solely for the research from an Institutional Review Board or Privacy Board. Further, the researcher and/or covered entity must not remove any protected health information.
- A covered entity must obtain the individual's written authorization for any use or disclosure of protected health information that is not for treatment, payment, or healthcare operations.
- A covered entity must obtain an authorization to use or disclose protected health information for marketing.
- A covered entity must make reasonable efforts to use, disclose, and request only the minimum amount of protected health information needed to accomplish the intended purpose.
- Each covered entity must provide notice of its privacy practices.
- A covered entity must maintain reasonable and appropriate administrative, technical, and physical safeguards to prevent intentional or unintentional use or disclosure of protected health information, including shredding documents before discarding them, securing records with lock and key or passcode, and limiting access to keys or pass codes.

Source: U.S. Department of Health and Human Services (2014). *Summary of the HIPAA Privacy Rule.* www.hhs.gov/ocr/privacy/hipaa/understanding/summary/; retrieved March 3, 2014.

Note: This information serves exclusively to orient readers to the highlights of the HIPAA Privacy Rule and does not represent legal interpretation or advice.

SHARING OF RESULTS

A key principle in scientific research is that the outcomes of one's work should be shared. While in the scientific community this is generally through publication of research results in a peer-reviewed journal, in many cases coaching evaluation methods may not be rigorous enough for this type of publication (though peer-review publication is certainly something to aspire to attain). This does not mean that results from effective programs should not be disseminated. Sharing information through trade magazines, social media and discussion boards, blogs, and newsletters on what has worked and what has not worked will help advance the coaching profession. It is important to note that when this information is shared, maintaining client confidentiality is of paramount importance. Client names or identifying information should only be used with the client's permission and with discretion.

PRACTICAL APPLICATIONS

3. The Diabetes Prevention Program serves as an excellent example of a coaching program with rigorous evaluation and widespread adoption, and which now qualifies for reimbursement by many insurance companies. This activity offers a guided evolution of this model program.

   Review the research study describing the methods and outcomes of the randomized controlled trial of the Diabetes Prevention Program, published in the *New England Journal of Medicine* in 2002. www.nejm.org/doi/full/10.1056/NEJMoa012512#t=articleTop

   Visit the Centers for Disease Control and Prevention's website, where the lifestyle-modification curriculum is available. www.cdc.gov/diabetes/prevention/recognition/curriculum.htm

   Review the "Application for Recognition" for the Diabetes Prevention Recognition Program (DPRP). Pay special attention to the reporting and evaluation requirements. www.cdc.gov/diabetes/prevention/recognition/standards.htm

   Review the "Funded Organizations" that have received grants to implement the Diabetes Prevention Program. www.cdc.gov/diabetes/prevention/about.htm#Funded

4. Review the Medicare bill, which, if passed, would require Medicare to pay for the Diabetes Prevention Program. www.govtrack.us/congress/bills/113/s452/text

   Write a brief paragraph summarizing your thoughts from this activity, including to what degree you feel it is relevant to you.

5. Visit the Institute of Coaching Center for Research (www.instituteofcoaching.org). The Institute of Coaching is committed to helping build the scientific foundation for coaching.

   Review the studies of grant recipients, journals that have published coaching research, and other resources available on this site.

   If you could develop a research study to evaluate your coaching, what would you study? How would you design the evaluation?

   Who might you partner with to assess the outcomes?

   How might you get funding to support this study?

6. Describe why you think coaching research and evaluation is or is not important to a practicing coach.

SUMMARY

Coaches are encouraged to build evaluation into the coaching plan. Its importance cannot be overstated, especially as the coaching profession advances and opportunities open in the healthcare community and at corporate worksites—two areas where evidence of effectiveness is highly valued.

EXPANSION QUIZ
Multiple-choice quiz available if you expand to the full experience

References

Kirkpatrick, D.L. (1959). Techniques for evaluating training programmes. *Journal of the American Society of Training Directors,* 13, 3–9, 21–26.

Kirkpatrick, J. & Kirkpatrick, W. (2010). *The New World Kirkpatrick Model.* www.kirkpatrickpartners.com; retrieved March 3, 2014.

U.S. Department of Health and Human Services (2014). *Summary of the HIPAA Privacy Rule.* www.hhs.gov/ocr/privacy/hipaa/understanding/summary/; retrieved March 3, 2014.

NOTES

Introduction to Section V:

STRATEGIES IN DIVERSE SETTINGS

Coaches work with clients in diverse settings, from worksites, clinics, and wellness or medical fitness centers to virtual forums including telephonic coaching, video conferencing, and email. Coaches themselves come from diverse backgrounds, often incorporating coaching into another professional role such as physician, nurse, dietitian, medical assistant, personal trainer, or community health worker. This section prepares the reader to successfully apply the fundamental coaching principles described throughout this book to diverse settings.

OVER THE COURSE OF THIS SECTION, COACHES WILL GAIN INSIGHT INTO COACHING IN THE FOLLOWING ENVIRONMENTS:

- Clinic, worksite, and wellness/medical fitness center
- Telephonic and virtual health coaching
- Group coaching
- Executive coaching

CHAPTER 14

CHAPTER 14

EMERGING COACHING OPPORTUNITIES:

WORKSITES, CLINICS, AND WELLNESS/MEDICAL FITNESS CENTERS

LEARNING OBJECTIVES

After reading this chapter, the coach will be able to:

- Outline emerging opportunities for coaches in worksites, clinics, and wellness/medical fitness centers
- Identify key metrics in working in worksites, clinics, and wellness/medical fitness facilities
- Develop a plan to approach worksites, clinics, and wellness/medical fitness facilities for potential coaching opportunities

The statistics are startling: Three behaviors—a lack of physical activity, tobacco use, and a poor diet—lead to four diseases: heart disease and stroke, lung disease, cancer, and type 2 diabetes. These four diseases are responsible for 50% of deaths (County of San Diego, 2010). This is commonly referred to as "3-4-50" and is a mantra of programs such as San Diego County's 10-year LiveWell San Diego initiative (www.livewellsd.org). Increasingly, there is recognition that efforts to improve nutrition and physical activity and to support smoking cessation can play a tremendous role in helping move the United States healthcare system toward a more sustainable and integrated future. But the old way of telling people what to do clearly is ineffective. The promise of coaching in supporting people to deploy their own strengths and motivations to make positive changes is intriguing—and key sectors are taking notice. As a result, coaching opportunities within worksites, clinics, and local wellness and medical fitness centers have emerged.

A MOVEMENT TOWARD WORKPLACE WELLNESS

With passage and implementation of the Affordable Care Act and its incentives for companies to adopt worksite wellness programs, opportunities for coaches within worksites have grown substantially.

THE LANDSCAPE

In 2013, the RAND Corporation published a comprehensive report on the state of workplace wellness programs in the United States. Its results were notable: about 50% of employers with more than 50 employees and about 90% of large employers (50,000+ employees) offer a wellness program (Mattke et al., 2013). The typical worksite wellness program includes a combination of programs including lifestyle interventions and health coaching, benefits like gym discounts, and structural changes such as healthier food options and more accessible stairs (Mattke et al., 2013).

A 2013 Kaiser Family Foundation report noted that of those workplaces that offer wellness programs, more than 55% of large companies and 33% of small companies offer health coaching to improve employee health (Kaiser Family Foundation, 2013). Most often, the coaching is provided virtually through telephone-based coaching through the employers' health insurance plans. Other times, coaching is offered on-site either in one-on-one or group coaching programs.

More than 75% of employers with wellness programs offer a lifestyle management program, most typically as a group program (Mattke et al., 2013). The most common topics of these sessions include nutrition and weight control, smoking cessation, fitness, alcohol and drug abuse, and stress management. Many worksites also offer disease-management programs for a variety of conditions, including diabetes, asthma, heart disease, depression, cancer, chronic obstructive pulmonary disease, and back pain. Typically, these programs are offered through telephone-based health coaching provided by the company's health plan (Mattke et al., 2013).

> Opportunities for coaches within worksites have grown substantially

AN EMERGING OPPORTUNITY FOR COACHES

The expansion of worksite wellness programs clearly opens an opportunity for trained coaches. But how does one best prepare for and pursue coaching opportunities within worksite wellness? The path can vary substantially based on the size of the company and its resources for outsourcing, the positions and roles within the company, and the interest level of the top leadership and human resources departments. This section offers three key strategies coaches may consider in exploring coaching opportunities in worksites. It is simply intended to be a starting point, and coaches interested in coaching in this setting are encouraged to continue their learning and take advantage of the many resources to learn more.

Speak Their Language

Employers report that they are driven by several motivators when it comes to wellness programs, including return on investment (ROI), health outcomes, employee retention, employee participation, and employee satisfaction (Kaiser Family Foundation, 2013). While many employers do not routinely evaluate their wellness program in a systematic way, they are driven by results. That is, if a coach can provide a case for why a program or coaching intervention is likely to positively impact any of the metrics above, a worksite is much more likely to express interest in learning more.

Offer a Program That Works

The RAND Study (Mattke et al., 2013) outlined several key features of the most successful wellness programs, including the following:

- *Effective communication strategies:* This includes broad communication outreach such as newsletters, intranet, flyers, word of mouth, email health fairs, and a wellness website. Successful programs also clearly communicate to employees the goals and anticipated outcomes.

- *Opportunity for employees to engage:* Successful programs are convenient, easily accessible, tailored to an individual employee's needs based on a needs assessment, and are aligned with the employee's preferences.

- *Leadership engaged at all levels:* Strong support of senior managers and whole-hearted buy-in of direct supervisors predicts success.

- *Use of existing resources and relationships:* Efforts such as engaging with a worksite health plan to expand wellness opportunities without increasing costs and use of in-house talent to contribute to wellness initiatives help to increase the diversity and breadth of wellness programs without negatively impacting the bottom line.

- *Continuous evaluation:* The best programs begin with a wellness needs assessment to identify the types of programs that are most likely to be successful, continue with ongoing feedback from employees, and end with a formal program evaluation.

Coaches are uniquely positioned to make the case for a comprehensive wellness program and develop a wellness proposal that includes many of the features that predict success.

Seek Out Opportunities

Opportunities to engage with workplaces and their wellness programs are many and varied, depending on business size, location, industry, and leadership (Table 14-1). For example, opportunities may exist in reaching smaller businesses, as they are the least likely to have any program in place. However, in many cases they may also be the setting where coaches will most likely face barriers to implementation. For example, employers without a program cite lack of cost-effectiveness, lack of resources, and low interest from leadership and employees (Mattke et al., 2013). At the same time, more than 25% of businesses without a wellness program are considering offering one in the near future (Kaiser Family Foundation, 2013). Alternatively, coaches may opt to approach larger companies that do not have wellness programs. The coach could make the case for how the wellness program can offer a competitive edge and boost employee engagement.

Table 14-1

A BREAKDOWN OF WORKSITES OFFERING LIFESTYLE OR BEHAVIORAL COACHING

Number of Employees	% With Lifestyle or Behavioral Coaching
3–24	30
25–199	40
200–999	54
1,000–4,999	69
5,000 or more	78
All small companies (3–199 workers)	33
All large companies (200 or more workers)	57
Region	
Northeast	37
Midwest	32
South	33
West	32
Industry	
Agriculture/mining/construction	25
Manufacturing	21
Transportation/ communications/utilities	69
Wholesale	28
Retail	17
Finance	53
Service	37
State/local government	8
Healthcare	25
All Companies	**33**

Data from: The Kaiser Family Foundation & Health Research & Educational Trust (2013). *Employer Health Benefits 2013 Annual Survey: Section 12 Wellness Programs and Health Risk Assessments.* Available at www.kff.org. Accessed March 8, 2014.

PRACTICAL APPLICATION

1. Keeping in mind the information provided in this chapter, and especially the 5 key features of a successful wellness program described on page 177, develop a proposal to a small business looking to start a workplace wellness program.

   Describe how your coaching services could match each of these needs.

   What would be the easiest elements to implement? Why?

   What would be the most challenging elements to implement?

   How might you overcome the challenges?

Of all types of programs offered at worksites, the most common are health promotion activities, especially in the areas of fitness and nutrition. Nearly 80% of companies with a wellness program offer a nutrition/weight intervention, such as group-based weight-management programs or telephone-based coaching. Programs with the highest employee engagement include yoga, guided meditation, and exercise programs (Mattke et al., 2013). Coaches who have a broad range of experience may be best positioned to propose a multifaceted wellness program, including coaching services, health information, and exercise programming. One way that coaches can help worksites assess their strengths and opportunities for improvement when it comes to workplace wellness is completion of the Center for Disease Control and Prevention's (CDC) Worksite Health Scorecard (www.cdc.gov/dhdsp/pubs/docs/HSC_Manual.pdf). This is also a credible tool coaches can use to help guide program recommendations.

Ultimately, the time is now for interested coaches to engage in workplace wellness initiatives, whether as an independent contractor, as a part of third-party vendor, or as an employee.

CLINIC

From the physicians, nurse practitioners, and physician assistants to medical assistants and licensed vocational nurses, each member of the clinical team benefits from the application of coaching skills. In fact, coaching is a mandated educational competency for the nurse practitioner, though in general this concept is poorly taught, explained, and enforced (Hayes & Kalmakis, 2007). As the healthcare system moves toward more patient-centered, team-based care and the clinic is more intimately linked to the community, individuals who are not historically an integrated part of the healthcare team, such as professional health coaches, registered dietitians, exercise professionals, and community health workers, may experience increased opportunities to engage in **clinical health coaching.**

THE PATIENT-CENTERED MEDICAL HOME AND ACCOUNTABLE CARE ORGANIZATIONS

Concurrent with implementation of the Affordable Care Act, practice-based and community-based transformations are well underway, including piloting of value-based care models such as **patient-centered medical homes, patient-centered medical neighborhoods, accountable care organizations,** and **accountable care communities.** Each of these entities aims to provide a higher quality of care to optimize patient health outcomes and realize healthcare savings. All of them focus heavily on team-based efforts to engage patients in the prevention and management of disease.

Arguably the most promising modality to do this is through adoption of a coaching model of behavioral change. This coincides with a realization that the "old" methods—advice-giving, health "education," fear tactics, threats, and disincentives—are ineffective at inspiring and supporting lasting behavioral change. Perhaps the most overt acknowledgement of coaching in this transition of medical care delivery is the inclusion of six core standards in order for a practice to achieve National Committee for Quality Assurance (NCQA) certification as a patient-centered medical home. Integration of coaching principles can help a clinic achieve each of these standards. The patient-centered medical home (PCMH) is defined by the NCQA as a "way of organizing primary care that emphasizes care coordination and communication to transform primary care into 'what patients want it to be'" (www.ncqa.org). The goal of the PCMH is to increase access to care, improve the quality of care, and lower the costs (the "triple aim"). Primary care practices can earn certification as a PCMH from the NCQA if they meet the criteria outline in Table 14-2, which shows how coaches help to fulfill the six standards for this certification. Integration of coaching principles as well as supporting a designated clinical health coach can help a primary care practice meet these standards. Figure 14-1 shows how the patient-centered medical home is integrated into the broader medical neighborhood, which can include the workplace and the wellness or medical fitness center.

Table 14-2

THE PATIENT-CENTERED MEDICAL HOME AND THE ROLE OF THE COACH

STANDARD	SUMMARY OF REQUIREMENTS	SAMPLE REQUIREMENT	COACHING APPLICATION
1. Patient-centered access	The practice provides 24/7 access to team-based care for routine and urgent needs of patients/families/caregivers.	Providing alternative types of clinical encounters	Patient communication via telephone, video chat, secure instant messaging, and group visits
2. Team-based care	The practice provides continuity of care using culturally and linguistically appropriate, team-based approaches.	Training and assigning members of the care team to support patients/families/caregivers in self-management, self-efficacy and behavior change	The practice supports care team members to receive training in evidence-based approaches to self-management support, such as patient coaching and motivational interviewing.
3. Population health management	The practice provides evidence-based decision support and proactive care reminders based on complete patient information, health assessment, and clinical data	Comprehensive health assessment, including behaviors affecting health	Assessment of risky and unhealthy behaviors such as physical inactivity, smoking status, nutrition, oral health, dental care, familial behaviors, risky sexual behavior, and secondhand smoke exposure
4. Care management and support	The practice systematically identifies individual patients, and plans, manages, and coordinates care based on need.	The care team and patient/family/caregiver collaborate to develop and update an individual care plan.	Incorporates patient preferences and functional/lifestyle goals; identifies treatment goals; assesses and addresses potential barriers to meeting goals; includes a self-management plan that is provided in writing to the patient
5. Care coordination and care transitions	The practice systematically tracks, tests, and coordinates care across specialty care, facility-based care, and community organizations.	Ensuring that patient needs and preferences for health services and sharing information across people, functions, and sites are met over time	Proactive contact includes offering patients appropriate care to prevent worsening of their condition and encouraging follow-up care. Follow-up care may include physician counseling; referrals to community resources; and disease or case management or self-management support programs.
6. Performance measurement and quality improvement	The practice uses performance data to identify opportunities for improvement and acts to improve clinical quality, efficiency, and patient experience.	The practice has an ongoing quality improvement strategy and process that includes regular review of performance data and evaluation of performance against goals or benchmarks.	The practice sets goals, identifies barriers, and acts to improve performance.

Data from: National Committee for Quality Assurance (2014). *Standards and Guidelines for NCQA's Patient-Centered Medical Home (PCMH) 2014.* Washington, D.C.: National Committee for Quality Assurance.

Figure 14-1

THE PATIENT-CENTERED MEDICAL NEIGHBORHOOD

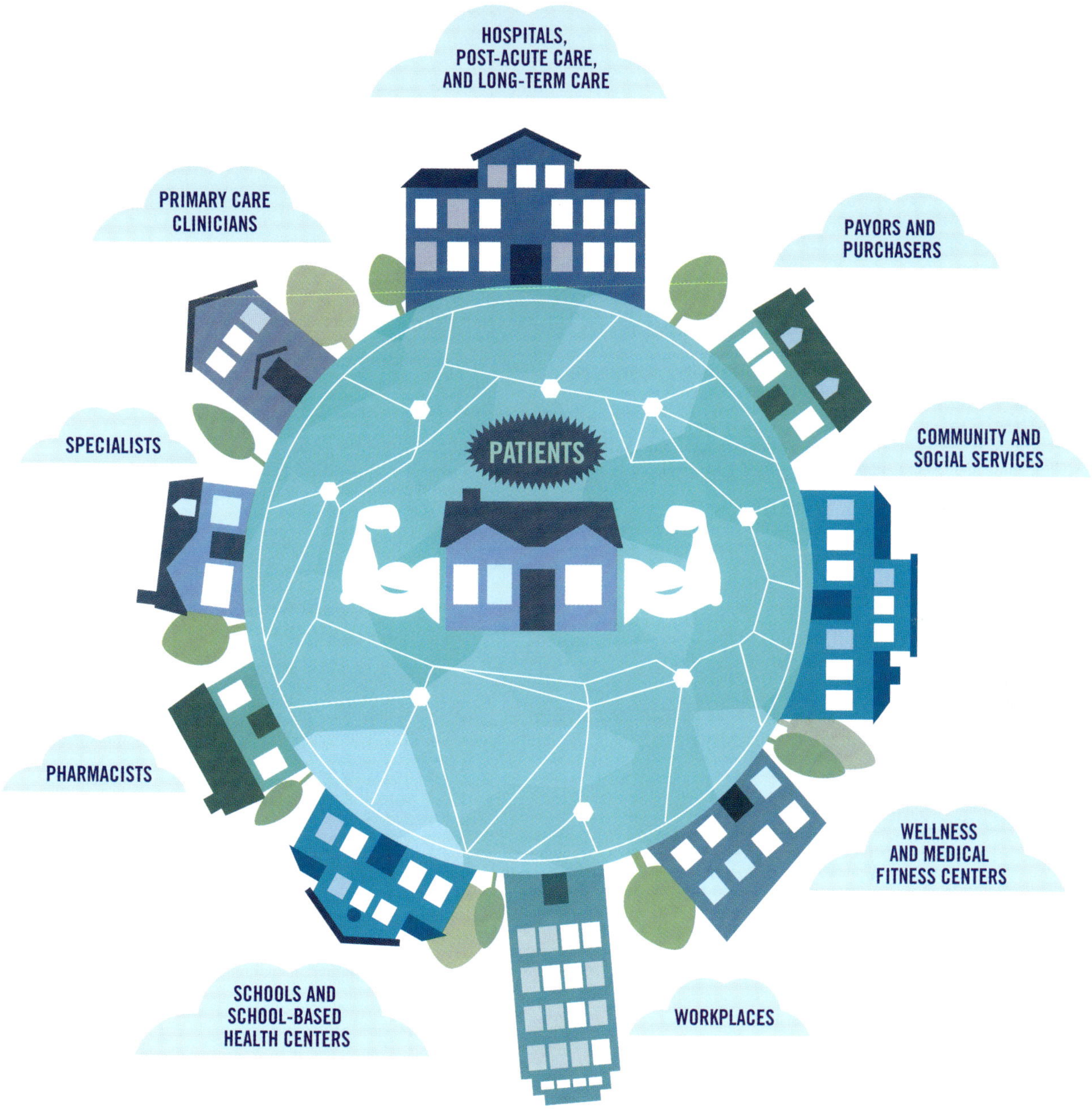

THE FIVE ROLES OF THE CLINICAL HEALTH COACH

Clinicians and researchers at the University of California-San Francisco and the San Francisco General Hospital Family Health Center have spearheaded the clinical health coaching model and integration of coaching into clinical flow. Practices may choose to implement this process by providing coaching skills training to existing members of the healthcare team, or by expanding the team to include a professionally trained health coach. While everyone on the team can benefit from training in coaching skills, so far the most effective practices have designated one person as the clinic's health coach (Bennett et al., 2010). Medical assistants often are the most appropriate team members to fill this role, as they are well-integrated into clinical flow and often are the team members most skilled at providing "linguistically and culturally concordant coaching" (Bennett et al., 2010).

Ultimately, the "clinical health coach" serves five key roles (Bennett et al., 2010):

- *Provide self-management support:* The American Academy of Family Physicians (AAFP) offers the following six tips to help a patient to achieve skills in **self-management** (AAFP, 2014):
    - ✔ Assess patient self-management abilities. That is, gain an understanding of the patient's current level of knowledge and skill in managing a given disease.
    - ✔ Use **motivational interviewing** to explore **ambivalence.**
    - ✔ Offer health coaching support, including helping the patient develop goals and action plans, disease-relevant skills such as blood glucose monitoring for patients with diabetes, and regular phone follow up.
    - ✔ Train patients in home monitoring, starting with assessing their current knowledge, skills, and **self-efficacy** and motivation to engage in home monitoring. From there, help to establish home monitoring goals and action plans. (Home monitoring activities include checking blood glucose for individuals with diabetes and measuring blood pressure for those with hypertension.)
    - ✔ Engage family members and caregivers in the self-management care plan. In other words, help to strengthen social support and accountability.
    - ✔ Bring it all together by implementing these steps and processes into the clinical work flow.
- *Bridge the gap between clinician and patient:* Studies report that 50% of patients do not understand the advice of their physician (Chodosh et al., 2005). Among those who do understand, few internalize and act upon the advice, such as the admonition to "eat less and exercise more" or even to take a given medication, with over 50% of medication prescriptions left unfilled (Sabaté, 2003). The clinical health coach serves the critically important, though underutilized, role of helping to assess a patient's understanding of the information, translate it into relevant terms, and engage in a patient-centered discussion about the issue at hand. The coach then ensures follow-up and helps to provide the patient with accountability for his or her changes.

> Engage in a patient-centered discussion

- *Help patients navigate the healthcare system:* The U.S. healthcare system is confusing and fractured. The clinical health coach plays a key role in helping patients navigate the system, helping to coordinate care and serve as a patient advocate.

- *Offer emotional support:* **Empathy** is an important coach quality and is especially important as patients face uncertain diagnoses, an intimidating healthcare system, and confusing information from providers. Clinical health coaches can help patients process their thoughts and feelings and focus them toward achieving a personal vision or goal.

- *Serve as a continuity figure:* As clinical health coaches connect with patients both inside and outside the office, they get to know the patients well and serve an important role in helping provide more continuous and complementary care.

INTEGRATION INTO CLINICAL FLOW

The **teamlet model** is the most widely studied and implemented approach to integration of health coaching in the clinical setting. In this model, the typical 15-minute primary care visit is extended by an additional 15 minutes—during which the patient receives a health coaching intervention. A physician is paired with a clinical health coach—typically a medical assistant or community health worker—who has received coach training as well as training in disease management and quality measures of prevalent chronic diseases such as prediabetes and obesity. The coach helps with medication reconciliation, assessment of patient understanding of information shared by the physician, and all of the components of the **ACE cycle of change,** depending on the patient's individual situation. The coach also increases accountability and success measures with patients between visit phone calls or emails.

PAYMENT AND REIMBURSEMENT MODELS

Several pilot studies of patient-centered medical homes and neighborhoods and accountable care organizations and communities are in progress. While healthcare reform is moving in this direction, most clinics still rely on a **fee-for-service payment model.** Coaching services are not routinely compensated, making integration of a health coach into the clinical flow a more difficult sell. However, some practices have experienced success in hiring medical assistant health coaches with the intent of freeing up physician time to see more patients. They have found that one medical assistant could serve the coaching needs for about three physicians. At a physician reimbursement rate of $40 per visit, each physician would need to see three additional patients per day to generate $57,600 in revenue—a number which would be more than enough to pay the salary of a medical assistant health coach. Other practices are experimenting with models using other types of coaching providers such as professional coaches and dietitians, though the cost tends to be increased. Ultimately, the practice of clinical health coaching is growing and evolving rapidly, creating many new opportunities for those prepared to engage patients in behavior change and in linking the clinic to the community.

A medical assistant could serve the coaching needs

PREPARING FOR A CAREER IN CLINICAL HEALTH COACHING

As opportunities arise for coaches to engage in clinical health coaching, a unique set of knowledge, skills, and attitudes are needed to be successful. The following are a few tips to get started:

- *Speak the language:* Coaches need to be able to "speak the language" of the clinical environment. Specifically, coaches should support coaching methods and assertions with peer-reviewed, published evidence; recognize the evolving landscape of the healthcare system and understand movements such as the patient-centered medical home and accountable care organizations; and value the importance of privacy, confidentiality, and professionalism. Coaches may do well to do develop an "elevator pitch," being careful to confidently present what they are able to do while being careful not to overstate claims for what coaching can or will achieve.

- *Understand disease management:* The reason for the rapid expansion of coaching in the clinical setting is to help improve outcomes for the most complex patients whose medical conditions are expensive when poorly managed, but affordable when managed well. Clinical health coaches should understand the medical goals for management of common chronic conditions such as obesity, type 2 diabetes, and asthma and be able to explain how coaching can help to achieve goal metrics.

- *Communicate effectively:* Many clinicians will be very cautious before referring patients to an unknown provider, or integrating such a provider into practice workflow, especially if the work of that individual will be done under a physician's medical license. Coaches should be prepared to communicate clearly the value and benefit of the coaching services, the coach's credentials, and methods for measuring impact and value. Additionally, the coach may benefit from applying the principles of coaching to the initial meetings with the clinic's practice manager or physicians to clearly understand their goals and objectives for the coaching services.

- *Develop relationships with clinicians:* Clinicians will be most willing to collaborate with other professionals that they know well. In many cases, the best place to start is with one's own physician or the physician of a family member such as a child or a parent. Engage in many networking events and seek out opportunities to work together.

- *Follow HIPAA guidelines:* Anyone working in a clinical setting who will interact with patient health information must adhere strictly to **Health Insurance Portability and Accountability Act (HIPAA)** guidelines. Coaches must be fully aware of these guidelines and follow them 100% of the time. More information on HIPAA guidelines is provided in Chapter 13.

- *Show your skills:* One way to begin to develop a relationship with physician providers is to show them the value of coaching, rather than telling them all about it. Helping a practice adopt healthier habits through physician coaching offers a great opportunity to help the practice leaders not only "walk the talk," but also see the coach's skills in action.

- *Go for it!* Approaching a physician practice and demonstrating interest in collaborating to improve patient outcomes may feel intimidating for many coaches, but if the coach is well prepared, this interaction can prove to be a game changer.

WELLNESS/MEDICAL FITNESS CENTER

As a cornerstone to many communities, and increasingly as a link from the clinic to the community, wellness and medical fitness centers are poised to play a leading role in the movement toward a coaching-based approach to behavioral change. From integrating coaching into existing roles such as that of a personal trainer or registered dietitian and creating a new role for professional health coaches to work with new members or those with any of a number of chronic diseases, to training membership teams and front desk staff in the essentials of quality communication and offering coaching-based programs such as the Diabetes Prevention Program at YMCAs, wellness and medical fitness centers are a natural place for behavioral change to occur. Individuals who gain coaching skills are best equipped to communicate more effectively with existing clients, broaden the network of potential clients, and ultimately, be more effective in supporting lasting behavior change. Table 14-3 highlights the multiple opportunities for integrating coaching into the medical fitness or wellness center.

Table 14-3

OPPORTUNITIES TO INTEGRATE COACHING INTO THE WELLNESS OR MEDICAL FITNESS CENTER

ROLE	DESCRIPTION
Professional health coach	Provide individual and group coaching sessions; refer to exercise professionals, dietitians, psychologists, and other providers as needed
Personal trainer	Integrate coaching principles into working with clients in goal setting; incorporate coaching into the first 15 minutes of a training session
Registered dietitian	Integrate coaching principles into working with clients in goal setting; incorporate coaching principles into meal planning and provision of information
Group coach	Employ coaching principles when leading group-based programs, engaging participants in the learning experience as opposed to "educating" or "teaching" them
Membership staff	Employ coaching principles to understand a potential member's interest in joining the facility; tailor information and discussion to the potential member's needs and identify how the facility can best serve those needs

2. Assume you are a professional coach interested in working in a clinical setting. Outline how you might prepare for and pursue this opportunity. Consider using the SWOT analysis presented in Chapter 17.

STRENGTHS	WEAKNESSES
OPPORTUNITIES	THREATS

3. Assume you are hired as a new health coach at a local wellness center. Your job is to orient all of the new members to the facility and engage in an initial coaching session to help each member identify a goal and additional resources to help achieve that goal. For instance, an overweight man may want to work with a personal trainer and registered dietitian to help him develop an overall fitness and nutrition program that might work for him down the road.

   What are your thoughts about this model?

   What special knowledge, skills, and attitudes would a health coach need to do this effectively?

   How would you make the business case to a wellness/medical fitness center in order to convince them to adopt this model?

SUMMARY

Whether in a workplace, clinical environment, wellness or medical fitness center, or elsewhere in the community, gaining coaching skills is certain to deepen the reach and impact of efforts to support lasting behavioral change and advance individuals and communities toward improved health.

EXPANSION QUIZ
Multiple-choice quiz available if you expand to the full experience

References

American Academy of Family Physicians (2014). *Educate and Experiment: Patient Self-management.* Retrieved March 9, 2014. www.aafp.org/practice-management/pcmh/patient-care/educate-self-management.html

Bennett, H.D. et al. (2010). Health coaching for patients. *Family Practice Management,* September/October, 24–29.

Chodosh, J. et al. (2005). Meta-analysis: Chronic disease self-management programs for older adults. *Annals of Internal Medicine,* 143, 427–438.

County of San Diego, Health and Human Services Agency, Public Health Services, Community Health Statistics Unit (October, 2010). *3-4-50: Chronic Disease in San Diego County.* Retrieved May 5, 2014. www.SDHealthStatistics.com.

Hayes, E. & Kalmakis, K.A. (2007). From the sidelines: Coaching as a nurse practitioner strategy for improving health outcomes. *Journal of the American Academy of Nurse Practitioners,* 19, 11, 555–562.

The Kaiser Family Foundation & Health Research & Educational Trust (2013). *Employer Health Benefits 2013 Annual Survey: Section 12 Wellness Programs and Health Risk Assessments.* Retrieved March 8, 2014. www.kff.org.

Mattke, S. et al. (2013). *Workplace Wellness Programs Study.* Santa Monica, Calif.: RAND Corporation.

National Committee for Quality Assurance (2014). *Standards and Guidelines for NCQA's Patient-Centered Medical Home (PCMH) 2014.* Washington, D.C.: National Committee for Quality Assurance.

Sabaté, E. (Ed.) (2003). *Adherence to Long-Term Therapies: Evidence for Action.* Geneva, Switzerland: World Health Organization.

Additional Resources

Agency for Healthcare Research and Quality Patient Centered Medical Home Resource Center (pcmh.ahrq.gov/): A comprehensive resource on all things related to the patient-centered medical home.

National Healthy Worksite Program from the Centers for Disease Control and Prevention (www.cdc.gov/nationalhealthyworksite/index.html): The National Healthy Worksite Program is designed to assist employers in implementing science- and practice-based prevention and wellness strategies that will lead to specific, measureable health outcomes to reduce chronic disease rates.

NOTES

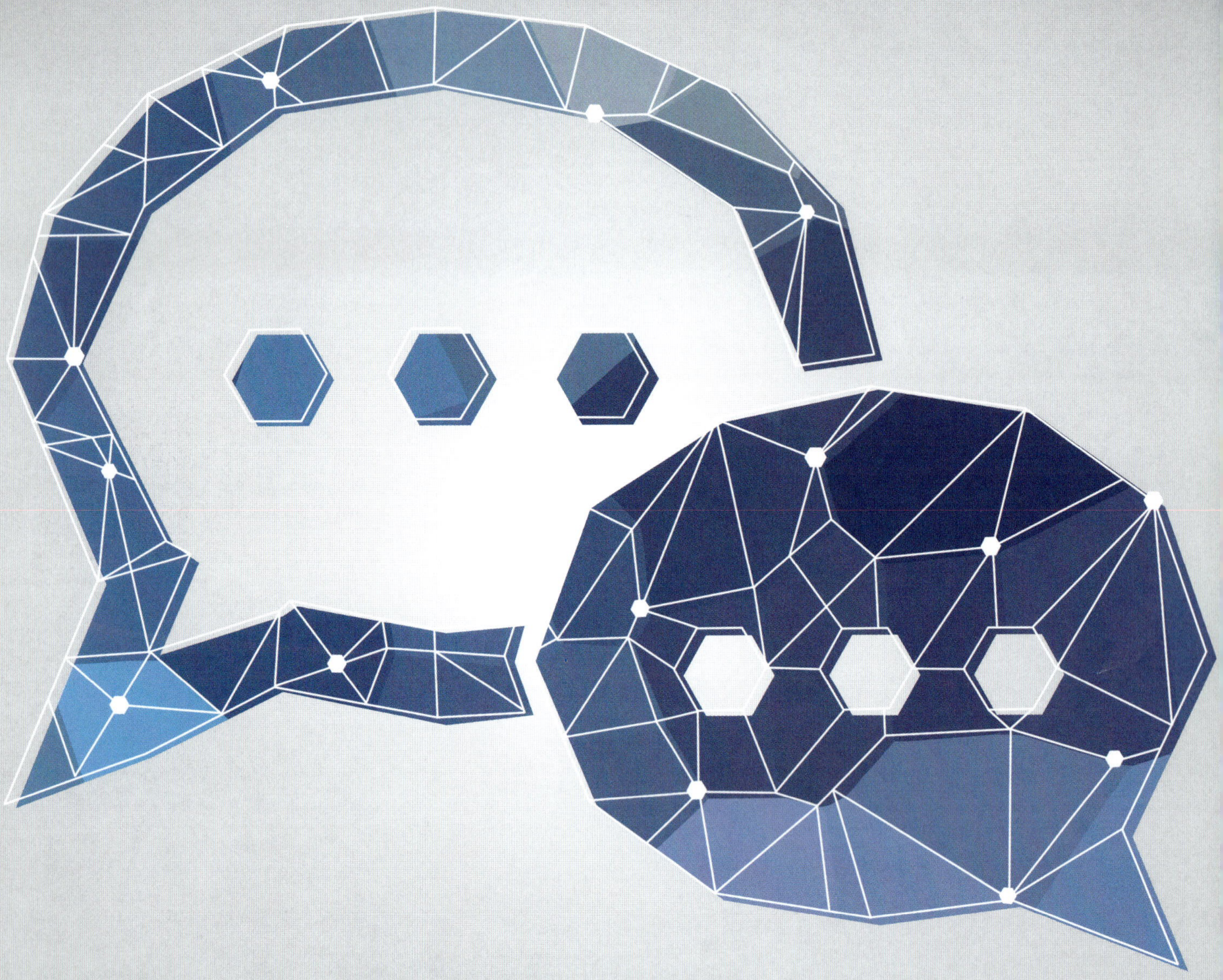

CHAPTER 15

CHAPTER 15
VIRTUAL COACHING

LEARNING OBJECTIVES

After reading this chapter, the coach will be able to:

- ________ Describe effective ways to use virtual coaching with clients
- ________ Complete a coaching session using various technologies including phone, email, text, and video
- ________ Describe the benefits and limitations of each technology
- ________ Outline how to expand a coaching business with virtual coaching
- ________ Build meaningful relationships with clients virtually

As more and more technologies emerge, the opportunities for coaches to have a positive impact on the health of individuals and communities as a whole expand exponentially. **Virtual coaching** is the implementation of the tools and technologies available via the telephone, internet, email, and mobile devices including tablets and cell phones to communicate with and coach clients.

The use of virtual coaching allows a coach to provide guidance to clients regardless of their geographic location. In addition, virtual coaching is an effective tool for follow-up with clients whom the coach already has met with in person. This chapter introduces the coach to multiple virtual coaching tools and techniques and sets the groundwork for a coach to fully integrate virtual coaching into a current or future coaching practice.

TECHNIQUES

As virtual coaching is a new and expanding area of coaching, few evidence-based recommendations are available. As such, much of the content in this chapter is based upon personal experience, trial and error, and best practices. Of course, the foundational principles of coaching—such as present and future focused, strengths based, and client-centered—apply equally as well to the virtual coaching experience. It is just the methods in which they are carried out that differ. Coaches are encouraged to experiment with different methods to find those that work best and are most suitable for a given coach's practice.

CASE STUDY

Lynette* is a woman in her mid-40s who was overweight and frustrated with her life. She was having knee problems that were complicated by her weight gain. Lynette understood the importance of a healthy lifestyle and how it impacted how she felt about herself, but she had lost confidence in her ability to make the lifestyle changes that she desperately needed to make.

I had the opportunity to meet Lynette at a health retreat in California where I was teaching a workshop on sustainable health behavior change. Following the workshop, Lynette approached me and said, "I wish I could take you home with me. I so desperately need your help to make changes in my life."

This comment opened the door for me to suggest that I coach her virtually instead of in person since we lived in two different states. She seemed surprised by that suggestion and said, "You mean you can do that?" Many current and potential clients are unaware that the option of a virtual health coach exists. They may also question the effectiveness of virtual coaching since it does not follow the traditional face-to-face coaching.

Lynette was excited to give this new approach of virtual coaching a try to see how it would work. Lynette was a virtual client of mine for five months. During that time, she found her own strengths and motivations, which allowed her to lose a significant amount of weight—she dropped from a dress size of 28 to a dress size of 12. She regained her zest for life and was able to successfully make her desired lifestyle changes.

*Name has been changed to protect privacy

"GETTING TO KNOW YOU"

A number of techniques were used to help Lynette achieve the results and success that she wanted. For our first session, I set up a 30-minute "Getting to Know You" discussion and a needs assessment interview to understand her needs and wants. I was able to do this face to face before we went our separate ways after the retreat; however, I often do this interview on the phone or via Google+ Hangouts with new virtual clients as well.

» It is recommended that coaches ask clients to set aside 30–45 minutes for their first "Getting to Know You" virtual appointment. The purpose of this appointment is twofold:

- *Build rapport:* This is an opportunity to let the client know that the coach cares about him or her, and his or her success. Have the client do the majority of the talking. Find commonalities that will build a strong connection. The coach should ask about the client's family, interests, job, pets, and whatever else may help them develop a friendship. Be sure to apply active listening skills.
- *Gain information:* This is an opportunity to find out what the client wants to accomplish by hiring a coach. This is also the time to gather information regarding the client's history and past experiences.

Below are some questions that coaches will find helpful to ask clients during the initial needs assessment interview:

1. If you had a magic wand and could make one wish regarding your health behavior and/or lifestyle change, what would it be?
   - ✔ This question allows your client to remove the emotional or mental barriers that may stand in the way of success. It also helps you to understand the "big picture" wants and goals of your client. With this knowledge, you are better equipped to guide your client in designing the most effective behaviors that will lead the client toward his or her "wish."
2. Look into the future 12 months down the road as you successfully move toward achieving (insert the answer to question 1). What would that look like for you?
3. Look into the future six months down the road as you successfully move toward achieving (insert the answer to question 1). What would that look like for you?
4. Look into the future three months down the road as you successfully move toward achieving (insert the answer to question 1). What would that look like for you?
5. Look into the future one month down the road as you successfully move toward achieving (insert the answer to question 1). What would that look like for you?

Questions 2–5 are open-ended questions that will assist both the coach and client in exploring the desired results that the client would like to achieve by working with a coach. Be sure to write down the client's responses and review them often during the client's journey to a healthier life.

COACHING TIP

If the timeline and desired results of a client are unrealistic, there is no need to address this issue during the needs assessment interview. The coach can follow up regarding what is realistic in subsequent sessions.

6. What are your strengths?
   - ✔ This is a very important question. Knowing this will help the coach build on the client's strengths and create what is called **success momentum** (see page 195).
7. What are your weaknesses?
   - ✔ If a coach were to leave any question out of this assessment, this would be the one. Although it is helpful to know what a client feels his or her weaknesses are, it is more important to focus on what he or she wants to achieve.
8. Is there anything else you would like me to know?
   - ✔ This question is a very effective way to allow a client to open up the discussion to topics or concerns that have not yet been addressed. It provides the client an opportunity to make the coach aware of other things that are going on in his or her life that will be helpful for the coach to know.

COACHING TIP

Have a pen and paper handy to record the responses of each client and to make notes. During the "Getting to Know You" appointment, coaches will need to make arrangements to get important forms and documents filled out, signed, and returned via email or fax. These forms may include Physical Activity Readiness Questionnaires (PAR-Qs), health questionnaires, liability waivers, medical releases, body-composition measurements, food diaries, etc. These forms and others can be found at: www.ACEfitness.org/healthcoachresources/pdfs/AssessmentForms.pdf.

Make a physical file for each virtual client. Keep very good notes and records about sessions with them: what was discussed, their challenges, coaching techniques used, and their progress. This file is also where coaches should keep the needed paperwork for each client, such as the coaching agreement and liability waivers. Be sure that these papers are in a secure password-protected file or lock box to maintain confidentiality and privacy.

CRAFT MODEL

THIS MODEL IS USEFUL DURING ANY KIND OF VIRTUAL COACHING, REGARDLESS OF THE TECHNOLOGY USED.

CASE STUDY CONTINUED

Once I completed the "Getting to Know You" interview with Lynette, we were able to set up a weekly 30-minute phone call. My original arrangement with Lynette was a three-month contract. She opted in for an additional two months at the completion of that agreement. This is not unusual for clients to do. They usually find that virtual coaching is a time-efficient method for them to engage with a coach.

Every Monday when I called Lynette, I would follow a virtual coaching model called the **CRAFT model.** This model is useful during any kind of virtual coaching, regardless of the technology used. CRAFT is an acronym that helps coaches systematically walk through a sequence of virtual coaching steps in a logical order. CRAFT stands for check-in; report progress; adjust and assign; feedback; and teach, train, and talk through.

Check-in

Check-in involves the coach and client starting the virtual coaching session by sharing something unique or unusual about themselves or something interesting that happened that week. The rules regarding "check-ins" are that they have to be done in 60 seconds or less and cannot be related to the coaching session. The check-in typically goes as follows:

Coach: Hi Jane. It's great to meet with you today for our virtual coaching session.

Jane: Hi coach.

Coach: Let's start our session with check-ins. (If it is the first time meeting with this client or group of clients, the coach will need to explain what a check-in is and the rules).

Coach: "My check-in is that I got a new dog this week. He's a chocolate Labrador and his name is Hershey."

Jane: "Wow. Cool. My check-in is I went to a family reunion this weekend and saw my brother who I haven't seen for a year."

Check-ins aid in building **rapport** and breaking the ice for each session. They give coaches more information about the client that can aid in coaching or building rapport. It is also a good practice to reference the check-in the client shared at a later point in time. When coaching a group, everyone takes a turn to share a check-in.

Report Progress

During this step of the virtual coaching session, the coach asks clients how they did during the week with what they are working on. This is an opportunity for them to report on their progress, challenges, and successes. This discussion may take some time, so plan accordingly.

Adjust and Assign

This is the time to make adjustments to a client's plan based on the progress reported. This is also the time to make and discuss new assignments that will help move the client toward his or her goal.

Feedback

After helping the client adjust the plan and/or agreeing on new actions, the next step is to ask for feedback. Questions such as, "How do you feel about that?" "Do you have any questions?" and "What are your concerns?" are appropriate. Any question that gives the coach a sense for how a client is feeling about the adjustments and/or new action plans is great.

Teach, Train, and Talk Through

The final step of the CRAFT model involves teaching or coaching as needed based on the feedback received from the client. This includes talking through the client's questions or concerns that surfaced during the feedback step. The coach may need to follow up with the client by emailing some information, nutrition tips, physical activity or exercise suggestions, or a video to watch.

> Resilience, optimism, and persistence

It is important to note that while the CRAFT model is an effective way of structuring communication in a virtual environment, it may be most applicable to goal-focused approaches to coaching in which clients have a clearly defined goal or aim of the coaching relationship. The coach working with clients who are more ambivalent about change may struggle with the CRAFT format at first. However, the CRAFT model seems to be effective in these situations as long as the coach and client have a clear focus and agenda for each session, even if this is not to set goals but to explore values that give rise to motivation to change.

ACCOMPANYING AUDIO:
Listen in on a short virtual phone coaching session with Lynette. See if you can identify the individual components of the CRAFT model in the coaching.

COACHING TIP

Have the CRAFT method written out on a piece of paper for easy reference and have it available while conducting virtual coaching sessions. If coaches follow this method, they will be able to cover all of this content in a quick and concise manner.

SUCCESS MOMENTUM

Helping clients create success momentum should be a primary goal for any coach. Success momentum occurs when a client experiences tiny successes, which in turn propel them onto a path of confidence. Success momentum is the key that unlocks the door to initiating other positive changes in their lives. It helps them to tackle other big challenges that they have not yet been able to face and move closer to their goals.

People who experience success momentum report a feeling of resilience, optimism, and persistence. These qualities will improve clients' lives in ways that are very powerful but that cannot be easily measured.

The result of success momentum is a natural process that occurs organically via the "ripple effect." The momentum that clients feel from their successes ripples out and positively impacts other areas of their lives, even those areas that are not specific to the stated goals.

Teaching clients to immediately celebrate their small successes will reinforce their forward movement and increase their progress exponentially. If a client learns to say a phrase to him- or herself such as "Yes! I rock" or "You got this" upon completion of even the tiniest new behavior, he or she will make faster progress toward the overall goals.

Most clients will not be familiar with the term success momentum, but they will be familiar with how it feels. The statements below reflect how clients have described the feeling of success momentum after experiencing very tiny victories:

- "I feel great.
- "I feel empowered!"
- "I'm feeling such a sense of accomplishment."
- "I feel happy and energized."
- "I am ready to take on more."

How do coaches incorporate success momentum and the ripple effect into virtual coaching? Consider the following email coaching session I had with a client who was completing a virtual Tiny Habits coaching experience. With the Tiny Habits program, which was developed by BJ Fogg, "habiteurs" aim to adopt new behaviors by anchoring a new habit—in its tiniest form—to an existing habit. For example, someone aiming to increase physical activity may start with "after I brush my teeth, I will do one jumping jack." Then, importantly, the person celebrates having done the habit. Refer to Chapter 10 and www.tinyhabits.com for more information.

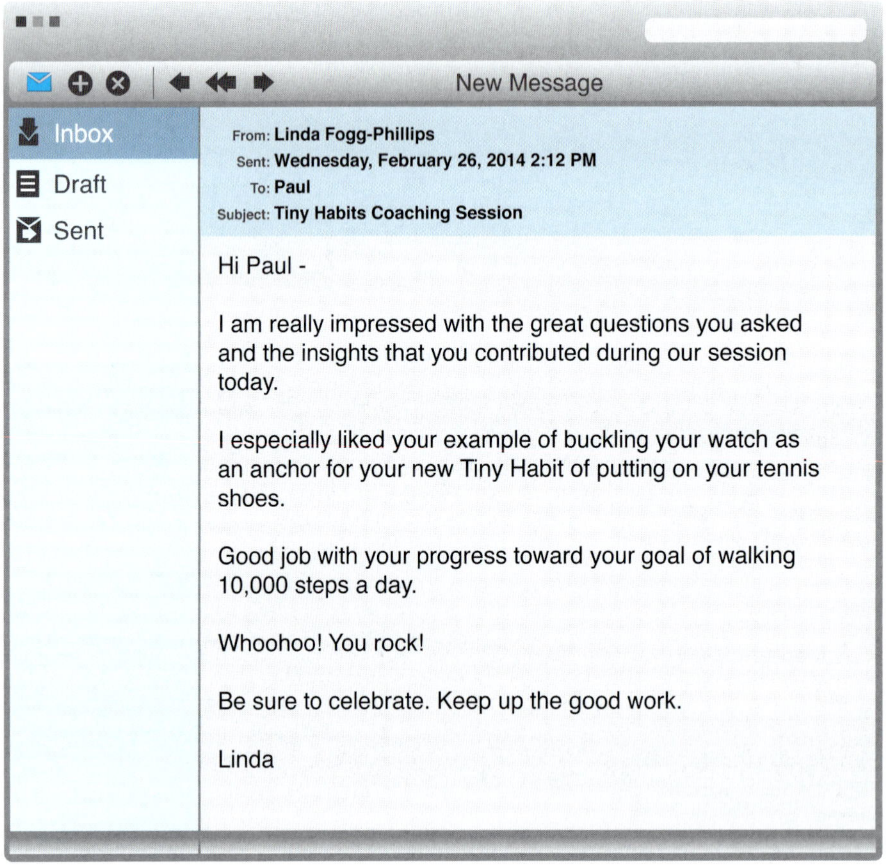

From: Linda Fogg-Phillips
Sent: Wednesday, February 26, 2014 2:12 PM
To: Paul
Subject: Tiny Habits Coaching Session

Hi Paul -

I am really impressed with the great questions you asked and the insights that you contributed during our session today.

I especially liked your example of buckling your watch as an anchor for your new Tiny Habit of putting on your tennis shoes.

Good job with your progress toward your goal of walking 10,000 steps a day.

Whoohoo! You rock!

Be sure to celebrate. Keep up the good work.

Linda

This email took me less than 60 seconds to write and send to Paul. During a virtual coaching session that took place earlier, I wrote down of some of the comments that Paul made that showed his understanding of the concept I was teaching and his progress toward one of his fitness goals. Notice that I very specifically referenced his comment in the email and tied it to his goal. Next, I celebrated his accomplishment of making progress toward his goal by writing "Whoohoo! You rock!"

Email is the perfect tool to use in virtual coaching for this kind of positive reinforcement and acknowledgement, as clients can read it over and over again. The impact and success momentum that it creates for the client each time he or she reads it is very powerful and a means of extending the coach's impact beyond the coaching session. Here is how Paul responded.

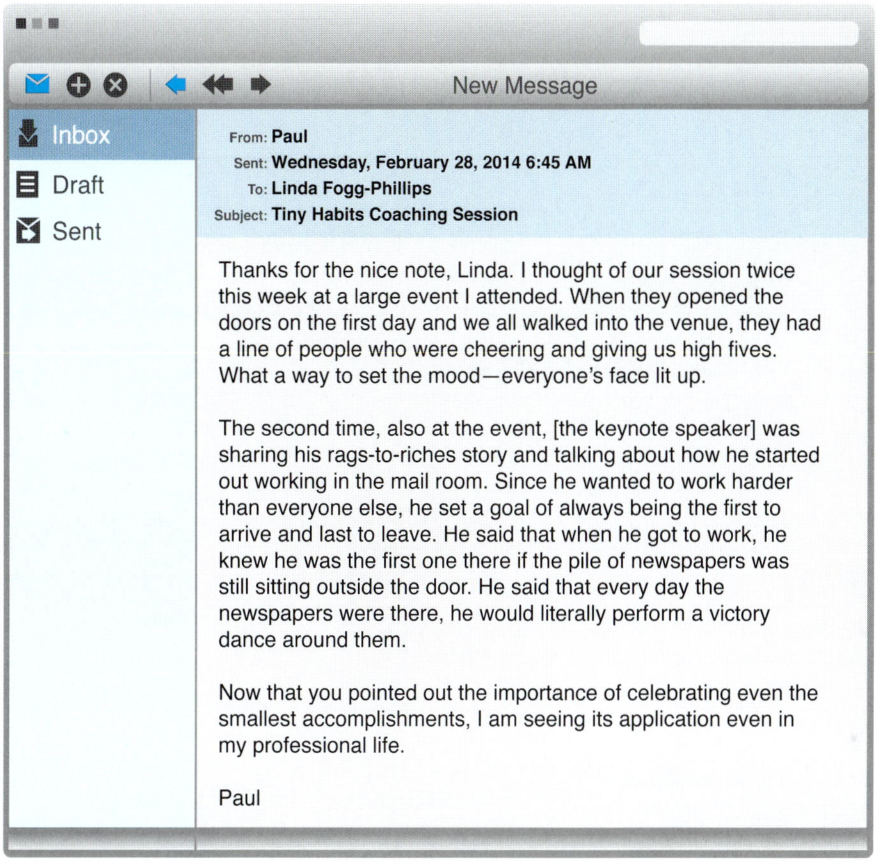

From: Paul
Sent: Wednesday, February 28, 2014 6:45 AM
To: Linda Fogg-Phillips
Subject: Tiny Habits Coaching Session

Thanks for the nice note, Linda. I thought of our session twice this week at a large event I attended. When they opened the doors on the first day and we all walked into the venue, they had a line of people who were cheering and giving us high fives. What a way to set the mood—everyone's face lit up.

The second time, also at the event, [the keynote speaker] was sharing his rags-to-riches story and talking about how he started out working in the mail room. Since he wanted to work harder than everyone else, he set a goal of always being the first to arrive and last to leave. He said that when he got to work, he knew he was the first one there if the pile of newspapers was still sitting outside the door. He said that every day the newspapers were there, he would literally perform a victory dance around them.

Now that you pointed out the importance of celebrating even the smallest accomplishments, I am seeing its application even in my professional life.

Paul

COACHING TIP

Make note of the client's specific comments during each virtual coaching session. Send the client a personal email complimenting him or her and referencing the comment. It is best if this email is sent within 24 hours of the virtual coaching session.

TECHNOLOGY AND TOOLS

Various types of technology and tools can be used for virtual coaching. The following is not an exhaustive list, but it covers the most common and effective tools.

COACHING TIP

By utilizing multiple technologies and tools while working with a virtual client, a coach will be able to engage the client on many levels. For example, if the virtual coaching sessions take place via telephone, use email and text to send additional information or to follow up before the next session.

TELEPHONE

Coaching via the phone may be the first thing that comes to mind when thinking about the term "virtual coaching." The phone is the easiest tool to use and the most familiar for both the coach and the client.

Virtual coaching appointments via phone can be readily set up without a lot of effort, as there is no reliance on other variables with technology (e.g., internet connections or knowing how to use new forms of technology). Clients will most likely have a cell phone, which increases the client and coach's accessibility to one another.

Most mobile phones have the ability to do a video call or Facetime. Using this feature when available is great because it allows the coach to see the nonverbal communication of the client.

COACHING TIP

Some clients may feel awkward participating in a video call. The coach must be sure that the client is comfortable with this format if before utilizing it.

There are many free conference call services available when coaching a group (instead of an individual) via phone, including www.freeconferencecall.com. By simply going to that site and entering their email address, coaches will be issued a conference call number and a PIN that they can give to clients for group coaching calls.

Most free services also have the ability to record the conference call. If coaches choose to record their calls, they must be sure to inform the group. Recorded calls are helpful for clients who are not able to attend the call, as well as for the coach's review.

Texting can also be used in virtual coaching. Texting can be very useful as a means to quickly follow up or check in with a client; however, it is not an effective technology to use for actual virtual coaching sessions. Texting can be used to "trigger" behaviors that coaches are helping clients establish.

COACHING TIP

If a coach does want to use texting as a virtual coaching tool, he or she should be sure to get permission from clients. Texting is best used as a check-in and accountability tool to see how a client is doing.

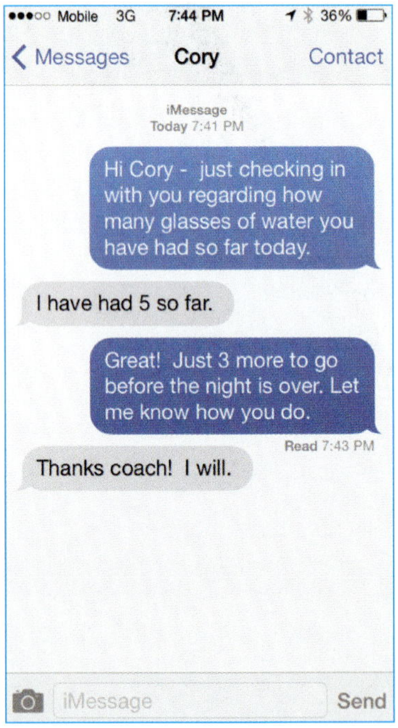

EMAIL

Email is an incredibly effective and efficient coaching tool. It is a great way to share information and give guidance. It is an easy tool for ongoing interaction with a client and an easy means of sharing links, sending forms, and collecting information.

My coaching team and I have effectively coached hundreds of clients from all over the world that we have never met in person. The foundation of our behavior-change program involves interacting via daily email. I am constantly amazed at the impact that a daily email interaction in a coaching situation can have. Even more amazing is how a strong relationship with those that you coach can be built through email alone.

If a coach is considering using email as the foundation for a coaching program, it is most effective if the program is designed to have daily email contact with each client. In essence, the coach is having an ongoing conversation with the client via email.

COACHING TIP

Coaching programs that are email-based should set a predictable pattern for the client, such as by sending out daily emails at the same time every day. It is important to respond to a client's emails in a timely manner, preferably within two hours of receipt.

GOOGLE+ HANGOUTS

Google+ Hangouts, which can be accessed via any computer, tablet, or mobile device with an internet connection, is a free video chat service from Google that works exceptionally well for virtual coaching. Google+ Hangouts enables both one-on-one video chats and group video chats with up to 10 people at a time (including the coach). Hangouts also have a chat window where participants can engage in written chats and make comments. Videos, slide shows, PowerPoint presentations, screen sharing, and document sharing is available while on a Hangout. Coaches can also use Google+ Hangouts for conference calling without the video feature if they prefer.

Google+ Hangouts also offers a "Hangouts On Air" feature for broadcasting live video conversations that are accessible to anyone with a web browser. Hangouts On Air can be recorded and archived for future viewing or uploaded to a YouTube Channel.

Google+ Hangouts is not only one of the most effective tools to use for virtual coaching, but one of the most versatile as well. Coaches will need to have a Google+ account to use the Hangouts feature, as will each participant.

BEST PRACTICES FOR USING GOOGLE+ HANGOUTS FOR VIRTUAL COACHING

- Inform clients of the time of the Hangout far enough in advance for them to be able to join.
- Invite clients to the Hangout 10 minutes before the coaching session is to start. Let them know that you will open the Hangout early in order to give them plenty of time to sign on and work out any technical difficulties.
- Do a Hangout test run with clients who have never used the Hangout feature before. This will allow you time to work out technical difficulties before a scheduled session and help clients become comfortable with the technology. A test run consists of making sure they can sign on when they receive your invite.
- Use a headset during your Hangout and instruct your clients to use one as well. This will help eliminate any background noise or echo.
- Conduct your Hangout virtual coaching session in a quiet location where you will not be interrupted.
- Be sure your face is well lit for the session. Natural lighting is best if possible. If natural lighting is not available, you may need to invest in some professional photo lights.
- Remove clutter or distracting objects that will show up in view of the camera on your computer during the Hangout. Run a test Hangout with just yourself to see what your client will see.
- Look directly at the camera when you talk to your clients on a Hangout, not at their picture on your screen. This is called "virtual eye contact" and makes a tremendous difference in terms of connecting with your client. This is something that you will have to practice and be conscience of. *Tip:* I have two googly eyes stuck on my computer on either side of my camera to remind me that is where I need to look.
- Place your computer (or the camera that you are broadcasting from) at eye level or above so that your client sees a straight-on view of your face. Views from lower than eye level will make you look like you have a double chin whether you have one or not. ▶

- If there are three or more participants in your Hangout virtual coaching session, mute your microphone when you are not talking and instruct your clients to do the same.
- Mute your camera if you do not want to be seen. This is a good practice to get into when you open your Hangout 10 minutes before the start time.
- Be aware that if you have the Hangout open before and after your Google+ Hangout virtual coaching session, you are broadcasting and can be seen and heard by anyone signed on.

Ultimately, each technology offers many benefits as well as limitations (Tables 15-1 through 15-6). Which method used will depend on the specific goals and requirements of the coaching relationship.

Table 15-1

BENEFITS AND LIMITATIONS OF VIRTUAL COACHING—TELEPHONE

Benefits	Limitations
Ease of use for coach and client	One dimensional—can only hear voice and cannot read body language
High accessibility to telephones/cell phones	No ability to visually demonstrate concepts being taught
Can communicate with clients regardless of location	Have to coordinate times for sessions
Immediate feedback and communication	Clients may be easily distracted or multitasking during coaching session
	Cost-prohibitive with international clients

Table 15-2

BENEFITS AND LIMITATIONS OF VIRTUAL COACHING—TELEPHONE WITH FACETIME OR OTHER VIDEO FEATURE

Benefits	Limitations
Ease of use for coach and client	Client may not be in a location that supports video connection via phone
High accessibility to telephones/cell phones	Cost-prohibitive with international clients
Can communicate with clients regardless of location	Have to coordinate times for sessions
Multidimensional—can see body language/facial expressions in addition to verbal communication	
Ability to visually demonstrate concepts being taught	
Increased ability to engage clients and thereby reduce distractions	
Immediate feedback and communication	

Table 15-3

BENEFITS AND LIMITATIONS OF VIRTUAL COACHING—TEXTING

Benefits	Limitations
Ease of use for coach and client	Cost-prohibitive with international clients
High accessibility to cell phones with texting capabilities	May not get immediate response
Can communicate with clients regardless of location	One-dimensional communication
Client can access when convenient	Cannot hear client's voice or see body language
Fast and easy	
No need to set appointment	
Immediate feedback and communication (if both parties are available)	

Table 15-4

BENEFITS AND LIMITATIONS OF VIRTUAL COACHING—EMAIL

Benefits	Limitations
Ease of use for coach and client	Cannot hear client's voice or see body language
Written communication—client and coach can refer back as needed	May not get immediate response
Can communicate with clients regardless of location	One-dimensional communication
Client can access when convenient	
Fast and easy	
No need to set appointment	
Immediate feedback and communication (if both parties are available)	

Table 15-5

BENEFITS AND LIMITATIONS OF VIRTUAL COACHING—SKYPE/VIDEO CALLS

Benefits	Limitations
Can see and hear client	Have to be familiar with technology
Can communicate with clients regardless of location	Need to have a Skype account (free)
Can visually demonstrate concepts	Need to set an appointment with the client
	Need an internet connection

Table 15-6

BENEFITS AND LIMITATIONS OF VIRTUAL COACHING—GOOGLE+ HANGOUTS

Benefits	Limitations
Can see and hear client—video conferencing for free	Have to be familiar with technology
Can set up group coaching for up to 10 people, including the coach	Need a Google+ account (free)
Can communicate with clients regardless of location	Need an internet connection
Can share written documents	Need a computer with a camera
Can share videos	
Can record session	
Can communicate with clients regardless of location	

VIRTUAL COACHING AND ESTABLISHING BOUNDARIES

When establishing the initial coaching agreement, coaches might consider including language outlining personal and professional boundaries. Virtual relationships can lead clients to invite coaches into types of relationships that might occur in a face-to-face relationship. For example, clients may send emails with expectations of an immediate reply, invite coaches to join other aspects of their virtual life (e.g. Facebook), or attempt to join the personal virtual world of their coach. As a result of this, it is incumbent on the coach to establish the "rules" or "boundaries" of the virtual therapeutic relationship. This might include having such boundaries stated in the coaching agreement and the coach discussing this up front when establishing the relationship.

GENERAL GUIDELINES FOR VIRTUAL COACHING PACKAGES

How coaches configure their virtual coaching packages is individual and needs to be based on the tools available, the goals of the client, and his or her comfort level with the technology/tools.

Other tools, such as personal activity devices and apps, are helpful to include in virtual coaching packages (i.e., have clients wear a Jawbone UP band, Fitbit, or Nike+ Fuelband and share their daily activity with the coach). In fact, it is highly recommended that coaches use multiple tools. Consider the following general guidelines:

Virtual Coaching Sessions Using Phone Calls Only:

- Hold sessions once a week, on the same day and at the same time each week.
- Optimum length of call: 30 minutes (allow 45–60 minutes for the first call)
- Optimum number of sessions: 12 over three months
- Minimum number of sessions: four over one month
- Texting can be added for additional support.
- Texting can be used daily as needed.

Virtual Coaching Sessions Using Email Only:

- Email contact should be daily, sent out at the same time every day.
- Emails should be as short as possible.
- Respond to clients' emails within 24 hours (within four hours is best).
- Optimum number of sessions: seven over one week
- Daily email coaching for longer than a month is not recommended.

Virtual Coaching Sessions Using Google+ Hangouts or Video Call:

- Hold sessions once a week on the same day and at the same time each week.
- Optimum length of Hangout or video call: 30–60 minutes (*Note:* The length of the Hangout/video call is determined by how much material the coach has to cover and the visual interaction employed. Be aware that the time goes very fast in this format. The more people on the Hangout/video call, the more time the coach will need to allow.)
- Optimum number of sessions: 12 over three months
- Minimum number of sessions: four over one month

PRACTICAL APPLICATION

1. Developing your skills as a virtual coach expands your reach and increases your marketability. You can even apply your virtual coaching skills with clients that you work with face-to-face as a follow-up to your in-person coaching.

   Virtual coaching provides a way to touch the lives of people from all walks of life and in all corners of the Earth. Try some of the technologies and tools discussed in this chapter. Enlist at least two volunteers to help you.

   Google+ Hangouts

   - Schedule Hangout practice with your volunteers.
   - At the predetermined time, invite your volunteers to a Google+ Hangout.
   - Once everyone is on the Hangout, use some of the features, such as screen sharing, document sharing, and the chat window.
   - End the Hangout and close the Hangout window.

   Describe your experience:

   Google+ Hangouts with Google+ Circles

   - Put your volunteers into a Circle on Google+.
   - Invite the Circle to your Hangout.
   - Once everyone is successfully signed onto the Hangout, you can end the Hangout and close the window.

   Describe your experience:

   Set up your free conference call number

   - Sign up for a free conference call number.
   - Share your call-in number with your volunteers.
   - Have a conversation and experiment with the record feature.

   Describe your experience:

SUMMARY

Virtual coaching—whether through phone, email, texting, or video conferencing—offers a useful and versatile way to engage clients in making a meaningful behavior change. Coaches are encouraged to experiment with these various methods and integrate them into their coaching to best meet theirs and their clients' needs.

EXPANSION QUIZ
Multiple-choice quiz available if you expand to the full experience

CHAPTER 16

CHAPTER 16
GROUP COACHING

LEARNING OBJECTIVES

After reading this chapter, the coach will be able to:

- Describe 10 principles of effective group facilitation
- Develop and prepare for a group coaching experience

For the coach, group coaching sessions serve as a natural extension of the coaching process, inviting coaches to employ the **ACE cycle of change**. When working in groups, attention is focused on a group comprised of many individuals, each with unique strengths and visions of how the experience will positively impact his or her life. It is incumbent upon the coach to help guide the individuals within the group on a change process that will become more rich and impactful as a result of the collective wisdom and experiences of the group's members. This chapter helps coaches identify, nurture, and practice the skills needed for effective group coaching.

MAKING THE CASE FOR GROUP COACHING

Group coaching offers several key advantages over one-on-one coaching, including increased cost-effectiveness and group support and empowerment. While the scientific evidence to support its efficacy is evolving, early studies have shown promise. An excellent article compiling research, expert opinion, and consensus as it relates to group coaching offered the following strengths and challenges of group coaching (Armstrong et al., 2013).

Strengths of group coaching:

- A "sense of community"; public commitment to a goal appears to strengthen commitment and accountability
- Increased willingness to consider new and different solutions to a given problem
- Streamlined provision of health information
- Increased reach and impact of the coaching intervention

Challenges of group coaching:

- Logistics, including availability, scheduling, and determining whether to offer an "open session" in which new members can join at any time, or a "closed session" in which the coaching intervention has a set start date and stop date
- Difficulty managing group dynamics
- High degree of skill and expertise required of the coach to effectively coach multiple individuals at once and also promote an optimal group dynamic

THE MOST IMPORTANT GROUP FACILITATION SKILLS

Individuals join groups seeking awareness, action, encouragement, empowerment, exploration, and acknowledgement on their behavior-change journey. An effective coach will help them engage with the group experience in order to achieve these ideals.

FIVE OBJECTIVES FOR A GROUP COACHING EXPERIENCE

Coaching a group requires refined skills not only in the process of coaching, but also in managing the group environment to create a place of trust, openness, and ready exchange of ideas that are helpful in moving the group toward its vision and goals. Generally, the most effective group coaches already have honed coaching skills through many one-on-one coaching sessions. As a group facilitator, the coach is responsible to:

1. *Create a feedback-rich environment where participants can benefit from the group wisdom.* The group coaching journey benefits when members feel empowered to share their thoughts and ideas with the goal of supporting change and progress toward the group's objectives.

2. *Encourage a variety of participants to share in order to maximize the collective group wisdom.* People join groups for various reasons. Many may choose a group environment to help buffer the focused attention created in a one-on-one environment. Others may join for the energy and excitement gleaned from being around many other people with a similar goal. The coach's role is to help direct the energy from the group experience toward achieving the goals and objectives of the group program while also using coaching skills such as open-ended questioning and reflective listening to help the more reserved members engage in the conversation.

3. *Respectfully challenge, encourage, and acknowledge group participants individually and collectively.* Through implementation of the **OARS model**—**open-ended questions, affirmations, reflections**, and **summarizing**—the coach applies **powerful questioning** to compel group members to derive their **internal motivation** for change and to share their insights and epiphanies with the larger group. This also provides an opportunity to share and celebrate successes, which can enhance the change process for many, even when the success was experienced by an individual.

4. *Help participants design customized action plans they can implement outside of the group sessions.* A challenge of group coaching is the diminished "air time" for any one individual. The group coach will need to employ tools and techniques to take advantage of the group experience to help individuals develop and implement their own change plans.

5. *Provide a forum where participants can be accountable for their results.* When goals and aspirations are made public, individuals are more likely to achieve those goals. A group coaching experience provides an outstanding venue for public sharing of goals as well as accountability in taking the steps to achieve them.

Help direct the energy from the group experience

10 GUIDELINES FOR FACILITATING GROUP LEARNING

To successfully meet these key objectives, the coach will benefit from honing some key facilitation skills. Carl Rogers (1969), a pioneer in the field of positive psychology and the principles of client-center coaching, offers 10 guidelines to effectively facilitate group learning. Though nearly half a century has passed since Rogers developed these guidelines, they continue to hold true today.

10 GUIDELINES FOR FACILITATING GROUP LEARNING

1. Establish and emphasize trust.
2. Elicit and clarify each individual's purpose for attending the group. Together, develop a purpose and goal as a group.
3. Identify each individual's primary motivation and drive for attending the class or group experience and help the client use that internal drive and purpose as the context for learning new information.
4. Organize and make accessible a wide range of learning resources for learners across various cognitive styles.
5. Serve as a flexible resource for the group. Whether as coach, lecturer, advisor, or colleague, the facilitator is willing to be flexible for the sake of helping the students achieve the most value from the learning experience.
6. Be open to both intellectual and emotional insights, feedback, and enthusiasm from the group.
7. As the group becomes established, adopt the role of serving as the voice of one equal part of the whole group, rather than the "leader" of the group.
8. The facilitator is open to share his or her feelings and thoughts with the group, and this is considered as one individual's perspective that the group may "take or leave."
9. The facilitator is keenly aware of deep or strong emotions of the group and is accepting of them.
10. The facilitator embodies a commitment to awareness of his or her own attitudes, and engages in the above principles with the group to the extent that the facilitator is willing and able.

Data from: Knowles, M.S. (1980). *The Modern Practice of Adult Education: From Pedagogy to Andragogy.* Englewood Cliffs, N.J.: Cambridge; Rogers, C. (1969). *Freedom to Learn.* Columbus, Ohio: Merrill.

ESTABLISHING GROUP NORMS

A key ingredient of a successful group coaching experience is the adoption of guiding principles or norms that everyone in the group agrees to honor. The coach or other group members can direct each other back to the norms if they have been violated, but more importantly, the process of developing and adopting these norms helps direct group behavior and lessens the probability that they will be violated.

While the members should come up with the group norms, the coach can provide direction and insights during the process. Examples of norms that groups may consider include:

- Focus on strengths.
- Provide honest feedback.
- Share resources.
- Acknowledge the uniqueness, individual context, and resourcefulness of all group members.
- Provide each other with accountability.
- Refrain from fixing, prescribing, or coercing.
- Display **empathy** and compassion for yourself and others.
- Speak from one's own experience (e.g., "This is what has worked for me" or "I have done it this way") rather than provide advice for how another should proceed.
- Promise confidentiality, except if someone is a danger to themselves or others.
- Acknowledge a willingness to defer to the facilitator, when needed.

While the coach may help guide the group members on the types of statements that they may consider, it is beneficial to engage the group in the creation of these "rules" so that all of the group members experience a greater commitment to them, and thus are most likely to remember to follow them and remind others to do the same.

THE GROUP COACHING EXPERIENCE

Coaching a group of individuals toward behavioral change initially can feel overwhelming and complicated. It may be easier to fall into the old habit of simply lecturing or providing health education to the group. However, for the benefit of each client, it is important to avoid falling into this trap.

THE ROLE OF PERSONAL PREPARATION, CLARITY, AND MINDFULNESS

Personal preparation is essential for group leadership success. Prior to focusing on the task at hand, coaches will benefit from making sure they are in the "right place" mentally and physically before beginning the session. This includes taking care of personal physical needs such as rest, nutrition, and hydration, as well as allowing adequate time to review notes from previous group sessions and the agenda for the current session.

As the coach prepares to lead a group experience, gaining clarity of mind is important so that he or she can provide full attention and energy to the group. The coach may ask him- or herself: Have I done my best to set aside projects or interpersonal concerns? Have I eliminated extraneous noise or visual distractions?

Become fully present for the group experience

Awareness is an important component not only of the behavior-change experience, but also for effectively coaching clients through that experience. A coach may consider employing techniques such as a few moments of quiet contemplation, conscious breaths, or a brief mental scan of one's body, emotions, and thoughts to become fully present for the group experience.

THE FOCUS AND CONTENT

The focus of a group coaching program is what unites the members. Whether the focus is on losing weight, improving care of a chronic disease, quitting smoking, managing stress, or another topic, it is incumbent upon the coach to clearly describe the program's focus in the marketing and recruitment of members as well as help to keep the group's attention on that focus.

The content of the program can help drive the focus while the coach also implements principles such as the ACE cycle of change. Coaches often will need to carefully balance the aim to "teach" a certain amount of information while still holding true to the coaching experience, including

The content of the program can help drive the focus

avoidance of the **righting reflex**, and engaging each member fully in the experience. Malcolm Knowles (1980), a leader in adult learning, described several effective strategies (Table 16-1).

Table 16-1

ALIGNING THE CONDITIONS OF LEARNING WITH THE PRINCIPLES OF TEACHING*

Conditions of Learning	Principles of Teaching
The learners feel a need to learn.	The teacher exposes students to new possibilities of self-fulfillment. The teacher helps each student clarify his or her own aspirations for improved behavior. The teacher helps each student diagnose the gap between his or her aspiration and his or her present level of performance.
The learning environment is characterized by physical comfort, mutual trust and respect, mutual helpfulness, freedom of expression, and acceptance of differences.	The teacher provides physical conditions that are comfortable (e.g., seating, smoking, temperature, ventilation, lighting, and decoration) and conducive to interaction (preferably, no person sitting behind another person). The teacher accepts each student as a person of worth and respects his or her feelings and ideas. The teacher seeks to build relationships of mutual trust and helpfulness among the students by encouraging cooperative activities and refraining from inducing competitiveness and/or being judgmental. The teacher exposes his or her own feelings and contributes resources as a co-learner in the spirit of mutual inquiry.
The learners perceive the goals of a learning experience to be their goals.	The teacher involves the students in a mutual process of formulating learning objectives in which the needs of the student, of the institution, of the teacher, of the subject matter, and of the society are taken into account.
The learners accept a share of the responsibility for planning and operating a learning experience, and therefore have a feeling of commitment toward it. The learners participate actively in the learning process.	The teacher shares his or her thinking about options available in the designing of the learning experiences and the selection of materials and methods and involves the students in deciding among these options jointly. The teacher helps the students organize themselves (e.g., project groups, learning-teaching teams, or independent study) to share responsibility in the process of mutual inquiry.
The learning process is related to, and makes use of, the experience of the learners.	The teacher helps the students exploit their own experiences as resources for learning through the use of such techniques as discussion and role playing. The teacher gears the presentation of his or her own resources to the levels of experience of his particular students. The teacher helps the students apply new learning to their experience, and thus to make the learning more meaningful and integrated.
The learners have a sense of progress toward their goals.	The teacher involves the students in developing mutually acceptable criteria and methods for measuring progress toward the learning objectives. The teacher helps the students develop and apply procedures for self-evaluation according to these criteria.

*Knowles described these as the "principles of teaching," but they could equally describe the "principles of coaching," in which the teacher is the coach and the students are the group members.

The coach's attention to the focus of the group experience as well as to the principles of coaching, including focusing on strengths, the future, and the change process rather than a focus on the past, deficits, and catharsis, can help keep the group experience well within the scope of a coaching intervention and avoid a spiral into a session resembling group therapy. Coaches must always be keenly aware of **scope of practice** and never engage in what may resemble "therapy." When a coach is uncertain, redirecting the focus toward a future focus and the change process can help keep the group moving forward. Coaches are advised to develop a network of professionals to refer to when needed, including a therapist or clinical psychologist.

LOGISTICS AND STRUCTURE

Taking the time and energy to focus closely on the logistics and details of a group experience is well worth the effort so that logistical problems do not end up derailing an otherwise successful group behavioral change journey. The following are a few tips and ideas to consider.

Design

Before promoting a group, consider the group's structure, including the following:

- Focus/agenda/purpose
- Dates and time
- Duration
- Eligibility
- Delivery (onsite, online, or telephonic)
- Location (addresses or dial-in number and pass code)
- Absences/tardiness/termination policies
- Fees and costs/refund policy

Promotion

- How will participants learn about the group?
- Will you rely on others to promote the group?
- How will technology be utilized?
- What features and benefits are most important?
- Who is the contact for questions?

Enrollment

- How do members join the group?
- Will there be an initial individual interview or session?
- What registration documents or materials are required and/or provided?
- How are fees paid?

Assessment

- How will you measure the value of the group experience?
- Will you provide pre– and post–health assessment instruments?
- How will you gather the data? How will you utilize the data?

Legal and Ethical Concerns

- What are you and your agency's policies regarding record keeping and confidentiality?
- What are the limits of confidentiality?
- How will you communicate your policies to the members?

GROUP COACHING FORMAT

Group coaching programs can vary considerably, from structured weight management interventions such as the MEND Childhood Obesity Program or the Diabetes Prevention Program to less structured wellness initiatives (see Table 16-2, page 217). While every group program will differ somewhat, the following is a general outline for how a group program may be formatted to provide optimal benefit for each member. Note that more structured, standardized programs may follow a different sequence and devote a fair amount of time to health education, based on adult learning principles emphasized in Chapter 12.

Initial session

- Introductions
- Pre-program assessment (may also be completed during the initial individual session)
- What would you like to achieve? What would you like to see happen in the next "X" weeks?
- Group "guiding principles" or "group logistics"
- Take-aways (e.g., What one new thing did you learn today?)

Subsequent sessions

- Brief check-in and attendance
- Optional: "Question of the Day"
- Optional: 0–5 rating on progress
- What would you like to focus on today?
- Successes
- Challenges
- What would support you to move forward?
- Action plans
- Take-aways
- Adjourn

Wrap-up sessions

- Ask about "key wins"
- Integrate key wins with intended results
- Ask about plans to sustain progress. How will you be supported? Who could hold you accountable? What could pull you off-track?
- Thank members for participating.
- Satisfaction survey: Provide an anonymous satisfaction survey at the conclusion of each meeting or series; let participants know that you value their input and feedback about the group coaching program.
- Post-program assessment: Ask participants to complete a second version of your program assessment (distribute during the final group or send via email or online survey).

EXAMPLES OF GROUP COACHING PROGRAMS

There are many successful models of group coaching programs. Some are delivered in person while others are implemented virtually. Some rely on professional trained coach facilitators, while others use peer coaches. Most last 60 to 90 minutes per session but may also be delivered in other formats, including several hours, all day, or over several days. Program duration may vary greatly from weekly sessions to monthly or less frequent sessions over a short period of time or up to a year or longer (Armstrong et al., 2013). Some programs may be highly structured while others may be relatively unstructured. Several examples of more structured group coaching programs are highlighted in Table 16-2.

Table 16-2

EXAMPLES OF STRUCTURED GROUP COACHING PROGRAMS

PROGRAM	FORMAT	OBJECTIVES	FOR MORE INFORMATION
MEND (Mind, Exercise, Nutrition, Do It!) Childhood Obesity Program	20-session family program that meets for two hours twice a week and is attended by the child and at least one parent or caregiver. The first hour is an interactive family session on nutrition and behavior topics, followed by one hour of fun exercise for the children while the parents meet for support and discussion on topics such as goals and rewards, label reading, and problem solving.	Help children (particularly those who are overweight) improve their health, fitness, and self-esteem	Mendfoundation.org
Diabetes Prevention Program	Individuals identified as having prediabetes are recruited to the program. Participants work with a lifestyle coach in a group setting to receive a 1-year lifestyle change program that includes 16 core sessions (usually 1 per week) and 6 post-core sessions (1 per month). Content includes nutrition and exercise information as well as problem solving and goal setting. Typically is delivered in-person, but increasingly virtual programs are offered.	Decrease risk of developing type 2 diabetes, support a 5–7% weight loss, and improve overall health outcomes	Cdc.gov/diabetes/prevention
Momenta Adult Weight Management Program	Developed for individuals who are overweight or obese based on body mass index. In-person 12-week course of weekly 1-hour sessions covering nutrition, physical activity, and behavior change, led by a highly skilled coach	5–7% sustainable weight loss, improved health outcomes and behaviors	Discovermomenta.com
Take Courage Coaching: Help for Chronic Pain	52-week program by telephone. Includes weekly 30-minute individual session and weekly group session.	Empower individuals to become more active participants in self-management of pain	Takecouragecoaching.com

PRACTICAL APPLICATIONS

1. You have been asked to start a coaching group for health seekers in your community. Design one or more groups using the guidelines presented in this chapter. How will you promote this group and enroll members? What assessment tools could you utilize? What legal/ethical considerations need to be addressed?

2 List and describe some practices that could help you prepare for a group coaching session. How much time might you allow? What do you need in order to be successful? What obstacles might interfere with your personal preparation?

3. Create a new list of your Top 10 Group Facilitation Skills, ranking them in order of importance.

SUMMARY

This brief overview of group coaching aims to lay the foundation for coaches exploring coaching in a group environment. It is with ongoing practice, reflection, and evaluation that the coach's skills will advance and the group coaching experience will be most likely to help foster optimal outcomes.

EXPANSION QUIZ
Multiple-choice quiz available if you expand to the full experience

References

Armstrong, C. et al. (2013). Group health coaching: Strengths, challenges, and next steps. *Global Advances in Health and Medicine,* 2, 3, 95–102.

Knowles, M.S. (1980). *The Modern Practice of Adult Education: From Pedagogy to Andragogy.* Englewood Cliffs, N.J.: Cambridge.

Knowles, M., Holton, E., & Swanson, R. (2011). *The Adult Learner: The Definitive Classic in Adult Education and Human Resource Development* (7th ed.). New York: Routledge.

Rogers, C. (1969). *Freedom to Learn.* Columbus, Ohio: Merrill.

CHAPTER 17

CHAPTER 17
EXECUTIVE COACHING

LEARNING OBJECTIVES

After reading this chapter, the coach will be able to:

- Provide a broad definition and description of the role of the executive coach
- Outline the foundational principles and considerations of executive coaching
- Complete a personal SWOT analysis

As worksite wellness programs expand and executives and senior leaders are called on to role model healthy behaviors, coaches may find increased opportunity to engage in executive coaching. Those coaches with a background in nutrition and fitness may be best positioned to help these leaders not only "walk the talk," but also develop strategies and initiatives that optimize employee health as well as organizational success.

LINKING WORKPLACE WELLNESS PROGRAMS WITH EXECUTIVE COACHING

According to a 2013 RAND Employer Survey, approximately half of American employers offer some type of worksite wellness program (Mattke et al., 2013). About one quarter of those who do not currently offer a wellness program plan to do so very soon (Kaiser Family Foundation & Health Research & Educational Trust, 2013). As healthcare costs have skyrocketed and legislation such as the Affordable Care Act has made offering such programs more attractive, a growing number of companies are supporting employee wellness initiatives.

The evidence is clear: A major determinant of a successful worksite wellness program is the degree of investment by senior leadership, including the chief executive officer (CEO) (Mattke et al., 2013). While executive coaching has not historically been considered a part of worksite wellness programs, a growing movement is calling upon chief executives to engage fully in these initiatives. Naturally, not every executive is a model of good health and not every executive feels comfortable providing the leadership and initiative to launch a comprehensive wellness program. As the definition of health broadens to include exercise, nutrition, **emotional intelligence** (i.e., **self-awareness, self-management, social awareness**, and **relationship managemen**t), emotional resilience, focus, conflict/relationship and stress management, **positive psychology,** goal setting, cognitive health, **self-efficacy,** work-life balance, and similar elements of well-being, the door opens for the coaches to collaborate with executives to optimize health and set the agenda for a healthy workforce, including themselves.

THE CEO PLEDGE℠

The National Coalition for the Promotion of Physical Activity (NCPPA) challenges chief executives to commit to a healthier workforce by signing the CEO Pledge. To date, nearly 200 companies have signed on. It is clear that a CEO's investment in health plays a crucial role in creating a healthier work environment. Executive coaches may consider using this Pledge as a starting point in helping executives establish goals and metrics to optimize the health of themselves and their employees.

CEOs who sign The CEO Pledge agree to implement at least six of the following strategies to create a culture of physical activity in their workplace(s). A mix of strategies from each category—behavioral, educational, and environmental/policy—is encouraged.

Behavioral Support

- Support "healthy meetings" such as stand-up or walking meetings, and/or meetings that incorporate stretching or other physical activity
- Offer a physical-activity program that includes motivational elements to inspire employees, such as employee competitions, team challenges, and recognition/rewards
- Establish a non-competitive physical-activity program, such as a "buddy program" or exercise groups
- Sponsor employee teams in organized fun runs/walks
- Integrate other innovative and effective ideas to increase physical activity

Educational Support

- Provide education and information to employees about the benefits of an active lifestyle
- Invite experts to conduct regular information sessions in the workplace on physical activity–related topics
- Promote the health and productivity benefits of avoiding long periods of **sedentary** behavior (e.g., sitting at a desk for an extended period of time)

Environmental/Policy Support

- Organize onsite fitness classes
- Reimburse employees for purchases of fitness equipment or physical activity–related programs
- Offer incentives for physical activity, such as gift certificates for equipment, and include such incentives in the employee benefit plan when appropriate
- Provide free or subsidized public transportation passes to encourage walking as part of a daily commute
- Give free or reduced rate memberships for bike share programs to encourage bikes as a form of transportation
- Increase the time allowed for lunch breaks or provide flexible scheduling to allow employees to be active during the workday
- Provide safe and clean facilities, such as showers, changing areas, and bike racks that support physical activity before, during, or after the workday
- Provide clean, safe, and attractive stairwells and encourage their use
- Create a map of indoor and/or outdoor walking paths that are safe, convenient, and easy to follow near the workplace
- Offer employees opportunities to wear casual, workout-friendly attire to work
- Create an onsite fitness area or reimburse/subsidize the cost of an offsite fitness center membership
- Encourage employees to take brief activity breaks throughout the workday
- Provide employees with the option to use "active office" furniture such as stand-up or treadmill desks, and stability balls

Reprinted with permission from the National Coalition for the Promotion of Physical Activity (www.ncppa.org). CEO Pledge is a service mark of the National Coalition for Promoting Physical Activity, Inc.

Coaches skilled in behavioral change can help an executive realize health and performance benefits and build the bridge connecting health and professional achievement. Employee development through executive coaching, long an important element in organizational improvement, now includes employee well-being and health.

WHAT IS EXECUTIVE COACHING?

Executive coaching, like other branches of coaching, is a collaborative, personalized, and goal-focused profession. It relies on many areas of study, particularly behavioral sciences, cognitive behavioral psychology, theories of learning, adult development, leadership and management science, communication strategies, business development theories, organizational and cultural development, finance and health, and transpersonal and **mindfulness** practices. The Executive Coaching Forum (2012) offers a useful definition:

"Executive coaching is an experiential and individualized leader-development process that builds a leader's capability to achieve short- and long-term organizational goals. It is conducted through one-on-one and/or group interactions, driven by data from multiple perspectives, and based on mutual trust and respect. The organization, an executive, and the executive coach work in partnership to achieve maximum impact."

Executive coaches are routinely called on to support growth in a number of key areas of leadership functioning, with encouraging results.

Executive coaching has been shown to improve an executive's ability to (Zenger, Folkman, & Edinger, 2011):

- Display honesty and integrity
- Exhibit technical/professional expertise
- Solve problems and analyze issues
- Innovate
- Practice self-development
- Focus on results
- Establish stretch goals
- Take initiative
- Communicate powerfully and broadly
- Inspire and motivate others
- Build relationships
- Develop others
- Collaborate and foster teamwork
- Develop strategic perspective
- Champion change
- Connect the group to the outside world

THE DIFFERENCE BETWEEN COACHING AND CONSULTING

It is important to differentiate executive coaching from consulting. Consultants often give direct advice, while the coach will use direct advice where appropriate, but more likely will be a partner helping the executive arrive at his or her own best solutions. Coaches are present- and future-focused in helping clients develop skills, improve performance, and plan for career enhancement.

Executive coaching is closely aligned to process consultation, which leading executive consultant Edgar Schein (1999) defines as, "the creation of a relationship with the client that permits the client to perceive, understand, and act on the process events that occur in the client's internal and external environment in order to improve the situation as defined by the client."

As with coaching, an important assumption of Schein's process consultation model is that the client continues to own the problem and the responsibility for its resolution.

THE DIFFERENCE BETWEEN COACHING AND MENTORING

While many executives may lean on mentors to help them improve their leadership skills, mentoring is quite different from coaching. Mentoring relationships generally include a more experienced and accomplished mentor who helps a younger, less experienced but promising mentee to navigate his or her professional and personal development, often drawing upon the mentor's experiences and insights in the process. This is in contrast to a coaching relationship, in which the coach is a guide who helps the coachee to establish focus, goals, and action plans. Unlike mentoring relationships, coaches need not have first-hand experience of the coachee's work. While mentors often provide direction and advice to mentees rooted in the mentor's experiences and expertise, it is through **powerful questioning** rather than provision of advice that coaches help clients establish a clear focus and develop their own insights and motivations for change.

COMMON METHODS

Executive coaches employ several methods of coaching. A few of the most common include the **GROW model,** appreciative inquiry, and the coaching method of leadership development.

THE GROW MODEL OF COACHING

Sir John Whitmore (2006), an esteemed executive coach and preeminent leader in leadership development, developed the popular GROW model of coaching (see Chapter 9). GROW stands for:

- **G** Goal setting for the session as well as short and long term
- **R** Reality checking to explore the current situation
- **O** Options and alternative strategies or courses of action
- **W** Will to move forward, including *what* is to be done, *when,* by *whom*

Whitmore (2006) defines coaching as "a management behavior that lies at the opposite end of the spectrum to command and control." He also emphasizes that the executive coach has the goals of building awareness, responsibility, and self-belief, and that coaching is a way of treating people, a way of thinking, and a way of being. He asserts that one day the word coaching will disappear from our lexicon altogether and it just will become the way we relate to one another.

Variations of the GROW model are commonly used in executive coaching. The process generally begins with the goal. The outcome is a **SMART goal** and the discussion may include questions such as:

- What would you like to discuss?
- What would have to happen for you to feel the time we've spent today is well spent?
- What outcome would you like from our discussion today?
- What do you want to focus on in the next three to six months?
- What would you like to be different after this discussion?

Next is discussion of the reality, with the outcome being to uncover specific details of the present situation to help focus on what needs to happen to develop solutions and options. Questions may include:

- What's the present situation?
- On a scale of 1 to 10, where are you now?
- When does this happen?
- How often?
- How have you tried to change this?
- What has worked and what has not worked?

The coach frequently discusses options next, developing solutions that might work with input and direction from the client. Questions might include:

- How can we get there?
- How can you move that from a 6 to an 8 in your scale?
- What are all the possible actions that you can see?
- Are there times when the problem does not occur?
- What's different about those situations?
- How have you stopped the problem from completely overwhelming you?

Specific actions and obstacles are frequently a part of the GROW model. Questions might include:

- What are the next steps?
- Do what?
- When?
- Precisely when will you take them?
- What support will you need?
- Do you see any obstacles?
- What might stop you or get in the way?
- How can you overcome this?
- How will you know that you're on track for success?

Finally, the coach helps the executive make a plan to move forward. Questions may include:

- What will you do now?
- How will you move forward?
- What will help increase your success?
- How often will you review your progress?

This model can be of great value when working with a business leader who has expressed a desire to improve his or own health or the overall health of the workforce. The conversation begins with the broad goal that gets explored in the context of the current work environment, followed by a discussion of opportunities for improvement as well as obstacles to implementation, and ultimately a specific plan to move forward, including target metrics, a plan for follow-up, and evaluation.

APPRECIATIVE INQUIRY

Another model that executive coaches draw on is from the work of Sue Hammond (1998). In this model, Hammond describes the executive coaching process as one that builds on what works in organizations rather than what does not. The focus is on what the organization wants to be, and is based on "the high moments of where they have been." Hammond suggests coaches look at the assumptions executives hold and build on the positive beliefs they have to help them move to their desired end-state. This model assumes:

> The focus is on what the organization wants to be

- In every society or company, something works.
- What we focus on becomes our reality.
- Reality is created in the moment and there are multiple realities.
- The act of asking questions of an organization or group influences the group in some way.
- People have more confidence and comfort to journey to the future when they carry forward parts of their past.
- If we carry parts of the past forward, they should be what is best about the past.

Executive coaches can apply this model to their coaching program using the tools of positive psychology and strengths-based coaching discussed earlier in this guide.

COACHING AS ONE OF THE FOUR BASIC LEADERSHIP STYLES

Paul Hersey, Ken Blanchard, and Dewey Johnson developed the original Situational Leadership model in 1969, which was later updated to *Management of Organizational Behavior* (Hersey et al., 2012). This book is a key text in graduate level courses on organizational behavior. The authors describe four basic leadership styles: directing, coaching, supporting, and delegating. These are not specifically about coaching, but the field of executive coaching has developed from this concept.

- **Directing** involves providing specific directions.
- **Coaching** involves directing and monitoring, but also explaining, soliciting, and supporting.
- **Supporting** involves facilitating, supporting, and sharing decision-making responsibility.
- **Delegating** involves the leader turning over responsibility for decision making and problem solving.

Executive coaches practice both the coaching style of leadership (with a greater emphasis on soliciting and supporting compared with directing and monitoring) and work collaboratively with their clients to explore the different leadership models and identify leadership styles and strengths.

THE EXECUTIVE COACHING EXPERIENCE

As with coaching anyone who desires to realize a vision, achieve a goal, or make a behavior change, every executive coaching experience is different based on many individual factors and preferences of the executive and the coach. However, the path to helping an executive achieve personal or business objectives is by way of some variation of the **ACE cycle of change**—increase awareness, identify choices, choose an option, build the plan, and execute—and then evaluate the outcome. This process—described in depth throughout this guide—is recapped and applied to the executive coaching experience below.

AWARENESS

During the awareness stage, the coach's primary aims are to establish **rapport,** build trust, and identify the executive's vision for him- or herself as well as goals for the coaching relationship. Coaches may use communication techniques such as **motivational interviewing** to help executives who are ambivalent about changes, the need for change, or the future to explore and work through this **ambivalence** to establish a clear vision and hope for the future. By the completion of this stage, the coach and client generally have a good understanding of whether they are a good match to proceed further. If they choose to move forward, the next step is to agree on a clear focus for the relationship and the terms of the coaching relationship. This typically is a written contract, including a confidentiality agreement and scope of work including coaching terms, procedures, and fees.

CHOICE

In the choice stage, the coach may assess the client's strengths and areas for improvement, and help the client develop goals and a plan to achieve them. This process may be informed by assessments; 360-degree feedback the coach collects from the client and others, which may include his or her peers, reports, supervisors, and customers; performance evaluation reviews; and/or direct observation. Through use of **open-ended questions, affirmations, reflections**, and **summarizing** (i.e., the **OARS model**), the coach helps the client process this information and reflect upon the perceptions of others in the organization. The coach may also gather information about organization and industry standards. Ultimately, this process helps to elicit goals, commonly expressed as "mission statements" or career interest measures.

> Assess the client's strengths and areas for improvement

EXECUTION

Next, in the execution stage, the coach helps the client commit to and proceed with an action plan to achieve the outlined goals. The coach helps the client develop a plan to fill knowledge gaps and ensure accountability and ongoing follow-up. As the client proceeds through the change plan, the coach employs excellent communication skills, including skilled use of open-ended questions, affirmations, reflections, and summarizing to help the client work through challenges, adapt goals when necessary, and strengthen internal commitment to change.

Coaching relationships can be relatively short, such as when helping a client achieve a specific objective (such as the launch of a workplace wellness program), or enduring, as when helping a client grow as a leader in pursuit of a long-term vision or ideal. In any case, ideally, throughout and at the end of the coaching relationship the coach will evaluate the outcome of the coaching, including the client's perception of the experience and the intended improvements to knowledge, behavior, and overall results.

BREAKING INTO EXECUTIVE COACHING: A SWOT ANALYSIS

A coach who is considering offering executive coaching services for the first time may see value in completing a SWOT analysis to recognize strengths, weaknesses, opportunities, and threats. This model was first described by Stanford's Albert Humphrey (2005) and is commonly employed in business environments. In fact, the model is based on Humphrey's work with several Fortune 500 companies.

A basic SWOT analysis is easy to perform. Begin by dividing a piece of paper into four sections and labeling them as depicted in Figure 17-1. The SWOT analysis can be used by a coach to assess him- or herself, to analyze a business or opportunity, or even to help a client explore a new opportunity or challenge. It is important to be as honest as possible about one's weaknesses, as this exercise will help the coach reframe weaknesses as new opportunities. For example, if a coach lists "lack of education" in a specific area as a weakness, this could be viewed as an opportunity to take a continuing education course, attend a workshop, or participate in a training program. When listing threats, the coach should include anything that might negatively impact either the coach or the business, from the emergence of a new competitor to a downturn in the general economic climate. The following is a quick rundown of some questions one might ask when conducting a SWOT analysis:

S STRENGTHS

- What advantages do I have that others do not?
- What do I do better than anyone else?
- What values do I believe in that help me succeed?

W WEAKNESSES

- What tasks do I avoid because I do not feel confident doing them?
- What will people around me see as my weaknesses?
- What personality traits are currently holding me back?

O OPPORTUNITIES

- What technologies can help me move ahead?
- What network of strategic contacts do I have or can I create?
- What needs in my company or in my industry are not being filled?

T THREATS

- What obstacles do I face in my work?
- What weaknesses could lead to additional threats?
- What technologies threaten my work?

Figure 17-1
SAMPLE SWOT ANALYSIS

STRENGTHS	WEAKNESSES
Undergraduate degree in business	Inadequate business-building know-how
ACE Certified Health Coach	Poor social media skills
Excellent one-on-one relationship-building skills	Anxiety about speaking to large audiences

OPPORTUNITIES	THREATS
Take a public speaking course	Social media applications ("apps") on lifestyle improvement, weight loss, and exercise
Market and emphasize value of personal one-on-one training/coaching	Attraction to group-fitness/weight-loss programs
Work with a social media and technology coach	Economic pressures limit the pool of new clients

PRACTICAL APPLICATIONS

1. From your perspective, describe the advantages and challenges of engaging in executive coaching. What are your main strengths? What are some potential learning opportunities to help you to be more prepared? Complete a personal SWOT analysis of this potential opportunity.

2. With a colleague, family member, or friend, role play how you might proceed with an initial coaching session with an executive of a small local business whose goal is to adopt healthier behaviors to serve as a role model for his employees.

SUMMARY

While executive coaching is an established profession, niche opportunities are developing as organizations increasingly value workplace wellness and a culture of health. In this evolution, coaches with a background and knowledge of health, nutrition, and fitness can play an important role not only in helping executives to optimize their own health, achieve personal and professional goals, and improve their leadership skills, but also in helping advance the overall health and well-being of the entire organization. This chapter provides a brief introduction to the field of executive coaching. Those who come from a health and fitness background who are interested in executive coaching are encouraged to review the Additional Resources list on the following page for ongoing learning and skill-development opportunities.

EXPANSION QUIZ
Multiple-choice quiz available if you expand to the full experience

References

The Executive Coaching Forum (2012). *The Executive Coaching Handbook: Principles and Guidelines for a Successful Coaching Partnership.* www.TheExecutiveCoachingForum.com

Hammond, S. (1998). *The Thin Book of Appreciative Inquiry.* Bend, Ore.: Thin Book Publishing.

Hersey, P. et al. (2012). *Management of Organizational Behavior* (10th ed.). Upper Saddle River, N.J.: Prentice Hall.

Humphrey, A.S. (2005). *SWOT Analysis.* www.businessballs.com/swotanalysisfreetemplate.htm

The Kaiser Family Foundation & Health Research & Educational Trust (2013). *Employer Health Benefits 2013 Annual Survey: Section 12 Wellness Programs and Health Risk Assessments.* Retrieved March 6, 2014. www.kff.org

Mattke, S. et al. (2013). *Workplace Wellness Programs Study: Final Report.* Boston, Mass.: RAND Health-RAND Corporation.

Schein, E. (1999). *Process Consultation Revisited.* Boston, Mass.: Addison-Wesley.

Whitmore, Sir J. (2006). *Coaching for Performance: GROWing People, Performance and Purpose.* London: Nicholas Brealey Publishing.

Zenger, J.H., Folkman, J.R., & Edinger, S.K. (2011). Making yourself indispensable. *Harvard Business Review,* October.

Additional Resources

Given the broad scope of knowledge executive coaches bring to their work, it is wise for those aspiring to move into this field of work to be familiar with key journals and publications that focus on executive coaching. These include:

- *Academy of Management Journal*
- *Coaching at Work*
- *Coaching: An International Journal of Theory, Research and Practice Consulting Psychology Journal: Practice and Research*
- *Harvard Business Review*
- *International Coaching Psychology Review*
- *International Journal of Coaching in Organizations*
- *International Journal of Evidence-based Coaching and Mentoring*
- *International Journal of Mentoring and Coaching*
- *Journal of Managerial Psychology*
- *Journal of Occupational and Organizational Psychology*
- *Leadership and Organizational Development*
- *Management Review*
- *Organizational Development Journal*
- *The Annual Review of Coaching and Consulting*
- *The Coaching Journal*
- *The Coaching Psychologist*
- *The Journal of Applied and Behavioral Science*

Additionally, coaches interested in obtaining further training in executive and leadership coaching are encouraged to search locally available training programs. Many colleges and universities provide certificate programs with intensive hands-on training and practice with leading experts. The International Coach Federation provides a listing of accredited executive coach training programs at www.coachfederation.org.

NOTES

APPENDIX A

APPENDIX A

INTERNATIONAL COACH FEDERATION CORE COMPETENCIES

The following 11 core coaching competencies were developed to support greater understanding about the skills and approaches used within today's coaching profession as defined by the International Coach Federation (ICF). They will also support you in calibrating the level of alignment between the coach-specific training expected and the training you have experienced.

Finally, these competencies and the ICF definition were used as the foundation for the ICF Credentialing process examination. The ICF defines coaching as partnering with clients in a thought-provoking and creative process that inspires them to maximize their personal and professional potential. The Core Competencies are grouped into four clusters according to those that fit together logically based on common ways of looking at the competencies in each group. The groupings and individual competencies are not weighted—they do not represent any kind of priority in that they are all core or critical for any competent coach to demonstrate.

A. Setting the Foundation

1. Meeting Ethical Guidelines and Professional Standards
2. Establishing the Coaching Agreement

B. Co-creating the Relationship

3. Establishing Trust and Intimacy with the Client
4. Coaching Presence

C. Communicating Effectively

5. Active Listening
6. Powerful Questioning
7. Direct Communication

D. Facilitating Learning and Results

8. Creating Awareness
9. Designing Actions
10. Planning and Goal Setting
11. Managing Progress and Accountability

A. SETTING THE FOUNDATION

1. **Meeting Ethical Guidelines and Professional Standards**—Understanding of coaching ethics and standards and ability to apply them appropriately in all coaching situations.

    1. Understands and exhibits in own behaviors the ICF Standards of Conduct (see list, Part III of ICF Code of Ethics).
    2. Understands and follows all ICF Ethical Guidelines (see list).
    3. Clearly communicates the distinctions between coaching, consulting, psychotherapy and other support professions.
    4. Refers client to another support professional as needed, knowing when this is needed and the available resources.

2. **Establishing the Coaching Agreement**—Ability to understand what is required in the specific coaching interaction and to come to agreement with the prospective and new client about the coaching process and relationship.

    1. Understands and effectively discusses with the client the guidelines and specific parameters of the coaching relationship (e.g., logistics, fees, scheduling, and inclusion of others if appropriate).
    2. Reaches agreement about what is appropriate in the relationship and what is not, what is and is not being offered, and about the client's and coach's responsibilities.
    3. Determines whether there is an effective match between his or her coaching method and the needs of the prospective client.

B. CO-CREATING THE RELATIONSHIP

3. **Establishing Trust and Intimacy with the Client**—Ability to create a safe, supportive environment that produces ongoing mutual respect and trust.

    1. Shows genuine concern for the client's welfare and future.
    2. Continuously demonstrates personal integrity, honesty, and sincerity.
    3. Establishes clear agreements and keeps promises.
    4. Demonstrates respect for client's perceptions, learning style, and personal being.
    5. Provides ongoing support for and champions new behaviors and actions, including those involving risk taking and fear of failure.
    6. Asks permission to coach clients in sensitive, new areas.

4. **Coaching Presence**—Ability to be fully conscious and create a spontaneous relationship with the client, employing a style that is open, flexible, and confident.

    1. Is present and flexible during the coaching process, dancing in the moment.
    2. Accesses own intuition and trusts one's inner knowing—"goes with the gut."
    3. Is open to not knowing and takes risks.
    4. Sees many ways to work with the client and chooses in the moment what is most effective.
    5. Uses humor effectively to create lightness and energy.
    6. Confidently shifts perspectives and experiments with new possibilities for own action.
    7. Demonstrates confidence in working with strong emotions and can self-manage and not be overpowered or enmeshed by client's emotions.

C. COMMUNICATING EFFECTIVELY

5. **Active Listening**—Ability to focus completely on what the client is saying and is not saying, to understand the meaning of what is said in the context of the client's desires, and to support client self-expression.

    1. Attends to the client and the client's agenda and not to the coach's agenda for the client.
    2. Hears the client's concerns, goals, values, and beliefs about what is and is not possible.
    3. Distinguishes between the words, the tone of voice, and the body language.
    4. Summarizes, paraphrases, reiterates, and mirrors back what client has said to ensure clarity and understanding.
    5. Encourages, accepts, explores, and reinforces the client's expression of feelings, perceptions, concerns, beliefs, suggestions, etc.
    6. Integrates and builds on client's ideas and suggestions.
    7. "Bottom-lines" or understands the essence of the client's communication and helps the client get there rather than engaging in long, descriptive stories.
    8. Allows the client to vent or "clear" the situation without judgment or attachment in order to move on to next steps.

6. **Powerful Questioning**—Ability to ask questions that reveal the information needed for maximum benefit to the coaching relationship and the client.

    1. Asks questions that reflect active listening and an understanding of the client's perspective.
    2. Asks questions that evoke discovery, insight, commitment, or action (e.g., those that challenge the client's assumptions).
    3. Asks open-ended questions that create greater clarity, possibility, or new learning.
    4. Asks questions that move the client toward what he or she desires, not questions that ask for the client to justify or look backward.

7. **Direct Communication**—Ability to communicate effectively during coaching sessions, and to use language that has the greatest positive impact on the client.

    1. Is clear, articulate, and direct in sharing and providing feedback.
    2. Reframes and articulates to help the client understand from another perspective what he or she wants or is uncertain about.
    3. Clearly states coaching objectives, meeting agenda, and purpose of techniques or exercises.
    4. Uses language appropriate and respectful to the client (e.g., non-sexist, non-racist, non-technical, and non-jargon).
    5. Uses metaphor and analogy to help to illustrate a point or paint a verbal picture.

D. FACILITATING LEARNING AND RESULTS

8. **Creating Awareness**—Ability to integrate and accurately evaluate multiple sources of information and to make interpretations that help the client to gain awareness and thereby achieve agreed-upon results.

    1. Goes beyond what is said in assessing client's concerns, not getting hooked by the client's description.
    2. Invokes inquiry for greater understanding, awareness, and clarity.
    3. Identifies for the client his or her underlying concerns; typical and fixed ways of perceiving himself or herself and the world; differences between the facts and the interpretation; and disparities between thoughts, feelings, and action.
    4. Helps clients to discover for themselves the new thoughts, beliefs, perceptions, emotions, moods, etc. that strengthen their ability to take action and achieve what is important to them.
    5. Communicates broader perspectives to clients and inspires commitment to shift their viewpoints and find new possibilities for action.
    6. Helps clients to see the different, interrelated factors that affect them and their behaviors (e.g., thoughts, emotions, body, and background).
    7. Expresses insights to clients in ways that are useful and meaningful for the client.
    8. Identifies major strengths vs. major areas for learning and growth, and what is most important to address during coaching.
    9. Asks the client to distinguish between trivial and significant issues, situational vs. recurring behaviors, when detecting a separation between what is being stated and what is being done.

9. **Designing Actions**—Ability to create with the client opportunities for ongoing learning, during coaching and in work/life situations, and for taking new actions that will most effectively lead to agreed-upon coaching results.

    1. Brainstorms and assists the client to define actions that will enable the client to demonstrate, practice, and deepen new learning.
    2. Helps the client to focus on and systematically explore specific concerns and opportunities that are central to agreed-upon coaching goals.
    3. Engages the client to explore alternative ideas and solutions, to evaluate options, and to make related decisions.
    4. Promotes active experimentation and self-discovery, where the client applies what has been discussed and learned during sessions immediately afterward in his or her work or life setting.
    5. Celebrates client successes and capabilities for future growth.
    6. Challenges a client's assumptions and perspectives to provoke new ideas and find new possibilities for action.
    7. Advocates or brings forward points of view that are aligned with client goals and, without attachment, engages the client to consider them.
    8. Helps the client "Do It Now" during the coaching session, providing immediate support.
    9. Encourages stretches and challenges but also a comfortable pace of learning.

10. **Planning and Goal Setting**—Ability to develop and maintain an effective coaching plan with the client.

1. Consolidates collected information and establishes a coaching plan and development goals with the client that address concerns and major areas for learning and development.
2. Creates a plan with results that are attainable, measurable, specific, and have target dates.
3. Makes plan adjustments as warranted by the coaching process and by changes in the situation.
4. Helps the client identify and access different resources for learning (e.g., books and other professionals).
5. Identifies and targets early successes that are important to the client.

11. **Managing Progress and Accountability**—Ability to hold attention on what is important for the client, and to leave responsibility with the client to take action.

1. Clearly requests of the client actions that will move the client toward his or her stated goals.
2. Demonstrates follow-through by asking the client about those actions that the client committed to during the previous session(s).
3. Acknowledges the client for what they have done, not done, learned, or become aware of since the previous coaching session(s).
4. Effectively prepares, organizes, and reviews with client information obtained during sessions.
5. Keeps the client on track between sessions by holding attention on the coaching plan and outcomes, agreed-upon courses of action, and topics for future session(s).
6. Focuses on the coaching plan but is also open to adjusting behaviors and actions based on the coaching process and shifts in direction during sessions.
7. Is able to move back and forth between the big picture of where the client is heading, setting a context for what is being discussed and where the client wishes to go.
8. Promotes clients self-discipline and holds clients accountable for what they say they are going to do, for the results of an intended action, or for a specific plan with related time frames.
9. Develops the client's ability to make decisions, address key concerns, and develop himself or herself (to get feedback, to determine priorities and set the pace of learning, to reflect on and learn from experiences).
10. Positively confronts the client with the fact that he or she did not take agreed-upon actions.

APPENDIX B

APPENDIX B
PERSONAL ADULT LEARNING STYLE INVENTORY*

INTRODUCTION

The theory of andragogy was developed long before the notion of learning styles became popular. In fact, the *Andragogy in Practice* model illustrates phenomena of adult learning styles and the *Orientation to Learning* principle highlights this dimension. When individuals become conscious of their learning style and facilitators become aware of the styles of their learners, learning motivation and effectiveness increase. This instrument has particular utility for professionals to assess their understanding of learning styles.

This inventory is for anyone involved in organizing and administering adult learning activities. You might be a trainer, teacher, group facilitator, administrator, educator, or anyone who works with adults in teaching/learning relationships. Your response to this inventory will give you some insight into your general orientation to adult learning, program development, learning methods, and program administration.

Self-assessments are not easy for anyone to make accurately. How we would like to be seen by others comes in conflict with how we really behave. Our vision of ourselves is likely to be somewhat optimistic. Please be as candid as possible in your responses so that you can obtain a better understanding of your human resource development (HRD) style.

Directions: Thirty pairs of items are listed on the next few pages. The statements comprising each pair are listed A and B. After reading each pair and considering your own approach, decide on the extent to which you agree with *each* statement. Place your response on the scale in the center of the page by circling *one* of the choices.

This inventory is designed to be used in a variety of settings; therefore, the words *facilitator* and *trainer* may be used interchangeably, as well as *learning* and *training*. Both words are included in the inventory and denoted with a slash mark ("/").

*Developed by Malcolm S. Knowles.

Use the following key:

A	=	I agree fully with statement A
A>B	=	I agree more with statement A than B
NANB	=	I do not agree with either statement A or B
B>A	=	I agree more with statement B than A
B	=	I agree fully with statement B

PERSONAL ADULT LEARNING STYLE INVENTORY

Developed by Dr. Malcolm S. Knowles

	A	A	A>B	NANB	B>A	B	B
1	There are a number of important differences between youths and adults as learners that can affect the learning process.	A	A>B	NANB	B>A	B	For the most part, adults and youths do not differ greatly in terms of the learning process.
2	Effective learning/training design puts equal weight on content and process plans.	A	A>B	NANB	B>A	B	Effective learning/training design is concerned with content first and process second.
3	Effective facilitators/trainers model self-directed learning in their own behavior, both within and outside the learning session.	A	A>B	NANB	B>A	B	Effective facilitators/trainers show learners that they, the facilitators/trainers, are content experts, with the knowledge and skills to be "in the driver's seat."
4	Effective learning/training is based on sound methods for involving learners in assessing their own learning needs.	A	A>B	NANB	B>A	B	Effective learning/training rests on the trainer's use of standard, valid methods for assessing learners' needs.
5	Client system representatives must be involved in the planning of learning/training programs.	A	A>B	NANB	B>A	B	It is the program developer's responsibility to provide clients with clear and detailed plans.
6	Program administrators must plan, work, and share decision-making with client system members.	A	A>B	NANB	B>A	B	Program administrators must have full responsibility and be held accountable for their plans and decisions.
7	The role of the facilitator/trainer is best seen as that of a facilitator and resource person for self-directed learners.	A	A>B	NANB	B>A	B	The role of the facilitator/trainer is to provide the most current and accurate information possible for learners.
8	Effective learning designs take into account individual differences among learners.	A	A>B	NANB	B>A	B	Effective learning designs are those that apply broadly to most or all learners.
9	Effective facilitators/trainers are able to create a variety of learning experiences for helping trainees develop self-directed learning skills.	A	A>B	NANB	B>A	B	Effective facilitators/trainers concentrate on preparing learning/training sessions that effectively convey specific content.
10	Successful learning/training designs incorporate a variety of experiential learning methods.	A	A>B	NANB	B>A	B	Successful learning/training designs are grounded in carefully developed formal presentations.
11	Client system members should be involved in developing needs assessment instruments and procedures that provide the data for program planning.	A	A>B	NANB	B>A	B	Learning/training program developers are responsible for designing and using sound needs assessment instruments and procedures to generate valid data for program planning.
12	Program administrators must involve their clients in defining, modifying, and applying financial policies and practices related to learning/training programs.	A	A>B	NANB	B>A	B	Program administrators must be able to explain clearly to their clients their financial policies and practices related to learning/training programs.
13	Effective facilitators/trainers must take into account recent research findings concerning the unique characteristics of adults as learners.	A	A>B	NANB	B>A	B	Effective facilitators/trainers must use the respected, traditional learning theories as they apply to *all* learners.
14	Effective learning requires a physical and psychology climate of mutual respect, trust, openness, supportiveness, and security.	A	A>B	NANB	B>A	B	Effective learning depends on learners recognizing and relying on the expert knowledge and skills of the trainer.

15	It is important to help learners understand the differences between didactic instruction and self-directed learning.	A A>B NANB B>A B	Learners should concentrate on the content of the learning/training rather than the method or methods of instruction.
16	Effective facilitators/trainers are able to get learners involved in the learning/training.	A A>B NANB B>A B	Effective facilitators/trainers are able to get, focus, and maintain the learners' attention.
17	Client system representatives need to be involved in revising and adapting learning/training programs, based on continuing needs assessment.	A A>B NANB B>A B	Learning/training program developers must develop and use ongoing needs assessments data, to revise and adapt programs to better meet client needs.
18	Program administrators must involve organizational decision-makers in interpreting and applying modern approaches to adult education and learning/training.	A A>B NANB B>A B	Program administrators must be able to explain clearly and convincingly modern approaches to adult education and learning/training to organizational policy makers.
19	Effective learning requires the facilitator/trainer to assess and control the effects that factors such as groups, organizations, and cultures have on learners.	A A>B NANB B>A B	Effective learning requires the facilitator/trainer to isolate learners from the possible effects of outside factors such as groups, organizations, or cultures.
20	Effective learning/training design engages the learners in a responsible self-diagnosis of their learning needs.	A A>B NANB B>A B	Effective learning/training can take place only after experts have diagnosed the real learning needs of learners.
21	Effective facilitators/trainers involve learners in planning, implementing, and evaluating their own learning activities.	A A>B NANB B>A B	Effective facilitators/trainers accept responsibility for the planning, implementation, and evaluation of the learning activities they direct.
22	Use of group dynamics principles and small group discussion techniques is critical for effective learning.	A A>B NANB B>A B	Effective learning centers on the one-to-one relationship between the facilitator/trainer and the learner.
23	Program developers must help design and use program planning mechanisms such as client system advisory committees, task forces, and others.	A A>B NANB B>A B	Effective program planning is the result of the program developer's efforts to interpret and to use the client system data they collect.
24	Program administrators must collaborate with organizational members to experiment with program innovations, jointly assessing outcomes and effectiveness.	A A>B NANB B>A B	Program administrators must take the initiative to experiment with program innovators and assess their outcomes and effectiveness.
25	In preparing a learning/training activity, the facilitator/trainer should review those theories of learning relevant for particular adult learning situations.	A A>B NANB B>A B	In preparing a learning/training activity, the facilitator/trainer should rely on certain basic assumptions about the learning process that have been proven to be generally true.
26	Effective learning/training engages learners in formulating objectives that are meaningful to them.	A A>B NANB B>A B	Effective learning/training requires that the facilitator/trainer clearly define the goals that learners are expected to attain.
27	Effective facilitators/trainers begin the learning process by engaging adult learners in self-diagnosis of their own learning needs.	A A>B NANB B>A B	Effective facilitators/trainers start by making a careful diagnosis of participant learning needs.
28	Learners must be involved in planning and developing evaluation instruments and procedures and in carrying out the evaluation of learning processes and outcomes.	A A>B NANB B>A B	Facilitators/trainers are responsible for planning and developing evaluation instruments and procedures and for carrying out evaluation of learning process and outcomes.
29	Program developers must involve client system members in designing and using learning/training program evaluation plans.	A A>B NANB B>A B	Program developers are responsible for designing and implementing sound evaluation plans.
30	Program administrators must work with organizational members and decision makers to analyze and interpret legislation affecting organizational learning/training programs.	A A>B NANB B>A B	Program administrators are responsible for making and presenting to organizational authorities analyses of legislation that affects organizational learning/training programs.

SCORING THE INVENTORY

Directions: Circle the numbers in each column that correspond to the answers you chose on the survey (see key below) and then add down the columns. Enter the sum for each column in the box provided. You will have six scores (subtotals). The, add the subtotals and place the sum in the Total box at the bottom.

A	=	5
A>B	=	4
NANB	=	3
B>A	=	2
B	=	1

I. Learning Orientation	II. Learning Design	III. How People Learn	IV. Learning Methods	V. Program Development	VI. Program Administration
1 5 4 3 2 1	6 5 4 3 2 1	11 5 4 3 2 1	16 5 4 3 2 1	21 5 4 3 2 1	26 5 4 3 2 1
2 5 4 3 2 1	7 5 4 3 2 1	12 5 4 3 2 1	17 5 4 3 2 1	22 5 4 3 2 1	27 5 4 3 2 1
3 5 4 3 2 1	8 5 4 3 2 1	13 5 4 3 2 1	18 5 4 3 2 1	23 5 4 3 2 1	28 5 4 3 2 1
4 5 4 3 2 1	9 5 4 3 2 1	14 5 4 3 2 1	19 5 4 3 2 1	24 5 4 3 2 1	29 5 4 3 2 1
5 5 4 3 2 1	10 5 4 3 2 1	15 5 4 3 2 1	20 5 4 3 2 1	25 5 4 3 2 1	30 5 4 3 2 1
				TOTAL	

GRAPHING YOUR RESULTS

To bring your results into sharper focus regarding your Andragogic or Pedagogic orientation, plot your results on the following graphs. Plot your Total score on the Pedagogy/Andragogy continuum below by placing an X at the appropriate point. Scores of 120–150 would suggest a stronger andragogical orientation. Scores of 60–30 would suggest a stronger pedagogical orientation.

Overall Results: *How Andragogic Am I?*

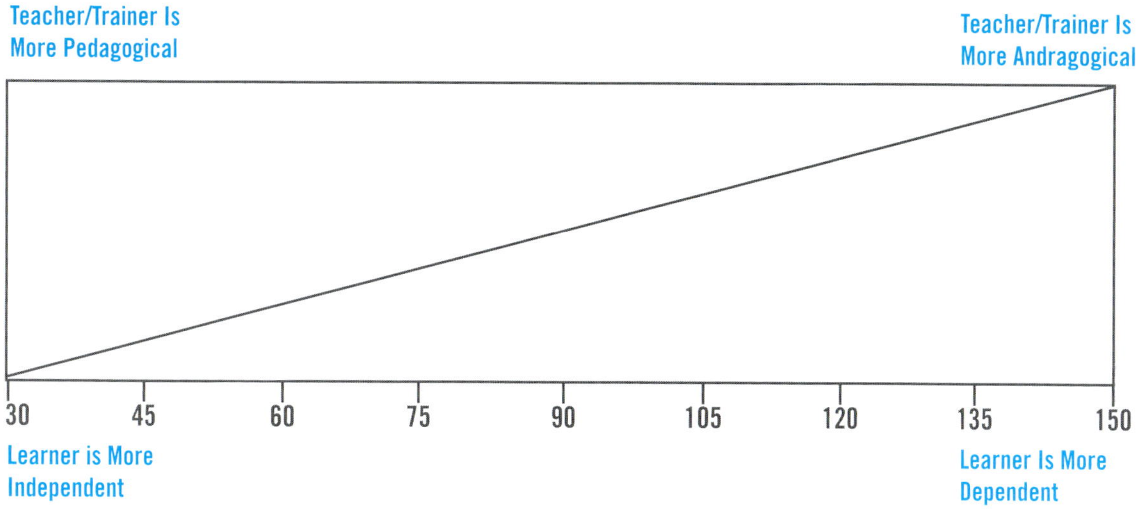

Component Results: *To What Extent Am I Andragogical in Each of the Six Areas?*

	Pedagogically Oriented	My Scores	Andragogically Oriented
I	5–10		20–25
II	5–10		20–25
III	5–10		20–25
IV	5–10		20–25
V	5–10		20–25
VI	5–10		20–25

INTERPRETIVE GUIDE

The *Personal HRD Style Inventory* is a learning instrument designed to help you asses the assumptions that underlie your teaching/training activities. These assumption may be useful or not useful, depending on the particular learner and the particular learning situation.

Teaching/learning assumptions may be categorized as *pedagogically* oriented or *adragogically* oriented. The body of theory and practice on which teacher-directed learning is based is often given the label *pedagogy,* from the Greek words *paid* (meaning child) and *agogos* (meaning guide or leader)—thus being defined as the art and science of teaching children.

The body of theory and practice on which self-directed learning is based is coming to be labeled andragogy, from the Greek word *aner* (meaning adult)—thus being defined as the art and science of helping adults (or, even better, maturing human beings) learn.

TRADITIONAL LEARNING: THE PEDAGOGICAL MODEL

The pedagogical model is the one with which all of us have the most experience. Teaching in our elementary schools, high schools, colleges, the military service, churches, and a variety of other institutions is largely pedagogically oriented. When we are asked to serve as instructors or prepare instruction for others, the pedagogical model comes quickly to mind and often control of our activities. That is easy to understand since pedagogy has dominated education and training practices since the seventh century.

Four assumptions about learners are inherent in the pedagogical model:

1. The learner is a dependent personality. The teacher/trainer is expected to take full responsibility for making the decision about what is to be learned, how and when it should be learned, and whether it has been learned. The role of the learner is to carry out the teacher's directions passively.
2. The learner enters into an educational activity with little experience that can be used in the learning process. The experience of the teacher/trainer is what is important. For that reason, a variety of one-way communication strategies are employed, including lectures, textbooks and manuals, and a variety of audiovisual techniques that can transmit information to the learner efficiently.
3. People are ready to learn when they are told what they have to learn in order to advance to the next grade level or achieve the next salary grade or job level.
4. People are motivated to learn primarily by external pressures from parents, teachers/trainers, employers, the consequences of failure, graded, certificates, and so on.

CONTEMPORARY LEARNING: THE ANDRAGOGICAL MODEL

During the 1960s, European adult educators coined the term *andragogy* to provide a label for a growing body of knowledge and technology in regard to adult learning. The following five assumptions underlie the andragogical model of learning:

1. The learner is self-directing. Adult learners want to take responsibility for their own lives, including the planning, implementing, and evaluating of their learning activities.
2. The learner enters an educational situation with a great deal of experience. This experience can be a valuable resource to the learner as well as to others. It needs to be valued and used in the learning process.

3. Adults are ready to learn when they perceive a need to know or do something in order to perform more effectively in some aspect of their lives. Their readiness to learn may be stimulated by helping them to assess the gaps between where they are now and where they want and need to be.
4. Adults are motivated to learn after they experience a need in their life situation. For that reason, learning needs to be problem-focused or task-centered. Adults want to apply what they have learned as quickly as possible. Learning activities need to be clearly relevant to the needs of the adult.
5. Adults are motivated to learn because of internal factors, such as self-esteem, recognition, better quality of life, greater self-confidence, the opportunity to self-actualize, and so forth. External factors, such as pressure from authority figures, salary increases, and the like, are less important.

IMPLICATIONS OF THE MODULES FOR TEACHERS/TRAINERS

A subscription to one model of learning or the other carries with it certain implications for the teacher/trainer. The basic concern of people with a pedagogical orientation is *content*. Teachers and trainers with a strong pedagogical orientation will be strongly concerned about what needs to be covered in the learning situation; how that content can be organized into manageable units; the most logical sequence for presenting these units; and the most efficient means of transmitting the content.

In contrast, the basic concern of people with an andragogical orientation is *process*. The andragogical process consists of eight elements: preparing the learners, considering the physical and psychological climate setting, involving the learners in planning for their learning, involving the learners in diagnosing their own needs for learning, involving the learners in formulating their own learning objectives, involving the learners in designing learning plans, helping the learners carry out their learning plans, and involving the learners in evaluating their own learning outcomes.

REFLECTION QUESTIONS

1. Taking the style inventory, how consistent are your results with what you imagined your style to be?
2. How would you like your style to grow and change in the future?

Source: Reprinted from Knowles, M.S., Holton, E.F., & Swanson, R.A. (2011). *The Adult Learner: The Definitive Classic in Adult Education and Human Resource Development* (7th ed.). New York: Taylor & Francis.

GLOSSARY

A-B-C-D-E model A model used in cognitive behavioral interventions to help a client change responses to events; stands for Activating event, Behavior, Consequence, Disputing, Effective reduction.

Accountable care community A collaborative, integrated, and measurable multi-institutional approach that emphasizes shared responsibility for the health of the community, including health promotion and disease prevention, access to quality services, and healthcare delivery; encompasses not only medical care delivery, but the public health system, community stakeholders at the grassroots level, and community organizations whose work often encompasses the entire spectrum of the determinants of health.

Accountable care organization Groups of doctors, hospitals, and other healthcare providers who come together voluntarily to provide coordinated high-quality care to their shared patients.

ACE cycle of change A model of behavior change in which a client experiences a nonlinear cycle of raised Awareness, Choice, and Execution; used to optimize a client's experience in each stage and subsequently increase the likelihood of long-term behavior change.

Action The stage of the transtheoretical model of behavioral change during which the individual is actively engaging in a behavior that was started less than six months ago.

Affirmation A statement of intended results spoken or written in the first person, present tense; offer of emotional support or encouragement.

Ambivalence A state of having mixed feelings about a change; arguing both for and against change simultaneously.

Andragogy The study of adult learning, consists of six core principles: adult learners need to know, learner self-concept, learner's experience, readiness to learn, orientation to learning, and motivation to learn.

Autonomy The capacity of a rational individual to make an informed, un-coerced decision.

Awareness The process by which a client first comes to identify that a behavior change is needed, and explores the advantages and disadvantages of beginning to pursue change.

Beneficence The act of doing good; kindness.

Change talk Statements reflecting a desire to change.

Choice The process by which a client who already has decided or intends to make a change commits to that change.

Clinical health coach A coach who works in a clinical setting helping patients to develop goals and action plans to optimally manage, prevent, or treat disease.

Cognitive ability An individual's degree of intelligence, can extend beyond intelligence quotient (IQ) to include multiple intelligences, such as linguistic, logical-mathematical, spatial, musical, bodily kinesthetic, understanding oneself, and understanding others.

Cognitive behavioral coaching (CBC) A method of coaching borrowed from cognitive behavioral therapy; aims to help a client intentionally change the way he or she thinks about life events; functions to facilitate behavior change.

Cognitive behavioral therapy (CBT) A form of psychotherapy that focuses on how thoughts and feelings influence behavior.

Cognitive controls Patterns of thinking about information.

Cognitive distortions Unproductive thought processes that can paralyze a client when making a positive and lasting behavioral change.

Cognitive style The approach to processing information; varies considerably among individuals, including such styles as visual, verbal, and tactile/psychomotor, among others.

Contemplation The stage of the transtheoretical model of behavioral change during which the individual is weighing the pros and cons of behavioral change.

CRAFT model An acronym that helps a coach systematically walk through a sequence of virtual coaching steps in a logical order; stands for Check in; Report progress; Adjust and assign; Feedback; and Teach, train, and talk through.

Decisional balance One of the four components of the transtheoretical model of behavioral change; refers to the numbers of pros and cons an individual perceives regarding adopting and/or maintaining an activity program.

Directing style A communication style in which the coach leads, tells, and decides; the coach is the main player and the client is a passive player. Triggers the "righting reflex."

Elicit-provide-elicit An approach to providing information in which the coach first asks permission to do so. When permission is granted, the coach follows with an open-ended question to understand what the client knows already (elicit). The coach follows with a small amount of highly relevant information (provide) and then checks back with the client to assess understanding and the response to the information (elicit).

Emotional intelligence The ability to recognize one's own feelings, as well as the feelings of others.

Empathy Understanding what another person is experiencing from his or her perspective.

Engaged life A type of happiness characterized by connection in work, relationships, and hobbies.

Engaging The first stage of motivational interviewing; the process of establishing a mutually trusting and respectful helping relationship.

Evoking A process of motivational interviewing in which the coach elicits from a client his or her own strengths and motivation to change.

Execution A process by which a client is engaging in the activities required to successfully achieve and maintain a desired change.

Fee-for-service payment model A traditional medical payment model in which physicians are reimbursed for each service provided (such as an office visit, test, and/or procedure).

Field dependent A cognitive control in which an individual relies more heavily on cues in the external environment when learning new information; field-dependent learners tend to thrive in group study sessions and interaction with outside sources when learning new information.

Field independent A cognitive control in which an individual learns best without regard to environmental factors; self-directed learning relies heavily on field-independent learning.

Focusing The second stage of motivational interviewing; the process by which the coach and client develop and maintain a specific direction in the conversation about change.

Following style A communication style in which the coach allows, listens, and understands the client; the coach is a passive player and the client drives the agenda.

Full life The end state when three domains of happiness merge, the pleasant life, the engaged life, and the meaningful life.

GROW model A goal-setting theory used to help clients establish behavior-change goals; stands for Goal, Reality, Options (or Obstacles), and Will (or Way forward); assumes the coach is not an expert in the client's situation.

Guiding style A communication style in which the coach helps to motivate, encourage, support, and assist a client in making a change; the coach is engaged but the client is the main player.

Health Insurance Portability and Accountability Act (HIPAA) Enacted by the U.S. Congress in 1996, HIPAA requires the U.S. Department of Health and Human Services (HHS) to establish national standards for electronic health care information to facilitate efficient and secure exchange of private health data. The Standards for Privacy of Individually Identifiable Health Information ("Privacy Rule"), issued by the HHS, addresses the use and disclosure of individuals' health information—called "protected health information"—by providing federal protections and giving patients an array of rights with respect to personal health information while permitting the disclosure of information needed for patient care and other important purposes.

Internal motivation Motivation that comes from internal states, such as enjoyment or personal satisfaction.

Justice A principle of fairness, especially in access to benefits and protection from harms.

Learning contract An important tool for self-directed learning in which the learner identifies a learning need, learning objectives, a plan for attaining the objectives, evaluation, and validation; helps to solidify learning and increase accountability.

Learning goal A clearly defined objective to improve knowledge, skill, or behavior.

Learning styles The range of preferred manners and methods of learning; no measures or descriptions of learning styles have been adequately validated.

Maintenance The stage of the transtheoretical model of behavioral change during which the individual is incorporating the new behavior into his or her lifestyle.

Meaningful life A type of happiness characterized by living with a sense of purpose and value.

Mindfulness The nonjudgmental awareness of the sensations, thoughts, and emotions of the present moment.

Motivational interviewing (MI) A method of questioning clients in a way that encourages them to honestly examine their beliefs and behaviors, and that motivates clients to make a decision to change a particular behavior.

Nonmaleficence The ethical principle of doing no harm.

OARS model A tool used to explore a client's values; stands for Open-ended questions, Affirmations, Reflections, and Summarizing.

Open-ended question A question that does not allow for a simple one-word answer (yes/no); designed to encourage a full, meaningful answer using the subject's own knowledge and/or feelings.

Patient-centered medical home A model of the organization of primary care that delivers the core functions of primary health care; encompasses five functions: comprehensive care, patient-centered care, coordinated care, accessible services, and quality and safety.

Patient-centered medical neighborhood Not necessarily a geographic location, but instead a set of relationships revolving around the patient and his or her patient-centered medical home, including community and social service organizations and state and local public health agencies.

Performance goal A clearly defined objective to improve functioning or performance in a particular area.

Planning The final stage of motivational interviewing; a client's readiness to begin planning for a change is signaled by increased frequency of change talk, decreased frequency of sustain talk, resolve, envisioning, and increased questioning.

Pleasant life A type of happiness characterized by a feeling of emotional contentment.

Positive psychology The scientific study of valued subjective experiences: well-being, contentment, and satisfaction (in the past); hope and optimism (for the future); and flow and happiness (in the present).

Powerful questioning The process of asking questions (such as the use of open-ended questions, affirmations, reflective listening, and summarizing) that elicit answers that provide deeper understanding of a person's feelings, emotions, fears, truths, and values.

Precontemplation The stage of the transtheoretical model of behavioral change during which the individual is not yet thinking about changing.

Preparation The stage of the transtheoretical model of behavioral change during which the individual is getting ready to make a change.

Rapport A relationship marked by mutual understanding and trust.

Reflection A feature of active listening in which the coach makes a best guess at the underlying meaning of what a client has said.

Relationship management The ability to manage emotions so as to attain specific goals.

Righting reflex The tendency to give advice, push recommendations, and offer solutions; makes sustainable behavior change less likely for a client who is ambivalent about change.

Scope of practice The range and limit of responsibilities normally associated with a specific job or profession.

Sedentary Doing or requiring much sitting; minimal activity.

Self-awareness The ability to perceive emotions in oneself and others accurately.

Self-efficacy One's perception of his or her ability to change or to perform specific behaviors (e.g., exercise).

Self-management Self-control; the ability to use emotions to facilitate thinking.

SMART goal A properly designed goal; stands for Specific, Measurable, Attainable, Relevant, and Time-bound.

Social awareness The ability to understand emotions, emotional language, and the signals conveyed by emotion.

Socio-ecological model (SEM) A tool that can be used to help the health coach better understand the health behaviors of their clients and more effectively structure behavior-change programs; examines interrelationships between individuals and the environments in which they live and work, as well as the many levels at which individuals are influenced, both in terms of support for healthy behaviors and barriers to improving health behavior.

Stages of change model *See* Transtheoretical model of behavioral change (TTM).

Success momentum Occurs when a client experiences tiny successes, which in turn, propel them onto a path of feeling confident and more likely to take on new challenges.

Summarizing A feature of active listening in which the coach states back to a client what the coach perceives to be the main points of what the client has said.

Sustain talk Statements reflecting a desire not to change.

SWOT analysis Situation analysis in which internal strengths and weaknesses of an organization (such as a business) or individual, and external opportunities and threats are closely examined to chart a strategy.

Teamlet model A model of provision of clinical health coaching services in which one or more health coaches are paired with one or more physicians. Often, the primary care visit is extended in that the coach sees the patient prior to the physician visit, together with the clinician, immediately following the visit, and between medical visits, usually by phone.

Transtheoretical model of behavioral change (TTM) A theory of behavior that examines one's readiness to change and identifies five stages: precontemplation, contemplation, preparation, action, and maintenance. Also called the stages of change model.

Values interview The use of open-ended questions, affirmations, reflections, and summarizing to explore a client's values.

Virtual coaching The implementation of the tools and technologies available via the internet, email, and mobile devices including tablets and cell phones, to communicate with and coach clients.

Whole-part-whole A method of instruction in which learners are introduced to the "big picture" of the topic, each part is discussed in turn, and then the parts are put back together in a discussion once again of the whole, or big picture; this style of teaching exemplifies the core principles of adult learning.

INDEX

C

U

V

W

ABOUT THE AUTHORS

Natalie Digate Muth, M.D., M.P.H., R.D., FAAP, is a pediatrician in North County San Diego and ACE Senior Advisor for Healthcare Solutions. She is dual board-certified in pediatrics and obesity medicine and is a Diplomate of the American Board of Obesity Medicine. She also serves on the Executive Committee of the Section on Obesity for the American Academy of Pediatrics. She holds credentials as a registered dietitian, Certified-Specialist in Sports Dietetics, and ACE Certified Health Coach. She is author of nearly 100 articles, books, and book chapters, including the *ACE Fitness Nutrition Manual* (ACE, 2013), *"Eat Your Vegetables!" and Other Mistakes Parents Make: Redefining How to Raise Healthy Eaters* (Healthy Learning, 2012), the textbook *Sports Nutrition for Allied Health Professionals* (F.A. Davis, 2014), and several chapters in the *ACE Health Coach Manual.* She holds a Bachelor of Science degree in Psychology and Physiological Science from UCLA, and a Master of Public Health and Medical Doctor degree from the University of North Carolina-Chapel Hill.

Michael R. Mantell, Ph.D., earned his Ph.D. at the University of Pennsylvania and his M.S. at Hahnemann Medical College, where he wrote his thesis on the psychological aspects of obesity. His career includes serving as the Chief Psychologist for Children's Hospital in San Diego and as the founding Chief Psychologist for the San Diego Police Department. Dr. Mantell is a member of the Scientific Advisory Board of the International Council on Active Aging, the Chief Behavior Science Consultant to the Premier Fitness Camp at Omni La Costa, a best-selling author of two books, including the 1988 original *Don't Sweat the Small Stuff, P.S. It's All Small Stuff,* an international behavior science fitness keynote speaker, an Advisor to numerous fitness-health organizations, and is featured in many media broadcasts and worldwide fitness publications. He has been featured on Oprah, Good Morning America, the Today Show, and has been a contributor to many major news organizations including Fox and ABC News. Dr. Mantell is a nationally sought after behavioral science coach for business leaders, elite amateur and professional athletes, individuals, and families. He is included in the greatist.com's 2013 list of *"The 100 Most Influential People in Health and Fitness."*

Billie Frances, M.A., is a Board-certified Life Coach, a licensed Marriage and Family Therapist, and a licensed spiritual counselor. She is on faculty at the University of Phoenix, a member of the National Wellness Institute, a past President of both the San Diego Professional Coaches Alliance and the San Diego Chapter of Marriage and Family Therapists, and presents on mindful coaching nationally. In 2000, Frances founded her own form of specialized coaching, "Guiding Mindful Change," with a vision of creating a network of certified coaches with the potential to positively change the lives of thousands. Guiding Mindful Change continues to set the standard for excellence in certifying qualified, ethical, and empowered professional coaches. Since 2004, Frances and the Employee Wellness Coaching team have provided telephone-based wellness coaching for the employees of several Fortune 100 companies.

Linda Fogg-Phillips, M.S., has a master's degree in Health Promotion and Exercise Psychology. Her work focuses on health behavior design, health coaching, and Tiny Habits®. Her family—she is the mother of eight children—is known as the Mobile Health Family and is frequently featured at health and technology conferences. She has been interviewed on local and national news such as ABC, CNN, and NBC, in addition to having a bi-weekly segment on Fox News. Fogg-Phillips is an author, speaker, personal trainer, and health coach.